W9-BCN-236

THE RISE OF THE VICTORIAN ACTOR

The Rise of the Victorian Actor

MICHAEL BAKER

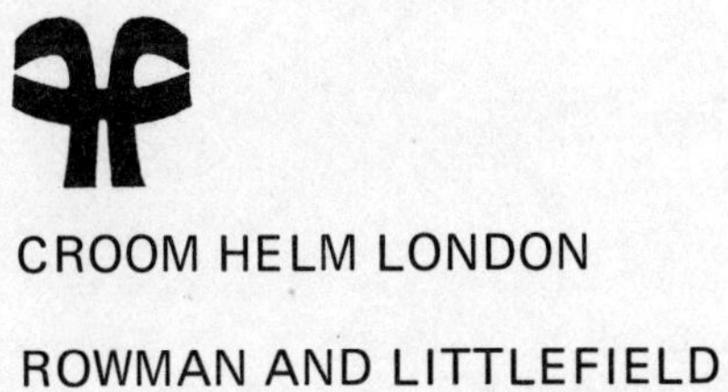

CROOM HELM LONDON

ROWMAN AND LITTLEFIELD

Croom Helm Ltd, 2-10 St John's Road, London SW11

British Library Cataloguing in Publication Data

Baker, Michael
The rise of the Victorian actor.
1. Theater and society – England – History
I. Title
301.44'4 PN2594

ISBN 0-85664-542-7

First published in the United States 1978
by Rowman and Littlefield, Totowa, New Jersey

Library of Congress Cataloging in Publication Data

Baker, Michael.
The rise of the Victorian actor.

Bibliography: p. 225
Includes index.
1. Theater and society – England – History. 2. Actors – England. I. Title.
PN2049.B34 792'.028'0941 77-25403

ISBN 0-8476-6033-8

To my parents

Printed and bound in Great Britain by
Redwood Burn Limited, Trowbridge & Esher

CONTENTS

ACKNOWLEDGEMENTS

This book first began as an Oxford B. Litt. thesis which was completed in 1976, and though additions and revisions were necessary for the purposes of publication, it nevertheless remains substantially unchanged. As such, it is perhaps natural that most of my thanks should go to those associated with the thesis stage of its preparation.

I am therefore particularly grateful to Dr Bernard Richards of Brasenose College, who supervised my work from afar and showed unfailing interest and enthusiasm over a number of years despite the problems created by my move to a full-time job. I would also like to thank Dr Brian Harrison and Dr Stephen Wall at Oxford, and Mr George Rowell of Bristol University. Each proved a source of help and guidance at different times.

There are many friends to whom I owe a debt of gratitude for putting themselves out on my behalf or for the stimulus and support they provided. I would mention in particular Serena Newmark, Roger Holdsworth, Andrew Purkis and Stephen Hickey.

Finally, I must acknowledge the great contribution made by my parents, whose quiet encouragement at all times was invaluable to morale and ultimately therefore to the completion of this work.

ABBREVIATIONS

I refer throughout the book to three Select Committee Reports on the theatre, in 1832, 1866 and 1892. The full titles of these Reports are somewhat unwieldy, so after the first reference I have abbreviated them, putting 'Select Committee Report', followed by the date and the relevant question number.

Thus the Report of the Select Committee on Theatrical Licences and Regulations, *Parl. Papers,* 1866, XVI, Q. 2924 becomes in abbreviated form: Select Committee Report, 1866, Q. 2924.

CHRONOLOGY

The following table provides a conspectus of the period, relating the theatre to other important events of the time. Dramatic works appear under the year of their first performance.

1831 Garrick Club founded. Law Society formed. Madame Vestris takes over the Olympic (till 1839).

1832 Select Committee on Dramatic Literature. Parliamentary Reform Act.

1833 Death of Edmund Kean. Dramatic Copyright Act. Bulwer Lytton's Theatrical Reform Bill debated. Factory Act ('Children's Charter'). Oxford Movement, Newman *et al., Tracts for the Times* (till 1841).

1835 Dickens, *Sketches by Boz*, first series.

1836 Dickens, *Sketches by Boz*, second series. Début of Helen Faucit. First train in London.

1837 Accession of Queen Victoria. Début of Barry Sullivan. Carlyle, *French Revolution*. Ben Webster takes over the Haymarket (till 1853).

1838 Anti-Corn Law League (Manchester). The *Era* started. Death of the popular showman 'Old Wild'. Dickens, *Nicholas Nickleby*. Beginnings of Chartism.

1839 Unsuccessful parliamentary resolution to abolish theatrical restriction in Lent. Chartist riots. General Theatrical Fund established.

1841 *Punch* started. Carlyle, *Heroes and Hero Worship.* Bradshaw's *Railway Guide.* Cook's tours.

1842 Canterbury Old Stagers formed. Mudie's Circulating Library.

1843 Theatrical Reform Act. Browning's *A Blot on the 'Scutcheon.* Macaulay, *Critical and Historical Essays*. Ruskin, *Modern Painters* (to 1860).

1844 Factory Act (restricting hours for women and children).

1845 Newman turns Roman Catholic. Methodist tract *The Sinner's Friend* reaches 140th edition.

1846 Repeal of the Corn Laws. Railway boom.

1847 G.H. Lewes, *Ranthorpe* (theatrical novel). Ten Hours Factory Act.

1848 First Royal Command Performances at Windsor. Geraldine

Jewsbury, *The Half-Sisters* (theatrical novel). Dickens, *Dombey and Son.* Public Health Act. Pre-Raphaelite Brotherhood formed. Revolution throughout Europe.

1849 Macaulay, *History of England* (to 1861). *Household Words* (ed. Dickens).

1850 Beginnings of music-halls. Tennyson, *In Memoriam.* Death of Wordsworth (Tennyson succeeds as Poet Laureate). Thackeray, *Pendennis.* Society for Promoting the Employment of Women formed.

1851 Great Exhibition. Macready retires. Helen Faucit retires. Charles Kean takes over the Princess's (till 1859). Elizabeth Lynn, *Realities* (theatrical novel).

1852 J.L. Toole makes his début. Albert Smith starts his one-man shows at the Egyptian Hall (till 1859).

1854 Dickens, *Hard Times.*

1855 Début of Marie Wilton (later Mrs Bancroft). Cambridge Amateur Dramatic Club founded. Madame Celeste scandalises as Harlequin. *Daily Telegraph* and *Saturday Review* start. The Dramatic Equestrian and Musical Sick Fund Association established.

1856 Début of Henry Irving. *La Traviata* scandalises.

1857 Matrimonial Causes Act (on divorce). Thomas German Reed starts his Gallery of Illustration entertainments (till 1873).

1858 Dramatic College instituted. British Medical Association established. Frith, *Derby Day.* Dickens begins his Public Readings (till 1870).

1859 Charles Kean retires. Darwin, *Origin of Species.* Death of Macaulay and Leigh Hunt. Samuel Smiles, *Self-Help. All the Year Round* (ed. Dickens).

1860 Boucicault's *Colleen Bawn* initiates the 'long run'. Windsor Strollers formed. *Cornhill Magazine* (ed. Thackeray).

1861 Charles Fechter in *Hamlet.* Débuts of Squire Bancroft and William Kendal. Death of the Prince Consort.

1862 Débuts of Ellen Terry and Charles Wyndham. George Eliot, *Romola.*

1864 Adah Menken plays Mazeppa at Astley's.

1865 Bancrofts take over the Prince of Wales (till 1880). Tom Robertson, *Society* (*Ours* 1866, *Caste* 1867, *Play* 1868, and *School* 1869). Swinburne, *Atalanta in Calydon. Pall Mall Gazette* and *Fortnightly Review* started. Lecky, *History of the Rise and Influence of the Spirit of Rationalism.*

1866 Select Committee on Theatrical Licences and Regulations. Henry

Morley, *Journal of a London Playgoer.*

1869 Arnold, *Culture and Anarchy.* J.S. Mill, *On the Subjection of Women*. Irish Church disestablished.

1870 Death of Dickens. Entry to the Civil Service by competitive examination. Début of Alma Murray. Elementary Education Act.

1871 Death of Tom Robertson. Purchase of Army Commissions abolished. George Eliot, *Middlemarch.* Abolition of religious tests at Oxbridge. Trade Unions legalised. Irving triumphs in *The Bells.* Attempts to disestablish the Anglican Church.

1873 Death of Macready, Mill and Bulwer Lytton. Pater, *Studies in the Renaissance.* Remington typewriters invented.

1874 *The World* (ed. Edmund Yates). Début of Johnston Forbes-Robertson.

1875 G.H. Lewes, *Actors and the Art of Acting.* Gilbert and Sullivan in partnership.

1876 Phelps proposes a National Theatre. Gustave Garcia, *The Actors' Art.* Edison's phonograph.

1877 The *Theatre* (ed. Clement Scott). Edmund Yates, *Celebrities at Home,* first series. Death of Walter Bagehot. Zola, *L'Assommoir.*

1878 Irving takes over the Lyceum (till 1899). Salvation Army founded. Hardy, *Return of the Native.* Electric street lighting in London. Début of Beerbohm Tree.

1879 Theatrical Reform Association and Church and Stage Guild founded. Shakespeare Memorial Theatre opened at Stratford. First London telephone exchange.

1880 Frank Benson's production of *Agamemnon* at Oxford. Gladstone PM. Death of George Eliot.

1881 Début of Lilly Langtry. Married Women's Property Act. Death of Disraeli and Carlyle. Henry James, *Portrait of a Lady.*

1882 Actors' Benevolent Fund founded. George Moore, *A Mummer's Wife* (theatrical novel).

1883 Gladstone offers a knighthood to Irving. *Dramatic and Musical Directory* started. F.J. Talma, *On the Actor's Art.*

1884 H.A. Jones, *Saints and Sinners* (first religious play of the century). Third Reform Bill.

1885 Oxford University Dramatic Society founded. J.K. Jerome, *On the Stage – and Off.*

1886 Theatrical restriction on Ash Wednesday abolished. Bradlaugh finally elected to the Commons. Bancrofts, *On and Off the Stage.*

1888 Westland Marston, *Our Recent Actors.* William Archer, *Masks or*

Faces? Début of Mrs Patrick Campbell. Death of Matthew Arnold. Eastman's Kodak box camera invented. Dunlop's pneumatic tyre invented.

1889 Ibsen, *A Doll's House* and *Pillars of Society*. London Dock Strike. Deaths of Browning and Wilkie Collins.

1890 Death of Dion Boucicault. Henry James, *The Tragic Muse* (theatrical novel). Death of Newman. First underground railway.

1891 Death of Barry Sullivan. Actors' Association established. George Gissing, *New Grub Street*. Hardy, *Tess of the D'Urbervilles.* Oscar Wilde, *Picture of Dorian Gray*. Free elementary education.

1892 Select Committee on Theatres and Places of Entertainment. P.H. Fitzgerald, *The Art of Acting.* Death of Tennyson. Kipling, *Barrack-Room Ballads.*

1895 Irving knighted.

1904 Royal Academy of Dramatic Art founded.

1905 Actors' Union established.

1920 Actors' strike.

1929 Equity founded.

INTRODUCTION

The purpose of this study is to trace the gradual emergence of acting as an accepted professional occupation in England. Central to this theme is the rise of the actor's social status, the rise of new middle-class professions, a revolutionary shift in cultural values, and the growth of the theatre into a flourishing social institution at the heart of a mass leisure industry. All these developments were part of a process which took place in the nineteenth century, and in particular during the Victorian period, a time of unprecedented theatrical change. For before 1800, and indeed well into the nineteenth century, the English stage was still generally a crude and haphazard affair: actors were few in number and the great majority performed as members of travelling troupes of one kind or another, either independently or on recognised local circuits, catering in fact for a predominantly rural population in much the same manner as the medieval Interlude players or the strolling bands of the Elizabethans. Even the indoor playhouse was a comparatively recent innovation, and though most towns could boast one by the end of the eighteenth century, many remained without a resident company and were used for only part of the year.[1] By 1900, however, the picture had changed dramatically and the theatre was recognisably modern in almost every respect.

I have chosen 1830 as a starting-point because it marks the end of one theatrical era and the beginning of another. By this date the monopoly of the Patent theatres was already very much in question and its abolition largely a matter of time; the removal of the Kembles and the imminent death of Edmund Kean[2] left the stage clear for a new generation of actors and managers who were to sweep away a style of theatre which, in its classical grandeur and gentlemanly ease, was essentially a survival of the eighteenth century. London in the 1830s witnessed an unprecedented theatrical boom: a host of 'minor' theatres sprang up or were revived[3] and there began several influential periods of management, notably Bunn's at Covent Garden (1833-5) and Drury Lane (1833-9), Webster's at the Haymarket (1837-53), Madame Vestris's at the Olympic (1831-9) and, not least, Ducrow's at Astley's (1830-41). All were factors which encouraged the spread of theatrical entertainment, improved the actor's standards of presentation, consolidated the institutional base of the theatre, and enabled actors to assert the distinctiveness of their occupation more confidently. Even in parliament the 1830s was a decade of exceptional theatrical activity, resulting in Bulwer's Bill to abolish the patent monopoly, and the Copyright Act of 1833, which finally gave dramatists some protection for their works in performance: it was an improvement in status which benefited the theatre as a whole, and it is no accident that the growing importance of the playwright in the nineteenth century ran parallel with the rising prestige of actors. Two further developments make the 1830s a significant era for the theatre: the change of monarch in 1837 and the building of the first railway networks.[4] With the accession of Queen Victoria royal patronage of the stage, largely defunct since George III's heyday, acquired a new lease of life. Its contribution to the growing respectability of actors and play-going cannot be underestimated. The coming of the railways, in particular the development of cheap rail transport, revolutionised social mobility. As a result, leisure facilities expanded enormously, becoming both more organised and more centralised. As we shall see, for the theatre in particular these changes had far-reaching consequences.

The year 1890 is a rather more arbitrary dateline, and I have not hesitated to seek out sources beyond this point where I felt they had a bearing upon the theme in hand. However, I did not regard it necessary to fix upon 1895 as a more appropriate dividing-line, this being the year when Henry Irving became England's first theatrical knight. In the first place, Irving's knighthood had already been offered, by the then Prime Minister Gladstone, as early as 1883.[5] And secondly, it would be generally true to say that the 1890s have a special literary flavour and cultural compactness which separate them from the preceding period. It is not easy to define the point at which the *fin de siècle* attitude emerged – some would trace its development back to Walter Pater, Arthur Hallam, Swinburne and as far as the major Romantic poets – but as a serious and consistent outlook it leaves its impression most intensely upon the years after 1890. Certainly in the field of drama the 1890s had a distinctive impact, fostering a new breed of playwrights, critics and even performers.[6] But by and large the theatre had already regained its fashionableness by 1890; it also exhibited by this date all the major characteristics with which it would pass into the twentieth century. Perhaps only in the sphere of women's work, revolutionised by the use on a large scale of the telephone and the typewriter, were the 1890s to effect a dramatic social change with later implications for the theatre. Certain major developments important to the full professionalisation of actors have to lie outside the scope of this study, notably the opening of national drama schools and the founding of a national theatre. Both were fore-shadowed before 1890, but they were essentially twentieth-century phenomena. In any case, it is arguable that by 1890 (or 1891, if we include the Actors' Association) the stage had gone as far as it could to model itself upon strictly professional lines. Thereafter, actors were more preoccupied with the struggles of unionisation.

It is my hope that this study will go some way to bridging a conspicuous gap in the history of British theatre in the nineteenth century. For apart from a number of standard general works,[7] by far the greater part of research into this period has been devoted to the literary or technical development of the stage. In other words, a good deal has been written about Victorian drama, the theatres where it was performed, and the style in which it was presented and staged, but relatively little about the people whose job it was to act the plays and the milieu in which they lived and worked. An examination of the stage which goes beyond the theatre, a social history such as Muriel Bradbrook's on the Elizabethan theatre,[8] is long overdue for the Victorian period.

I have divided the book into eight separate chapters. I have not attempted to cover the period 1830-90 chronologically, but instead examine different aspects of the actor's world and its relation to society to show how each in turn contributed to acting's rising status. This concurrent method inevitably entails a certain overlapping, but I have kept repetition to a minimum, and, on the assumption that the reader is familiar both with the period in question and the broad lines of theatrical development within it, I have not wasted space by retelling the background to the events employed in the argument. Clearly, over such a large period it has not been possible to refer in detail to some developments which played their part in raising the actor's standing, but on the whole these can be found in standard works and are now familiar to theatre historians. Thus I have not elaborated upon the individual efforts of certain theatrical managements whose contribution to improved standards of performance and presentation, as well as of audience comfort, accelerated the process of rehabilitating the actor. While these deserve mention, and get it where necessary, it seemed to me more important to break new ground and, in particular, to discuss the corporate efforts of actors to raise their calling.

A word about the source material and my general approach. One of the difficulties about theatre research in the nineteenth century is the extremely scattered nature of the available sources and the disparateness of contemporary theatrical activity. It is not always easy to know who are actors and who are singers and dancers, since the versatility of the Victorian theatre was such that distinctions between the performing arts were invariably hazy; indeed, the legal definition of a 'stage-play' was never satisfactorily resolved in the course of this period. It is possible to detach the theatre from opera and, until roughly 1850, from ballet, but actors clearly had links with showfolk at one end of the period and with music-hall performers at the other. But such difficulties were recognised by contemporaries and are part and parcel of our story, for the regular play-actor's search for occupational distinctiveness, and hence higher status, necessarily compelled him to disown those categories of performers whom he regarded as 'inferior'. In fact, in illustrating the rise of the professional player we are also resolving the question of definitions.

The scattered nature of theatrical sources poses more intractable problems. One significant development in this period is the growth of a specifically theatrical press, but as many different libraries hold separate issues of the same journal or newspaper, comprehensive coverage is often difficult. Moreover, many whole periodicals remain in the United States or were destroyed in the British Museum during the war.[9] I have therefore tended to rely upon a small number of established journals, such as the *Era* and the *Theatre*, which are well-known and easily obtainable in their entirety. These do tend, however, to give a better coverage of the London theatre than elsewhere. The same is true of theatrical memoirs, which I have used extensively. The latter have many drawbacks, often being less than objective, self-indulgently anecdotal and factually incorrect; moreover, most relate to the author's life on stage rather than off, and tend to reflect the careers of successful actors or actresses rather than the middling or struggling performer. This imbalance raises serious problems of interpretation on a national level, especially with regard to the living and working conditions of actors, which clearly varied enormously in different theatres as well as different parts of the country. In fact, there is an imperative need for more research at the local and individual level if we are to obtain a satisfactory picture of theatrical conditions over the country as a whole. Some progress has been made in this direction, notably by the Society for Theatrical Research, and I have tried to weigh this material against more familiar evidence to reach a comprehensive assessment.

Clearly, any social history of the theatre must seek out non-theatrical sources as well. Here I have made extensive use of the personal diaries or memoirs of many different public figures both high and low,

I have explored contemporary social surveys, examined religious tracts, and analysed the more considered comments on the theatrical scene passed by serious and fashionable journals alike. Last, but not least, there is a wealth of material relating to actors in parliamentary evidence, ranging from the censuses to the vitally important Select Committee Reports on theatrical licensing, the first major examination of the actor's occupation by the legislature in the theatre's history. In short, the sources I have used are almost all in print and should be familiar to social and theatre historians alike; the approach, however, I believe to be a fresh one, throwing new light on the theatre's place in Victorian society.

Finally, I would like to make brief mention of the theatrical novel. This much neglected branch of Victorian literature[10] offers a vivid glimpse of the prevailing social attitudes to acting and actors, or rather actresses, who are the most popular subjects in this genre. The stage novel really requires a book to itself, for any satisfactory treatment of fiction as social history must take into account the many variables posed by individual authors and their methods. Space does not permit this in the present study. However, I have felt it important not to dismiss the evidence of this genre altogether, and so where a novel genuinely illuminates the social position of actors, I have not hesitated to quote from it.

1 THE STAGE AND THE PROFESSIONS

It would be no exaggeration to say that, in general, the actor of 1830 was a social and artistic outcast and the theatre an outlawed sector of private enterprise. In this respect the status of the professional stage in England had scarcely changed for over two hundred years.

Of course, the scope and framework of theatrical activity had developed considerably during this period. A written dramatic tradition had emerged and with it more sophisticated techniques of presentation. The building of provincial playhouses in the second half of the eighteenth century had encouraged new urban audiences outside London, and had placed play-acting in many areas in a fixed, indoor setting for the first time; this in turn led to the growth of new acting companies and gave rise to established theatrical circuits in some regions of the country.[1] By the end of the seventeenth century women had replaced boys as actresses and quickly established themselves on an equal footing with actors, a development which was not only of great dramatic significance but boosted the superior attraction of the theatre over other forms of entertainment.[2] Finally, the growing economic self-sufficiency of the better companies hastened the end of aristocratic patronage of actors; after 1750 the player depended increasingly for his livelihood upon the box-office.

Yet this growth was not matched by the development of an organised theatre. Theatrical undertakings remained wholly unregulated, and theatres were simply autonomous businesses. Actors were casual labourers in an extremely fluctuating market; one, moreover, which had to contend with more than its fair share of social disapproval and official intolerance. By the beginning of the nineteenth century fashionable audiences were deserting the playhouse in favour of the opera, and the all-class audiences of Elizabethan times gave way to predominantly working-class or lower-middle-class spectators and a handful of connoisseurs. The Church, which had fostered drama in its early days, now worked to prevent the building of theatres and the social recognition of actors. Performances were regularly suppressed during Lent and Holy Week, and theatre-going denounced as unchristian. Government recognition of the stage had not been accompanied by government support. The patent system, instituted in 1661 and confirmed in 1737, remained in force until 1843, despite its growing obsolescence from the end of the eighteenth century onwards. Designed to safeguard the 'legitimate' drama by restricting competition, it had the reverse effect while imposing severe handicaps upon both dramatists and the great majority of actors who never reached the patent companies. With the establishment of the Lord Chamberlain's Office under the Licensing Act of 1737, the theatre submitted to a censorship unknown in other branches of public life. Originally carried out for political reasons, this censorship remained, excused as a safeguard of the nation's morals, while other mediums were free to be as scurrilous as they wished.[3]

These conditions survived well into the nineteenth century and were symptomatic of the way in which the English theatre had always been treated, not as a desirable social amenity, as in France and Germany,[4] but as a disreputable luxury. The social status of actors was correspondingly low. Under the law unlicensed players could still in 1830 be classed as vagrants and vagabonds, a position inherited from as far back as 1572. And despite the social success of most celebrated actors and actresses, acting was not a career deemed suitable for a 'gentleman', still less for a 'lady', nor would any self-respecting member of the educated upper or middle classes lightly countenance an association with 'the actor class'. Marriage into the theatre at this level was greeted with nothing less than horror.[5] So if actors themselves tended to refer to their occupation as a 'profession' or as 'art', such exalted terms were conspicuously absent amongst society at large. The early nineteenth-century tragedian William Macready wrote:

> My experience has taught me that whilst the law, the church, the army, and navy give a man the rank of a gentleman, on the stage that designation must be obtained in society (though the law and the Court decline to recognise it) by the individual bearing. In other callings the profession confers dignity on the initiated, on the stage the player must contribute respect to the dignity of his art . . . I had to live to learn that an ignorant officer could refuse the satisfaction of a gentleman on the ground that his appellant was a player, and that, whilst any of those above-named vocations, whatever the private character, might be received at Court, the privilege of appearing in the sacred precincts was too exclusive for any, however distinguished, on the stage.[6]

Macready's assessment was an accurate one for the early Victorian actor, but it failed to recognise that the stage had little in common with accepted notions of a profession. Nor was this position exclusive to actors. Similar social stigmas attached to all artistic occupations. To a lesser or greater degree, painting, sculpture, poetry, authorship and music all lacked those attributes deemed necessary to qualify for a place within the charmed circle formed by the traditional career professions. The two foremost 'learned' professions of the eighteenth century – the Law and the Church – derived their ultimate strength from their constitutional importance. Doctors and the officer class of the armed forces had a long-standing tradition of service to the State. The arts could make no such claims. Moreover, unlike these professions, they were generally unprofitable and went unrecognised by the law. Their power was negligible, being small in numbers and wealth, and having little influence over public opinion.[7] But above all the traditional professions bestowed gentility. Their members were generally men drawn from a superior class and possessing superior education, preferably a classical schooling, a qualification which could be more important than professional training itself.[8]

On this latter count other occupations besides the arts were disqualified as professions in the early nineteenth century. Engineering, for example, which was central to a growing industrial society, nevertheless smacked too much of artisan origins and purely technical skill to be afforded the same honours as doctoring and the law.[9] But on the score of gentility, the arts were particularly suspect. Appearing to require no learned expertise nor to provide any useful service, and having no set work routine or conventional standard of ethical conduct, artists laid themselves open to the charge of 'idleness' and 'bohemianism'. The author and journalist Edmund Yates, himself the son of an actor, characterised English bohemians of the 1850s as young, gifted and reckless, working by fits and starts, 'never except under the pressure of necessity'; above all, they had 'a thorough contempt for the dress, usages and manners of ordinary middle-class civilisation'.[10] By this token few successful Victorian artists could be described as bohemians; indeed, the very precariousness of artistic life acted as a strong inducement to acquire the conventional trappings of respectability. However, the unorthodox lifestyle of a minority of artists undoubtedly coloured the reputation of the group as a whole, bringing it into direct conflict with the prevailing moral code. There was nothing new in the so-called cult of sensibility with which artists were associated, but its emphasis upon the claims of natural impulse threw it into sharp relief against the prevailing Victorian spirit of earnestness, self-restraint, thrift and hard work.[11] The struggle between these two opposing sets of values persisted throughout the nineteenth century, and was never satisfactorily resolved in the case of the artist. His social standing consequently remained more or less controversial. As a careers guide of 1870 put it, though art was now 'respectable', the notion lingered that artists were 'not quite *comme il faut* persons'; or, as another social commentator observed:

> The keen-scented, eminently decorous British public perceives a certain aroma of social and moral laxity in the atmosphere of the studio, a kind of blended perfume of periodical impecuniosity and much tobacco-smoke.[12]

What this meant in practice was that artistic careers were rarely encouraged – though the successful artist might well receive equal honours to those bestowed upon members of the professions. Painting, for instance, could be an acceptable pastime for an educated man but hardly a career. 'The polite world', Thackeray remarked in the 1850s, 'permits a gentleman to amuse himself with [the Muse of Painting], but to take her for better or for worse!'[13] Consequently, men who adopted artistic vocations did so generally after a number of false starts in other occupations considered more suitable to their station in life. Certainly, no respectable parent would have marked his son down for future success as a painter, author or actor, an attitude which prevailed even among artists themselves who commonly sought to direct their own children to a more regular and gainful means of livelihood. The financial precariousness of the arts, which especially for the beginner compared unfavourably with the professions, undoubtedly had an important influence on this prejudice.[14] But ultimately it was the fact that an artistic career did not of itself bestow standing which accounted for society's lingering reluctance, right through the century, to entrust its sons to such a course in life.

The superior prestige of the traditional professions remained unchallenged throughout the nineteenth century, but new professions arose as the concept of a profession changed to meet the needs of an increasingly urbanised society. By 1860 the three chief principles upon which the modern profession is based were already being recognised: qualification by examination, legal acknowledgement of the right to practice, and the right of a professional body to internal self-regulation. Together these principles conferred that sense of exclusiveness which the professional so much desired. Gradually the older professions adapted to the new criteria, so that by the 1870s competitive entry had become the rule for the law, medicine, the Civil Service and the Army.[15]

The spread of the professional idea was accompanied by an upgrading of the arts. The popularity of acting, music, painting, and in particular authorship, as occupations rose dramatically between the 1840s and 1860s.[16] By 1861 the census had begun to classify the arts as 'professions' for the first time. But there is no easy connection to be made between the growth of the new professions and the reclassification of the arts. In fact, the initial growth in the numbers of artists as a group largely pre-dated full acceptance of the new professional idea. So the situation was rather more complicated than it first appears. Two trends seem to have been at work in the field of the arts at this time. On the one hand, there was a levelling process gradually developing whereby artistic occupations, and literary work in particular, were starting to acquire commercial characteristics as a result of a growing market demand for their services and products. Thus artists of all kinds no longer needed to work in a vacuum but could cater for a public, as architects, draughtsmen, designers and illustrators on the one hand, novelists, bookmen and journalists on the other. The explosive rise of a cheap popular press from the mid-fifties was crucial to this development and, as we shall see in chapter 8, had particular significance for the status of the stage. But prior to this democratising process, and then running alongside and often at odds with it, was a more élitist notion of the artist. This view saw him as different from other mortals, not because he was poor, idle, immoral and eccentric, but because he had a more intense sensibility than other men and therefore could only be judged by purely aesthetic criteria. At the same time as some artists were coming to think of themselves as producers of a commodity on a par with others in the great buying and bargaining universe, others were describing themselves as specially endowed and spiritually enlightened – and explicitly above such considerations. For this attitude was not simply a professional one, but was a cultural judgement, a view that art somehow embodied certain life-enhancing human values which were felt to be threatened by the advance of modern industrial society.[17]

It was a concept of the artist which the Romantics had expressed in some form, but it was taken a stage further by, first, J.S. Mill, Carlyle, Ruskin and Dickens, and then later by Arnold and Pater. Mill and Dickens embodied both views of the artist to some extent, for Mill believed poetry was quite compatible with being written for the commercial market[18] and Dickens was himself a successful popular novelist and journalist. But both subsequently turned against the utilitarian spirit of the age. As early as 1838 Mill had concluded that Benthamism, the guiding light of his intellectual upbringing, could do little for either the individual or the spiritual interests of society,[19] and in his *Autobiography* (1873) he condemned its neglect of feeling and imagination as an element in human nature.[20] Dickens takes a rather similar standpoint in both *Dombey and Son* (1848), where there runs an extended debate over the values of sterile business success versus the vital human qualities of uncommercial pursuits, and *Hard Times* (1854), which in bold, unvarnished terms points the accusing finger at Bounderby and Gradgrind. More specifically, Dickens championed theatre-going, proclaiming the benefits of 'sound, rational amusement' as an escape from the business of life [21] – though few artists would have gone along with this, as we shall see. In Carlyle and Ruskin the transition from aestheticism to social criticism is yet more explicit. For Ruskin great art was the work of 'men in a state of enthusiasm', 'men who feel strongly and nobly'.[22] The moral emphasis was important, for the good artist was not merely talented, but possessed special qualities of apprehension through which the essential truth and beauty of life was revealed. But such an artist had limited scope and influence in a social climate where the virtues of industrialism were constantly extolled. And so in pondering on the role of the artist, and in turn identifying the arts as the yardstick of social health, Ruskin arrived naturally at a critique of society, and a scathing one at that. 'The great cry that rises from all our manufacturing cities, louder than their furnace blast', ran his indictment, 'is all in very deed for this – that we manufacture everything there except men'.[23] For Carlyle too the subordination of man's spiritual interests to the demands of the machine age had gone too far. 'Mechanism' had become a complete habit of mind, at the expense of the notion of 'internal perfection',[24] an analysis echoed by Arnold's verdict in *Culture and Anarchy* (1869) that 'the idea of perfection as an *inward* condition of the mind and spirit is at variance with the mechanical civilisation in esteem with us'.[25] Carlyle's hero was the 'Man-of-Letters', whom he regarded as 'our most important modern person', a guiding light to the confused world 'in its dark pilgrimage through the waste of Time'.[26] It was this artist's neglect that lay at the heart of all that was wrong with modern society.

So the specific development which arose from all these writers' criticisms of industrialised society – and the trend was also at work in that yearning for the past expressed in Pugin and Tennyson, the Young England and Oxford Movements, and the Pre-Raphaelites – was the notion of a cultural ethic, a body of values identified with the arts and learning which transcended, and was superior to, the ordinary progress of society. Pater, in his *The Renaissance* (1873), went even further (though in a negative sense) by reducing the cultural idea to a single part of it, 'the love of art for art's sake';[27] here the 'artistic view of life' was supreme. But it has to be said that such intellectual movements were slow to influence the ordinary world in which Manchester School economics could be seen to be profitable and beneficial, making Britain the commercial master among nations. If the importance of the artist was increasingly recognised, it remained difficult to place him in any conventional scale of values. Those who tried – and this in itself indicated at least some reassessment of the arts – tended simply to stretch the existing system of values to accommodate artistic production. Thus Samuel Smiles in *Self-Help* (1859), for example, included a chapter on 'Workers in Art' where he sought to demonstrate, through the example of famous painters and composers, that success in artistic endeavours depended just as much upon perseverance and 'unremitting labour' as did achievement in more mundane fields. But in practice the arts had little in common with either the old status professions or the new principles of professionalism. A formal training and apprenticeship or distinctive technical expertise were not indispensable requirements for a good artist (though they could be for a mediocre one, and significantly the run-of-the-mill artist lay at the heart of the rising notion of arts careers). His success was valued less in proportion to the knowledge he could display of the tricks of his craft than by the manner in which he transcended technique and created something original. The status of the arts therefore depended greatly upon the individual artist and the impact wrought by his originality.[28] This made it extremely difficult to apply the same standards to the arts as to the rising new professions such as the law, doctoring, surveying, accountancy or the civil service. It ruled out the principle of competitive qualification and made a nonsense of any legally enforceable right to practise. The Fine Arts and music had their respective Academies by 1830,[29] and these institutions were acknowledged as professional bodies of national importance, but they were unable to prevent artists who did not have their seal of approval from earning a living or being successful or indeed from challenging their authority from time to time (as the Pre-Raphaelites did).

The census reports in this period throw a revealing light upon the difficulties of classifying the status of the arts. The census commissioners clearly were uncertain of the standing of artists in all fields, and it is significant that this group is frequently reclassified in different censuses. In 1841 it is ranked below the traditional professions under the general label of 'Other Educated Persons';[30] by 1861 it emerges as a sub-division of the professional classes for the first time,[31] but the classification seems largely optimistic in view of the diverse and ill-defined groupings which it covers (the claim to professional status of people such as acrobats, pugilists and organ-grinders would have been dismissed as ridiculous by contemporaries). By 1881 further reclassification is necessary under the more discriminating labels of 'Artists' on the one hand and 'Literary and Scientific Persons' on the other.[32] Even at this date, however, the census commissioners are at pains to point out the extremely heterogeneous nature of the artistic group, stressing that little real value can be placed upon their recorded numbers: 'who can say', they ask, 'how many of the 7,962 persons who were returned as Artist Painters were really such, and how many were house decorators, who had magnified their office?'[33] It was a question which applied with equal force to literary men, musicians and other artistic groups.

In the pursuit of professional status, the actor's difficulties were therefore part and parcel of the wider struggle experienced by the arts generally in Victorian England. But there is no doubt that of all the arts the stage was the least favoured and started its assault upon the bastions of professional power hampered with the most formidable handicaps. Its growth as a profession was thus especially slow and erratic. It was a peculiarity which did not go unnoticed by the actor's supporters as the other arts began to gain in respectability. Speaking at Charles Kean's farewell dinner in 1859, the Duke of Newcastle found it curious, 'in this land of literature and art, while poets, sculptors, and painters receive some portion of approbation . . . that that branch of art, the most difficult to arrive at excellence in, should be cast in the shade and treated with obloquy, or at any rate, with indifference'.[34]

The truth was that acting was like no other occupation. It was unique even among the arts. Social commentators who specialised in giving careers advice to an ambitious middle-class market invariably found themselves at a loss when they came to the stage. One concluded that, so far as acting was concerned, 'there is nothing to be said upon it, so entirely does it seem to be beyond the usual rules.'[35] For, exclusive as it was, bound by tradition, steeped in jargon, technical in its business, and requiring great practice, nevertheless acting could not be said to possess any of the normal attributes of an organised occupation. The actor could draw upon no specialised training schools nor even fall back upon an accepted body of theory to improve his practice. There was no recognised means of entry to the stage, there were no institutions to its name, and the actor received no public honours other than the fleeting approbation of an audience.

Training schools had been tried in the theatre's past but had been localised and short-lived. This was not surprising in view of the fact that lack of expertise and even ability had rarely prevented a man from becoming an actor. Above all, it was commonly accepted that an actor was born with his skills; it was left to practice itself to sort out the sheep from the goats. The fact that acting was traditionally a family business and many actors had been born into the theatre tended to support this view. Vocal tuition could be had from the elocution class, but its benefits were dubious and its teachers often charlatans; in any case, elocution was not the exclusive preserve of the actor, for in an age when rhetoric played an indispensable part in public life it was a skill which was in great demand from, among others, lawyers, MPs, lecturers and clergymen. Despite its traditions, the stage had no institutional symbol of its heritage in the form of a Royal Academy or a Royal College. The theatres themselves were its only institutions, and these, though acknowledging from time to time the superiority of certain among their number, remained independent of each other and often highly individualistic. As we shall see, attempts to establish national theatrical bodies or institutions were singularly unsuccessful before 1890, and this lack of coherence was to make the stage as great an oddity as a 'profession' as it had been as an 'occupation'.

By professional standards, one of the least favourable aspects of an acting career was its lack of exclusiveness. In the absence of training schools and any regular body of professional knowledge, anyone could become an actor. In the better theatre companies there were more rigorous standards of entry; under the patent system, for instance, the royal houses of Covent Garden and Drury Lane had traditionally taken new recruits from the 'nurseries' of the provincial Theatres Royal. But many managements, more anxious to make money than to set a high artistic standard, were less than scrupulous about whom they engaged.

Supporting casts in particular were given little attention, on the grounds that the 'star' players were the main attraction and therefore the only performers who really mattered. A stage aspirant could thus secure an engagement for any number of reasons other than ability: because he possessed a good set of 'props', because he knew the manager or had the right 'contacts', because he was related, because he had the right looks or bearing, or because he was simply the cheapest labour available (eager amateurs would get subordinate parts on a star billing by offering their services virtually free).[36] This system was taken to its logical extreme by some provincial companies which nightly hired the local inhabitants or the local soldiery for their supporting casts or as 'supers'; it was a practice which enabled a manager to keep a small permanent company and, accordingly, low overheads.

But such unrestricted entry to an occupation was wholly opposed to the professional idea. Here again the conditions of the contemporary stage put actors at a severe disadvantage to other artists. From a strictly professional standpoint, authorship, painting and music were also 'open' callings, but any new-comer to these branches of art required at least a demonstrable knowledge of his craft if he was to earn a living from it. They were, in short, artistic occupations which demanded 'palpable study', as the critic F.C. Burnand put it.[37] Not so the stage, at any rate under Victorian conditions. The fact that the theatre had traditionally hired its fair share of illiterates and casual labour gave the impression that acting, far from being an 'art', was one of the most accessible unskilled occupations. It was a common assumption in the first half of the nineteenth century that anyone with any ambition could succeed in a stage career. 'Almost every young person', observed G.H. Lewes, 'imagines he could act, if he tried'.[38] Acting was an easy option, being considered a job which offered 'a certain resource for all who are unfit for anything else, or too lazy to learn the rudiments of a laborious calling'.[39] It could also be a last resort, before unemployment, the workhouse, or enlistment in the services.[40] At this level, there was little to distinguish the actor's 'calling' from the mass of unskilled occupations open to the illiterate and able-bodied poor.

The stage had other disadvantages by comparison with the Fine Arts. Had the theatre presented only 'legitimate' drama, that is, Shakespeare and the classics, entry would necessarily have been more restrictive and acting considered more eligible as an art. This objective had been the original intention of the patent system, which sought to protect the 'legitimate' drama by legal discrimination against any other form. By the 1830s the system was well in decline, however. The patent theatres themselves were no longer presenting 'legitimate' fare alone, and actors moved easily from Shakespeare to pantomime; indeed, the most successful performers in the early Victorian theatre were not the great tragedians whose names have survived to posterity, but rather their lesser colleagues whose versatility in many different forms of theatre made them an invaluable commercial proposition. Even dancers were an integral part of the actor's presentation, fulfilling an indispensable role as sprites and demons in pantomimes and musical spectaculars. With the decline of classical ballet by 1850, many dancers graduated to the dramatic stage, to become among the lowest paid theatrical rank and file, aspiring no longer to the position of prima ballerina but to a speaking part and the status of an actress.[41]

The hazy distinctions between the performing arts – in itself a reflection of the lack of regulation – meant that regular play-actors were readily associated with the lowest branches of their occupation, where acting as such might be little more than agility. The association was not unwarranted in view of the fact that actors frequently shared the stage with acrobats, equestrians and clowns, and in many cases had probably graduated to a dramatic career from the crude beginnings of the circus-ring or the show-booth. Edmund Kean, for example, had started life as a tumbler, while the remarkable career of Fred Robson (1821-64), who was equally at home as a singer, comedian or tragedian, showed how easily actors could travel across theatrical boundaries. When the music-halls came on a large scale, it is quite clear that there was a vigorous trade in actors back and forth between the halls and the theatres.

Versatility, the hallmark of Victorian acting, reflected the enormous influence exercised by the stock system which, though limited, served to provide a genuine craft basis to the theatre. Outside the theatre, however, the stock apprenticeship was not regarded as a professional training of any worth. The poor standards of so many stock companies partly account for this reaction. But it was also the case that the actor's skills were misunderstood or underrated. Versatility went against the professional idea which implied specialisation – which bestowed in its turn exclusiveness. Thus the actor's association with all levels of theatrical entertainment was seen not as a training which would give him the widest possible experience, and therefore improve his technique, but as a social weakness which lowered the tone of his calling. The precariousness of an acting career did not help matters. Had players passed through their crude apprenticeship to remain dramatic performers for the rest of their careers, some merit might have accrued to the stock training. As it was, however, the system could not guarantee stability, and casualties of waning popularity could find themselves sinking back through the theatrical ranks to the poverty and obscurity of slumland 'penny gaffs' or provincial strolling bands.

These proletarian connotations of theatrical life were enhanced by one other peculiarity of the actor's occupation. Alone among the arts, the stage depended upon the collaboration of many variable human instruments: to produce a play required more than simply actors. The performer therefore rubbed shoulders as a matter of course with managers and dramatists on the one hand, and with stage-hands, scene-painters, wardrobe women and carpenters on the other. If some of these staff were educated and artistic people, it was obvious that the great majority were far from being anything of the kind. This situation was rare in the other arts, orchestral musicians apart.[42] The painter, author or musician/composer could usually undertake his work single-handedly, in isolation and in his own time. He was in short 'his own man', and provided he could make a reasonable living, this independence gave him a certain social standing. The actor, tied to a manager and merely one element in the production of his art, had no such independence; he suffered accordingly in the game of social honours.

The peculiar openness of acting as an occupation, with its mixture of literate and illiterate, gentleman and artisan, is reflected in the particular difficulties which the census commissioners experienced when they came to classify actors. The 1851 census is especially revealing. In 1841 actors had been grouped with other artists as 'educated persons', a testimony to the crudeness of the early censuses, but also perhaps to the more 'gentlemanly' image of actors bequeathed by the Georgian theatre. A decade later, however, actors had lost this position among the arts, – now grouped as a sub-division of the professions in Class IV – and had sunk to a place in Class XI alongside those 'engaged in the higher class of mechanical and chemical arts' and those who were 'intimately connected with artists and men of science'.[43] Even this rather broad classification did not wholly satisfy the census commissioners, however, for they admitted that 'the higher order of actors belongs naturally to Class IV'.[44] On the one hand, therefore, actors ranked on a level with the skilled artisan, for Class XI included engravers, civil engineers, draughtsmen, watchmakers, and surveyors, and on the other with men of education like historians, architects, natural philosophers and teachers of literature and science. By 1861 the position had again changed. Now the commissioners gave up any attempt to draw detailed distinctions between performers, instead bestowing a professional classification upon the whole field of amusement, including equestrians, conjurors, acrobats, ventriloquists and pugilists.[45] Such a broad grouping as this was based on little but convenience, but all these occupations shared one common distinction: their members were paid directly for their services. This was an important determinant of social standing in the Victorian era, and the conspicuously commercial character of theatrical undertakings again singled out the actor from among his fellow artists.

In an age when state-subsidised theatre was inconceivable, all Victorian theatres had to be run as private commercial enterprises. It took – and still takes (with the exception of film-making) – more customers, more money, and more artists to create and maintain a play than any other work of art. This alone doomed the patent system to failure from the outset. To work properly, the patent theatres needed a subsidy; as it was, they were left to compete with the more lucrative burlettas and extravaganzas of the 'minors', which forced up their expenses and lowered both prices and standards. In his early days the actor had enjoyed the sort of selective patronage from the nobility which other artists were granted. By the mid-eighteenth century the stage had, with few exceptions, to fall back upon the box-office. The impact upon the actor's position as an artist was decisive and exceptional. Alone among artists, the actor was now obliged to present his work to a mass audience, which paid for his services directly and in cash; his livelihood and his success or failure became dependent upon the immediate reactions of this audience. It was a change which instantly removed the theatre from the more rarified aura of aristocratic protection and courtly favour and placed it within reach of the counting-house. In short, the stage was henceforth a trade, providing a service to the public under the same conditions which prevailed in any other sector of private enterprise.

For the Victorians, important considerations of social standing followed upon this transformation. Although wealth was considered a necessary ingredient of professional status, too close a connection with money smelt of 'commerce', and was a positive disadvantage.[46] In general, Victorian actors were far from wealthy and their incomes were derived from direct cash payments, in most cases upon a weekly basis. Try as they might to talk in terms of 'salaries', most actors were basically wage-earners. Even in the professional world, some social commentators maintained, professions where fees passed directly from client to practitioner, such as medicine, were ranked beneath professions where they did not, such as the Bar.[47] It meant that even the highest paid actors, however distinguished, had to be content with something less than full professional acceptance; they were still, like their poorer colleagues, mere 'servants of the public', a term which, ironically, had always been used within the theatre with a certain mock self-deprecation, but which for Victorians had literal connotations of social inferiority. 'The Englishman', remarked a foreign visitor to early Victorian England, 'does not consider those whom he pays as his equals even though it be a famous artist to whom he must give £1,000 for his portrait.'[48]

In fact the painter was more fortunate than the actor. He might be paid a fee by his client, but his services produced a commodity which was solid and lasting, and in the course of time possibly a sound investment as well; more important, though, the painter's 'product' could be appreciated in the comparative calm of the home or the art gallery. The setting for the musician's or writer's work, in the concert-hall or library and home respectively, was equally respectable, isolated as it was from the artist's actual origins, however humble or squalid. The actor had no such advantage. He had to present his work where he practised, within the public setting of a theatre, and under the conditions which prevailed in the early and mid-Victorian years this involved the spectator in a greater or lesser degree of discomfort, both to his person and to his sensitivities.

Moreover, what was true of appreciation also extended to participation. All the arts with the exception of acting could be pursued as a livelihood within the genteel surroundings of the domestic hearth. This was certainly the case with authorship and painting, if less so with music and singing, but even the latter arts could find a paying market in the contemporary passion for concert parties and musical soirées. Significantly, these were fields of art which were foremost in accepting women workers when other male preserves remained resolutely shut to them. Acting, however, could not be carried out professionally on a domestic level (save as solo entertainment), and prejudice against the professional theatre made amateur acting taboo in middle-class households. Upper-class families were less scrupulous on this score and amateur dramatics were a favourite pastime in some aristocratic circles throughout the period,[49] but great care was taken to distinguish these efforts from professional undertakings (reviewers of public amateur productions frequently drew pointed and unflattering comparisons with the low standards of the professional stage) and to minimise their professional associations. Ironically, as professional standards rose and the stock system declined, the amateur theatre became one of the chief recruiting grounds for the Victorian stage, but by this date it was amateurism of a semi-professional nature, organised not from the home but on a coherent basis in education institutes and in theatres of its own.

What literature and the Fine Arts lacked in social respectability, they could, increasingly, redress with intellectual weight. The stage had no such intellectual credentials, certainly not before the 1870s. Indeed, it had so few that even its fellow arts adopted condescension and ridicule in their references. In Victorian fiction, chiefly before 1860, the uneducated actor, the pretentious dramatist and the grasping manager were stock fictional types, a satirical tradition which lingered on in theatrical novelettes to the end of the century and beyond.[50] It was a literary style born of the assumption, which was widespread among mid-century intellectuals, that the actor was inferior to the writer, just as the singer or musician was inferior to the composer. It was a distinction based upon the belief that the actor or musician was not of himself capable of artistic originality; he was simply the paid instrument of the artist's intentions. Unlike other arts, therefore, acting was ascribed no independent interpretative or educative merit.

It is significant that nearly all literary supporters of the Victorian theatre were champions of the drama rather than acting, of the dramatist rather than the actor. The critic G.H. Lewes observed:

> we exaggerate the talent of an actor because we judge only from the effect he produces, without enquiring too curiously into the means. But, while the painter has nothing but his canvas and the author has nothing but white paper and printer's ink with which to produce his effects, the actor has all other arts as handmaids . . . these raise him upon a pedestal; remove them, and what is he? He who can make a stage mob bend and sway with his eloquence, what could he do with a real mob, no poet by to prompt him? He who can charm us with the stateliest imagery of a noble mind, when robed in the sables of Hamlet, or in the toga of Coriolanus, what can he do in coat and trousers in the world's stage? . . . Reduce the actor to his intrinsic value, and then weigh him with the rivals whom he surpasses in reputation and in fortune.[51]

Lewes's statement overlooked the fact that most actors acquired neither reputation nor fortune and it underrated the more lasting achievement of the writer or painter; but it was a view which found echoes in the deep-seated conviction of many early and mid-Victorian men of letters that their art was superior to the actor's but received less recognition. In his *England and the English* (1833), the dramatist Bulwer Lytton considered that 'in the great game of honours', men of letters ranked beneath 'those who amuse us'.[52] This was not strictly true on a social level, even at this date, but Lytton's view was jaundiced by the current low status of the writer in the theatre where he was undoubtedly a victim of the whims of both actors and managers. Other contemporary literary figures expressed a similar condescension towards the stage. Forster, the biographer and friend of Dickens, deplored the author's proposed public readings in 1858 on the grounds that it was a 'substitution of *lower* for *higher* aims, a change to *commonplace* from more *elevated* pursuits, which had so much of the character of a public exhibition for money, as to raise, in the question of respect for his calling as a writer, a question also of respect for himself as a gentleman.'[53] It was a plea which fell on stony ground, but Dickens, a scrupulous cultivator of a respectable public image, took care to perform alongside like-minded intellectual colleagues when he embarked upon his career as an amateur actor.

The anti-intellectual bias of the Victorian stage was not hard to find. While the other arts were all closely associated (many leading artists in different fields were mutual friends – exemplified by the Pre-Raphaelite Brotherhood) and formed something of a mutual admiration society, with critiques and reviews of each other's work providing a staple ingredient of newspapers and journals, the theatre stood in a critical vacuum. Until the 1880s, with few exceptions, standards of dramatic criticism were uniformly poor, if not nonexistent; the London theatre possessed a handful of critics worth the name, but in the provinces there were few reviewers competent enough, as one contemporary put it, 'to judge either the merits of a play or the talents of the players'.[54] In the 1830s, 1840s, and 1850s critical discernment in the theatre was at a particularly low ebb; certainly there were no individual critics to shoulder the mantle bequeathed by earlier figures such as Hazlitt, Lamb and Leigh Hunt – and even their writings smacked more of literary criticism than popular newspaper reviewing (Hunt's praise of actors was rarely unbegrudging and Lamb had little confidence in the theatre's ability to tackle serious drama). Most reviewers of this period did no more than provide their readers with a brief résumé of the plot, adding a few vague and generalised comments as to whether the performance was 'well done' or not; according to the mid-Victorian critic Henry Morley, there was a tendency to overpraise,[55] which cannot have encouraged more discriminating standards. In general, the view persisted throughout the mid-Victorian period that dramatic criticism required no special qualifications, and as a result press coverage of the stage tended to be minimal, careless and ill-informed. It was the critic's misfortune, lamented the journalist and manager John Hollingshead in 1867, 'to work at a time when the drama is not much respected by intellectual people'. He added:

> Some editors who have very lofty notions of the place they occupy

> amongst the governing powers of the world, affect to speak of actors as 'those people', and pretend not to care much how their dramatic reporting is done as long as they are not troubled with complaints and corrections.[56]

The absence of critical standards within the wider press merely confirmed the lack of interest in such matters within the theatre itself. Consequently, before the 1870s the stage was exceptional among the arts in its failure to develop a regular press of its own.[57] The *Dramatic Register of 1853*, anticipating its own demise after three years, complained that people had no interest in 'the Drama' beyond amusement, and it reiterated the conclusion of *The Stage* in 1849 (which closed down after only fourteen numbers) that over the last thirty years some one hundred theatrical periodicals had failed.

If it occasionally flirted with the theatrical world, at bottom educated and intellectual society despised it as vulgar and frivolous. Prevailing dramatic taste was not such as to excite literary enthusiasm. Lamb's observation of 1812 that serious dramatic writing was unpalatable to contemporary audiences[58] held true by and large for the entire period 1830-90. From time to time individual theatres, such as Charles Kean's Princess's, Phelps's Sadler's Wells, and Irving's Lyceum, were hailed as 'the temple of the Drama', but the exalted title proclaimed the isolated position of these houses and concealed the fact that their productions of classical drama fell far short of the expectations of cultured spectators.[59] Victorian stagings of Shakespeare have had, both then and now, more than their fair share of attention, but the Bard was rarely successful box-office in the nineteenth century, and when he was, the attraction was less the play than the production or the players.

It was characteristic of the Victorian stage's flamboyant style that at the beginning and end of our period there was much-vaunted talk of a 'dramatic renaissance'. However, while the theatre certainly became more literate in the course of the century, it hardly became more literary, and such claims had a hollow ring when set against the overwhelming predominance of melodrama, farce, burletta, pantomime, light opera, musical extravaganza and sensational spectaculars. Bulwer Lytton's 'superior melodramas', on which the 'renaissance' of the 1830s and 1840s was largely based, were inseparable from the acclaimed performances of Macready. At the other end of the epoch, equally, the superior prestige of the Lyceum's productions, while setting exemplary standards of professionalism, was nevertheless based upon a wholly traditional artistic programme which owed its impact to inventive stagings and the charismatic talent of Irving and his nucleus of 'star' players; there was often more effect than sense in Irving's acclaimed productions, and intellectual critics, aware of a growing avant-garde movement on the dramatic horizon, did not hesitate to say so.[60] Passing judgement upon the late Victorian 'renaissance of the drama', a critic pronounced in 1888:

> It is much to be regretted that the English theatre of today fails to enlist the services of more Englishmen of letters of the first rank . . . The well-known aphorism of Ducrow, to 'cut the dialect and come to the 'osses', has obtained a well-nigh universal acceptation.[61]

The Macready and Irving eras in the theatre were fortunate in possessing these two outstanding actors: both were untypical members of their profession, being in particular of more intellectual temperaments than most actors and therefore on friendly terms with the literary giants of their day. Significantly, their heyday corresponded with the high points of dramatic criticism and witnessed at least some attempts to bridge the gap between theatre and literature;[62] in this light the optimism of the 'renaissance' years was perhaps excusable. By contrast, the intervening period possessed no great English classical actors (though some talented foreign ones), and the emphasis upon spectacle and sensation in the theatre became so overriding that even low and high comedy, exemplified by Planché's extravaganzas on the one hand and pieces such as 'Cool as a Cucumber' and 'Box and Cox' on the other, regularly played to miserable houses at the Lyceum in the 1850s.[63] The verdict of educated observers upon these years in the theatre was summed up by Henry Morley's cryptic comment that audiences wanted only pieces 'which are all leg and no brains'.[64] Tom Robertson's 'society dramas' went some way to redress the balance in favour of 'brains', but it is debatable whether the plays were a greater draw than the technical proficiency with which they were performed and the unprecedented elegance of the theatre in which they had their premières. In any case, by the end of the 1870s the Robertson craze had shot its bolt, and audiences were soon turning their attention markedly towards yet another form of 'illegitimate drama', musical comedy and 'the sacred lamp of burlesque'. To intellectuals and theorists of the 'new drama' alike this renewed burst of theatricalism on the stage appeared vulgar and frivolous, and its evident popularity only added fuel to their scorn and despair.[65]

The barrister and former actor Montague Williams reckoned that within the theatrical hierarchy of his day the playwright's standing was lower than the call-boy's.[66] Such hyperbole is characteristic of the theatrical memoir, but in this case it accurately conveys the prevailing 'showbusiness' spirit of the contemporary stage world, which, devoid of literary values and social purpose, intellectual and artistic society found unbearably philistine. The Victorian theatre was undeniably the actor's domain at a time when actors were not generally conspicuous for either their education or their professionalism. In his capacity as performer and manager, the actor both formulated artistic policy and carried it out. He cast the play, directed it and even rewrote it at will, with little or no reference to the author (Shakespeare included). It was a system of play production geared almost entirely to the actor's requirements, and in particular to the leading actor whose supremacy in the theatrical hierarchy ensured that even classical drama became little more than a suitable vehicle for projecting his own talent.

This bias extended to the whole style of performance. Before the growth of intimate theatres and genteel audiences, the player acted against a constant uproar, hushed only during the purpler passages. Such conditions discouraged high standards of ensemble playing and inspired audience favourites to the practice of up-staging their fellows[67] and engaging in a sort of personal contest with spectators designed to win applause from climactic passages throughout the play. For their part audiences commonly 'called for' their favourites to appear before the curtain not only at the end of the play, but during the course of a scene or at the conclusion of a well-rendered speech. It was a tradition of spectator participation which had much in common with contemporary election meetings; indeed, early Victorian actors were championed by rival groups of supporters as riotously as anything seen at the hustings.[68] It was further confirmation of the 'vulgar' character of the theatre, and educated audiences stayed away or went to the opera instead.

This essentially 'popular' theatre, which thrived upon the grandiloquent gesture, the primitive emotion and the inventive stage trick, did not lend itself to serious dramatic writing. A 'theatre of ideas' was impossible when a sustained high level of performance was thwarted by constant interruptions and distractions (Macready, for example, found the intermittent applause of audiences unnerving and exhausting, to the detriment of what he called 'the proper mental balance').[69] But even without this stormy relationship between actor and spectators, serious drama stood little chance of being satisfactorily presented when basic technical standards remained generally poor. Here again the theatre, until the 1870s, lacked an important ingredient of professional status recognised by contemporaries: it was simply 'unprofessional' in conducting its own business.

For, by modern standards, Victorian stage productions, with few exceptions, were badly prepared. This was not always the result of incompetence; lesser companies, especially outside London, were often short of money and commercial pressures induced an unfavourable reliance upon quantity rather than quality in their weekly output. Still, many managements approached their task with conspicuous carelessness, with the result that rehearsals were skimped, miscasting was widespread, scenery and costumes were inadequate and inaccurate, and originality was suppressed by an inflexible dependence upon traditional stage 'business'.[70] The 'star system' discouraged the notion of ensemble playing, and supporting casts accordingly received little or no direction beyond what was necessary to heighten the impact of the lead players, a practice which grew rather than lessened as the provincial circuits, threatened by rival attractions in the 1840s and 1850s, began importing performers of national status. It is of some significance that in the London theatre the Victorian managements which did not engage the most outstanding actors, and were therefore less troubled with the 'star system', were also those which set new standards of 'professionalism' and initiated fresh trends in dramatic taste; these developments single out the Olympic of Madame Vestris, Phelps's Sadler's Wells and the Bancrofts' Prince of Wales.

The poor level of competence in the early and mid-Victorian theatre provided satirists with a field day, and it is in the works of fictional writers that the full force of the intellectual's condescension towards the stage is best measured. In the 1830s and 1840s the tone of these novelists remains good-humoured and sardonic. If theatrical characters in the writings of Dickens, Thackeray and lesser novelists such as Albert Smith are invariably eccentric, pretentious and wholly ignorant of 'professional' standards, nevertheless they are depicted with a sympathy bordering upon affection.[71] But the theatre's ill-treatment of dramatists is, significantly, a favourite theme. It is central to Smith's *The Fortunes of the Scattergood Family* (1845) and to G.H. Lewes's *Ranthorpe* (1847). In the former, there is little sign that the playwright or the play is given much consideration in the theatre: three days 'was declared quite sufficient space of time to get up the most elaborate minor-theatre drama ever written, including scenes, dresses, incidental music, and lastly, being of least consequence, the words of the author'.[72]

By the end of the 1840s, however, the novelist's tone has hardened, being more directly censorious and overtly critical of theatrical standards. The actress heroine of Geraldine Jewsbury's *The Half-Sisters* (1848) is disconcerted to find that her fellow-players do not consider 'their profession as an art to be reverently cultivated – only a means of getting a livelihood.'[73] She is finally overwhelmed by the 'coarse, gaudy, glaring accessories' inseparable from theatrical undertakings, and abandons her stage career for the safety of a respectable marriage. Writers at this date are still capable of seeing the comic side of theatrical incompetence: 'The piece was played, the applause bestowed . . . nothing went amiss; if we except one obstinate quarter of a house with trellis-work and trees, which would stand obtrusively in the midst of a Louis quatorze drawing-room'.[74] But the ultimate message of such fiction has become perceptibly moral, pointing up the gulf between the illusory glamour of stage representation and the actual coarseness of the performers: 'And then they went on and played at heroes and queens in all the stately lordliness of virtue and refinement; and when they came off they drank porter and made unseemly jokes, and acted to the life their enduring roles of degradation and vulgarity'.[75]

This change of tone at the mid-century mark reflected the wider hardening of moral attitudes which accompanied the Evangelical revival as well as the conspicuous dearth of theatrical talent left by the passing of the Macready era. Gone forever was 'that essentially friendly relation which used to exist between the actor and his audience'.[76] In retrospect, as we shall see in a later chapter, this development was to prove the necessary stimulus to higher and more professional standards in the theatre.

If the novelist was often deliberately caricaturing the stage of his day, nevertheless sentiments such as those expressed above find clear echoes in the recorded experience of educated actors and actresses. For the intelligent Victorian performer with serious artistic ideals encountered just as much frustration and disillusionment as his fictional counterpart. And there emerged the curious spectacle of a handful of leading theatrical lights disowning the very occupation from which they had earned their fame and fortune. Macready, for example, personified that rarity of the Victorian stage, an intellectual actor. Schooled in a 'liberal' education and trained initially for the Bar, he brought with him into the theatre all the instincts of the cultured Victorian gentleman. He remained accordingly a reluctant participant throughout his career, appalled by the 'unprofessional' conduct of the majority of his colleagues. Their conversation he found 'generally of a puerile and uninteresting character',[77] and in 1836, on the occasion of a run at the

Theatre Royal, Bristol (where one of the company had been drunk on stage), he despairingly confided to his diary: 'I come from each night's performance wearied and incapacitated, compelled to be a party to the blunders, the ignorance, and wanton buffoonery, which . . . degrades the poor art I am labouring in.'[78] And on 3 June of the same year, in a speech to the Garrick Club, he alluded to 'the want of fidelity to the cause of the art in the actors themselves'.[79]

Fanny Kemble was another theatrical misfit; indeed, her almost academic disposition makes her one of the most unusual actresses of her day; her views took their cue from the 'liberal' intelligentsia with which she associated.[80] She was thus not only scornful of the stage which she knew, but, in response to the outlook particularly associated with educated women of her day, was positively hostile to what she saw as the ethical effects of an acting career. The constant theme of her letters and diaries is that acting is detrimental to nobility of character, inducing vanity, pretension and that ceaseless striving for effect which so characterised the style of the contemporary actor in performance.[81] It was a line of attack which formed the common basis to much typical theatrical fiction in the 1850s, bestowing as it did a moral complexion upon the everyday ineptness and vulgarity of contemporary theatrical standards.

The frustrations of a stage career were not confined to a handful of serious-minded celebrities only. Records of the experience of rank-and-file performers are scarce before the 1870s – no doubt largely because educated actors were comparatively few before this date – but there are indications from later sources that the middle-class newcomer to the stage went through an ordeal quite as traumatic as anything undergone by the genteel heroines of the theatrical novelette. The 1880s, the decade when theatrical memoirs first became fashionable and prolific, produced a number of rank-and-file acting reminiscences which suggest that the early generation of educated, middle-class recruits was bitterly disappointed by a theatrical career. Though these works usually reflect the experience of performers who failed to reach the top, a fact which jaundiced their views to some extent, nevertheless they share a common concern and disillusionment with the low 'professional' standards of the theatre as they knew it, which seems entirely genuine and wholly representative of educated reactions of the day. 'An intellectual life among intellectual people' was one young lady's ideal of an acting career. It was rudely shattered by her first engagement: 'In the company there is no one of whom I could make a companion, even for an afternoon . . . It is not their social standing I care about, but their utter absence of refinement or culture, their vulgarity, their way of looking at things'.[82] And she was quick to note one of the chief defects of the provincial stock system, the inadequacy of rehearsal: 'My real rehearsals are usually at night, when I am playing the part'.[83] The musical comedy star Louis Bradfield (1866-1919) had a similar shock when he made his début in the provinces in 1885: 'the profession I do like immensely', he told his brother Will in a letter, 'but the professionals I do not like. Really I never in all my life saw such dissipation. All last week & this there has been somebody drunk'.[84]

'Corin' (pseudonym of a failed actor named Lind), the author of a somewhat sensational account of stage life which claims that the 'black sheep' described represent 'at least sixty per cent of the players of this country', attributed the vulgarity of the actor's world to its social isolation:

> Many a good play has been shelved to gratify the whim of a successful actor, who has condemned the whole work because he couldn't find a part in it to please him. Actors and actresses are, as a rule, excessively narrow-minded; they live in a contracted sphere, called the theatrical world, and few ever step beyond its confines. They talk little else but shop from morning till night. In the green-room, when there are no new casts to discuss, they amuse themselves by criticising other artists behind their backs.[85]

Lack of education had always been a traditional criticism of actors. But it was a charge made with increasing force from the 1860s, partly because general standards of literacy were rising, inside the theatre as well as out, and partly because the spread of 'society' drama began imposing new demands upon the actor's skills, demands which he was ill-prepared to fulfill with traditional 'training'. This gave rise to barely concealed condescension on social grounds from some commentators,[86] but it was generally agreed that the English actor's ignorance of high society made him no match for the more refined playing exhibited by his French counterpart. Indeed, it is some measure of the low standing in which the English stage was held by contemporaries that the French theatre was regarded so highly (as were all foreign performers, notably on the operatic stage[87]). It was a striking preference for an age when, in most aspects of public life, the British were so intensely patriotic and xenophobic.

What early and mid-Victorian intellectuals and cultured people really demanded of the theatre was that it should be 'elevating', or as the poet

Charles Swain put it in 1852 in lines dedicated to the tragic actress Helen Faucit,

> Bid the Stage show, as of old,
> Something of that classic mind
> Which makes Heroes of mankind![88]

There seemed little evidence that this function of the drama was being fulfilled in 'the great mill of the "rank, popular" playhouse' where, according to Elizabeth Barrett, 'noble works' were simply 'ground to pieces between the teeth of vulgar actors and actresses'.[89]

It was all too clear that the modern playwright was little more than a hired hack who was obliged to work in surroundings unconducive to genuine creative work. By contrast, the novel, the essay, the painting or the poem demanded no such compromise with commercialism, with riotous audiences, with squalid neighbourhoods and unlettered actors. For the artist of sensitivity, in fact, the theatre was too closely associated with the mob culture which appeared to have grown up with industrial society to offer him any serious attraction. Carlyle's contempt for the 'masses' and their 'amenability to beer and balderdash' reminds us of the essentially anti-democratic tone of many of the Victorian champions of culture, and it seems clear that in this respect the theatre was regarded as symptomatic of that lowering of standards which the Romantics and their followers laid at the door of industrialism. Thus, although writers were not immune to the stage's glamour and tried their hand as dramatists from time to time, they were not prepared to maintain that day-to-day relationship with the theatrical world which was necessary for success and which had characterised the careers of the leading English dramatists of the past. 'I, for one,' expostulated Elizabeth Barrett, 'would as soon have "my soul among lions" '.[90] Consequently poets who wrote plays (and several tried, including Shelley, Browning and Tennyson) made little allowance for their practical staging. Indeed, the period produced that unique feature of English literary history, the play written to be read rather than acted. The glorification of Shakespeare's works aided this process, obscuring the fact that the Bard had been wholly a man of the theatre, both as an actor and manager. Thomas Hardy was not therefore the first to speculate, at the turn of the century, whether 'mental performances alone may not eventually be the fate of all drama other than that of contemporary or frivolous life'.[91] By this date, men of letters had rallied to the stage, inspired by the vision of a theatre at the centre of intellectual and artistic life (though, by continental standards, this burst of literary activity seems short-lived and half-hearted). Before 1890, however, there was no such 'renaissance', and even Arnold's famous appeal – 'the theatre is irresistible, organise the theatre'[92] – went largely unheeded by the literary and artistic world.

On several fronts, then, the theatre suffered grave disadvantages by comparison with the professional world, old and new, on the one hand, and with other spheres of artistic endeavour on the other. This is not without significance, for both the professional and the artist upheld a common sense of exclusiveness not shared by the actor. As we have seen, implicit in the notion of 'culture' was its opposition to the market and its reliance upon a special class of persons, 'intellectuals', a 'spiritual aristocracy', the 'cultivated few', all of them meeting in the creative artist. Ever since the Renaissance it had been possible to conceive of the artist as genius, as a personality who transcended tradition, theory and conventions, even the work itself. This went far beyond any concept of professionalism, but at its most basic level the idea of the artist as a person of special qualities and, implicitly, of some learning and cultivation, was not so far removed from the special 'learning' required for doctors and lawyers. In this respect, the existence of royal academies and artistic knighthoods before 1830 is extremely significant. Art, it seems, did possess 'status' in certain circumstances in a manner not so very different from the traditional professions. The connection is more difficult to make with the new Victorian professions, for the artist as part of an élite was directly opposed to the idea of arts careers. The latter, however, were vitally important in bringing the theatre back into the artistic fold, as will be shown in chapter 8. But as a strict professional the actor was always to have shortcomings, even as he became more educated and more competent. The very nature of the actor's art and the character of theatrical undertakings militated against any satisfactory form of professional security such as other professions knew. Thus while the theatrical establishment became increasingly aware of its professional defects, it had difficulty finding the same remedies as other occupations with professional aspirations. For this reason, several of the goals which actors, in emulation of other professions, sought to achieve in this period were not reached by 1890 or for many years afterwards. Nevertheless, as we shall see, the stage had by 1890 – characteristically, perhaps, for an occupation which dealt in illusion – successfully altered its public image to give the appearance that it was a responsible profession. This could not have been achieved without significant changes in attitude both inside the theatre and out. Foremost among these was the change in moral attitudes, which traditionally had cast the stage as the villain among the arts. It is to this area of anti-theatrical prejudice that we must now turn, for it exercised a disproportionate influence upon the actor's social reputation and persistently characterised English treatment of the theatre in this period, as in the past.

2 ACTORS AND ETHICS

The actor's struggle to achieve professional respectability in the Victorian age would have been less difficult had it merely been a case of raising standards of proficiency. A far more intangible obstacle to overcome, however, was the prevailing moral taboo which covered the acting world. To a greater or lesser extent, this taboo was directed at other fields of art as well, but nowhere was it more steadfastly maintained than on the subject of theatres and actors. Generations of Victorian parents acknowledged, both consciously and subconsciously, that it was the chief ground upon which they forbade their children either to attend theatres or go on stage. Indeed, this influence was so powerful that public respectability became in this period an obsessive preoccupation with actors to the detriment of artistic development. Equally, however, it is clear that if the stage was to acquire the respect accorded to other professions, it had first to resolve the ethical doubts raised by its opponents. For, whatever the reality and, indeed, however carefully they guarded their reputations, Victorian actors were left in no doubt that contemporaries judged them to be morally suspect. 'Contrasted with types of honourable men in business or the various professions', recalled the actor Robert Courtneidge, 'the dissolute actor stood out in bold relief as characteristic of his fellows'.[1]

Ironically, the charge of moral corruption laid against the stage was so universal and indiscriminate that it is not always easy to identify the grounds upon which it was made. As we have seen in chapter 1, the life-style of the artist was, at least up to 1860, out of tune with the austere temper of the age. This climate, again, affected the actor in particular, for it raised the fundamental question whether his occupation, that of entertaining others, could qualify as honest work. It could scarcely do so under the terms of those contemporary prophets of earnestness who preached the gospel of 'unremitting labour' and self-denial.[2] Nor was it acceptable to the commercial middle class of early and mid-Victorian England, for whom 'idleness' was an unforgivable economic sin, whether it was found among upper or lower classes. 'Persons whose profession it is to amuse others . . .', declares a businessman in Geraldine Jewsbury's *The Half-Sisters* (1848), 'cannot in the nature of things expect to take a very high position. Men cannot feel reverence or respect for those who aspire to amuse them.'[3] A similar point of view is experienced in the attitude of Bounderby and Gradgrind in Dickens's *Hard Times* (1854). Sleary's performing company is regarded as little more than the object of vulgar curiosity; for Bounderby, they are 'the kind of people who don't know the value of time', while Jupe's plight is merely confirmation for Gradgrind of the consequences attendant upon such a pursuit.[4]

These were not Dickens's feelings on the subject and the moral of *Hard Times*, if any, is expressed in Sleary's philosophy that 'people mutht be amuthed . . . they can't be alwayth a working nor yet they can't be alwayth a learning'.[5] But Dickens's advocacy of 'a little more play' in the bleak Victorian working day was not to receive a sympathetic hearing until the mid-sixties; and indeed, though he was for a relaxation of the rigid work ethic, it was not contemplated in a generous democratic spirit but as a rather paternalist scheme in which the theatre would canalise and tame the ignorance, violence and depravity of the urban working masses. This feeling Dickens shared with many writers and critics connected with the theatre, and it accounts for the unmistakable note of satisfaction in their admiration of the wonders Phelps had performed with popular audiences at Sadler's Wells: 'there sit our working classes in a happy crowd', observed the drama critic Henry Morley, 'as orderly and reverent as if they were at church'.[6] If this was the tone of progressive theatrical people, the social pressures which fell upon the conscientious early Victorian actor must have been considerable under average conditions. Despite his enormous success, Macready was one notable actor who experienced persistent qualms about the validity of his occupation. He confided to his diary in the 1840s: 'I employ at least nine hours a day in the theatre in labour, to say nothing of my writing, reading, and thinking on my business elsewhere. My money is not got without some equivalent of toil. Thank God, that I can work for it.'[7]

But the notion that acting was idleness does not itself explain the tone of horror and hysteria detectable in contemporary strictures against the stage. The severity with which the prevailing moral code was applied to theatrical entertainment must have stemmed from deeper suspicions about the very nature of the dramatic medium and the influence it could wield upon its audiences; there must have been immediate signs that this influence threatened to undermine the very basis of the nation's moral health.

It should be remembered that, before the 1870s, the Victorian theatre was essentially popular. The bulk of its audiences were drawn from the lower and working classes, the uneducated and the poor. It was this section of the community which was traditionally the furthest removed from all those influences and restraints that were held to constitute the acceptable limits of conventional behaviour. As a preponderant influence in their lives, greater than either school or religion, the theatre assumed an inordinate importance in the contemporary struggle to establish the moral order. Indeed, clergymen clearly regarded it as one of their most powerful rivals in the battle for hearts and minds. Its persistent popular appeal appeared to lend it a power which other mediums did not possess. This belief was implicit in the censorship exercised by the Lord Chamberlain's Office, a unique piece of government intervention which, significantly, continued to operate throughout the nineteenth century without serious challenge, even from the theatre itself. If this control was employed on political grounds from time to time, there is no doubt that its principal area of concern was morals. The need for dramatic censorship was justified on the grounds that acted entertainment drew a mass audience and its impact was more realistic and immediate than that of other mediums; an immoral play was thus held to be potentially more damaging than an immoral book.[8] What was peculiar about the influence of a theatrical performance, explained one late Victorian observer, was its reliance upon 'the contagious sympathy of a crowd'; this had the effect of multiplying the emotional reaction of the spectator to dangerous proportions.[9] Hence 'a mind ready to explode will only be made more inflammable by the shows of the stage'.[10] The prevailing view was that if censorship was to be abolished in the theatre, playhouses would soon become 'the scenes of riot and disturbance.'[11]

These assumptions were compounded by the fact that the most popular theatrical fare was 'amusing' and 'frivolous' rather than instructive or ennobling. Churchmen in particular were concerned about the low educational potential of the stage that this implied, fearing harmful consequences for an essentially illiterate audience. In some quarters these fears went yet deeper, with plays being stigmatised as directly subversive of religion, the rule of law and parental control.[12] In this respect, even Shakespeare did not escape criticism. The Dean of Carlisle, for instance, considered that the genius of the Bard should not obscure the fact that 'morality, modesty, and religion find occasion of censure' in his works.[13] The explanation was not hard to find, he added, since Shakespeare had been an actor as well as playwright and 'thus accustomed while yet a young man to much that was evil'.[14] The Reverend Thomas Best, a Sheffield clergyman who preached an annual sermon against the stage between 1817 and 1864, was even more specific. He was convinced that scenes of villainy enacted on the stage actually disposed the spectator to commit crimes, on the ground that his corrupted mind 'goes with him . . . and is ever ready, even against his will, to renew and increase the original mischief'.[15] Curiously, the presence of theatrical censorship did not diminish the persistence or force of these arguments. Indeed, in a perverse twist of logic, it was averred in some quarters that the very existence of the Lord Chamberlain served to prove the corrupting influence of acting, just as the existence of Bowdler confirmed the evils of Shakespeare.[16] This distortion of cause and effect was, however, central to the deep moral apprehensions expressed about the theatre's influence. To the average Victorian observer most theatres in towns and cities before 1870 gave the worst of appearances. They were dingy and dilapidated, residing in the neighbourhood of slums and notorious rookeries in the bigger cities; this applied even to the more important theatres, but it was especially the smaller houses and 'penny gaffs' which gave cause for concern. Many of these were unlicensed and appeared to attract a large criminal element. Worst of all, they appealed particularly to the children of the poor, and many observers, secular as well as religious, saw them as the breeding grounds of juvenile delinquency. James Grant considered the London 'gaffs' 'no better than so many nurseries for juvenile thieves',[17] while the Home Office inspector who visited Liverpool's borough gaol in the early 1840s submitted that 'Perhaps in no other town in the United Kingdom has the demoralising influence of low theatres and amusements upon children been so decidedly experienced as at Liverpool.'[18]

For early Victorians evidence such as this required no analysis. The knowledge that known delinquents frequented theatres was sufficient to prove that such establishments were at least in part the source of the evil. By extension of the argument, there was no limit to the corruptions which emanated from the stage, and accordingly every conceivable mischief was laid at the door of theatres and every sort of vice attributed to theatrical spectators. Thus a major argument of the anti-theatrical camp during the parliamentary debates of the 1830s over the proposed abolition of the patent system was that more licensed theatres risked increasing the scale of violence and immorality in the cities. In the Lords debate on Bulwer Lytton's bill in 1833, the Bishop of London drew a lamentable picture of one theatrical neighbourhood: 'the value of property had deteriorated, houses could not be let, offences multiplied, and the district alarmed by riots by night'.[19] Even fifty years later the same argument was being employed in some quarters. 'Find a theatre', declared the Reverend Augustus Lyne, 'and not many steps off you find the haunts of drunkenness, impurity, and unholiness'.[20]

The intensity of the theatrical taboo, especially in the early Victorian period, took root in the profound anxiety of contemporaries that the traditional moral order was the target of exceptional assaults. Nowhere was this concern felt more deeply than in the sphere of sexual morals. On all sides it appeared that the sexual impulse was undermining conventional restraints. French-imported fiction and drama, pointedly called 'the literature of prostitution', grew in popularity in the 1850s and 1860s, and was seen as encouraging adultery and divorce.[21] There was growing criticism of marriage and the traditional virtues of womanhood, as reflected in public discussion of women's 'rights', the philosophies of free love, and the prominence of actual cases which exemplified this trend (e.g. the liaisons of J.S. Mill and Harriet Taylor, of G.H. Lewes and George Eliot, and the households of John Chapman and Thornton Hunt[22]). Above all, there was a visible evidence that sexual promiscuity was widespread and on the increase, as recorded in surveys of prostitution, illegitimacy (the 1851 census reported 42,000 illegitimate children in England and Wales) and the social habits of the man-about-town.[23]

The theatre appeared to be at the centre of these subversive developments. Before the 1860s it had conspicuous links with prostitution, and much of its entertainment was considered over-sensual and obscene.[24] Soliciting in playhouses had been a long-standing practice in the theatre's history, but it particularly upset the Victorians. Even the best houses were not immune to it, as two Indian visitors to Covent Garden discovered in the late 1830s.[25] Indeed, the West End theatrical districts, especially in the vicinity of the Haymarket and Regent Street, were the most notorious haunts of London prostitutes in the early Victorian years. As the theatres in these neighbourhoods closed each night and poured their audiences on to the streets, soliciting became rife. Dr Acton proposed that the police should keep these areas free of prostitutes during the half-hour which followed the closure of the theatres, to allow the 'throngs of orderly company' to make their way home unmolested.[26]

Contemporaries felt no hesitation in blaming the stage as a major cause of prostitution. Ryan singled out the 'penny gaffs' for particular responsibility in this respect, and Logan considered the contribution of the theatres as second only to intemperance.[27] But the emotive tone of such accounts belies the supposedly scientific spirit in which they claimed to investigate the subject. The reluctance of theatre managements to take active steps against soliciting within their premises clearly owed something to the fact that the presence of prostitutes increased the sale of half-price tickets and was a draw for some section of their customers. But there is no evidence that the theatres exercised a greater attraction for prostitutes than other establishments, such as saloons, public houses, pleasure-gardens and supper rooms, which drew large numbers of people intent upon an evening's amusement and relaxation. Acton thought that the late-night refreshment houses and coffee shops of the Haymarket area were an important cause of soliciting in this theatrical neighbourhood, and his ultimate conclusion was that prostitution stemmed not from amusements but from deeper social ills such as inadequate wages and overcrowding.[28]

The average Victorian observer, however, entrusted his judgement to his moral sensitivities. These told him that a large share of acted entertainment was offensive to decency and conducive to a breakdown of public restraint in sexual matters. As we shall see in chapter 5, criticism here was particularly directed against the performances of actresses and dancers, whose scantily-clothed appearances in burletta, burlesque and extravaganza appeared to strike at the heart of conventional ideals of modesty and womanly reserve. But the subject-matter of drama also gave cause for grave concern. In this respect, audience and critics could be more prudish than the censor.[29] The realistic treatment of disease and drunkenness frequently met with a barrage of criticism, a reaction which helps to explain the scandalised reception which later greeted Ibsen from conventional theatre critics. The *Saturday Review*, passing judgement on the play *Retribution* in 1856, found it 'questionable in taste, inasmuch as it brings disease on the stage, and dramatises the progress and symptoms of pulmonary consumption.'[30] Some twenty years later Charles Reade's *Drink*, adapted from Zola's novel *L'Assommoir,* was the centre of similar furore. The *Theatre*'s critic recorded the disgust of many spectators at Charles Warner's realistic portrayal of the drunken Coupeau and wondered whether such a subject was artistically proper.[31] 'Zolaism' was seen as a particularly dangerous dramatic trend, and the influx of a number of dramatisations of this author's novels heightened the growing debate of the time whether, as Joseph Knight put it, 'the facts of real life carry with them an inherent right to reproduction in art.'[32] Few critics before 1890 felt that 'real life' had any such right on stage, certainly not where vice was depicted. Thus the heroic whore rarely failed to shock contemporaries and earn sharp rebuke. The first London performance of *La Traviata* in 1856 was heavily censured in the press,[33] and the dramatised version of Zola's *Nana*, appearing nearly thirty years later, was stigmatised as a 'bold, unvarnished tale of sin and infamy.'[34]

The rigidity of Victorian theatrical judgements cannot be fully explained without some reference to contemporary religious belief and the hostility of the churches to the whole concept of acted entertainment. Indeed, in an age when so much public discussion and private thinking was pietistic in tone, clerical influence over social attitudes towards the stage was bound to be considerable. Religious bodies of all denominations were without doubt the staunchest opponents of the theatre in this period. This opposition had a long history in the English theatre's development, reaching a high point during the Puritan Commonwealth when the theatres were forcibly closed down. In the nineteenth century clerical hostility took on a renewed lease of life under the stimulus of a widespread religious revival, which was especially influential in the years roughly between 1840 and 1880. The Anglican Church restored thousands of churches, built hundreds of others, and increased the numbers of its clergy from over 17,000 in 1851 to nearly 22,000 by 1881. Even more striking was the progress of Nonconformist belief, which had been growing rapidly since the turn of the century and was to prove in this period the most implacable opponent of the stage.[35] By the 1850s, when Evangelical influences were at their height and a tract such as 'The Sinner's Friend', first published in 1821 by the Methodist layman J.V. Hall, had sold more than 800,000 copies, it is no surprise to find that some observers attributed the widely acknowledged decline of the theatre to 'the growth of puritanical feeling'.[36]

By the nineteenth century clerical opposition to the stage had already secured a high degree of official acceptance. Theatres were compelled by law to close their doors on all religious feast days, notably Ash Wednesday and throughout Passion Week. Closure could also be commanded for royal or state funerals, as in 1843 to mark the death of the Duke of Sussex.[37] Despite constant protests from theatre managements, and some active attempts to reduce this restriction upon theatrical life (a parliamentary resolution condemning restriction in Lent was successfully passed in March 1839, but subsequently quashed by the Home Office), this arrangement survived intact almost until the end of this period. Religious subjects were indiscriminately banned by the Lord Chamberlain's Office, and all references, scriptural or religious, were invariably excised or changed, however mild. H.A. Jones's *Saints and Sinners*, which appeared at the Vaudeville in 1884, was probably the first play of the century to take religion and the clergy as its subject-matter, but it did not escape without heavy censure in the press.[38]

Anti-theatrical pronouncements were by the nineteenth century so traditional a part of clerical polemics that churchmen who made them took it for granted that their congregations understood the taboo. Indeed, among the Dissenters opposition to the theatre in any form was raised almost to the status of an article of faith, constantly repeated in sermons and their own press in the most emotive rhetorical style. References to the stage were invariably sweeping and indiscriminate: thus it was an 'unmixed evil' or 'a school of immorality and vice'. Again, the frequent republication of anti-theatrical tracts throughout the period suggests that the clerical stance was essentially backward-looking rather than a response to contemporary conditions. Individual churchmen might point to the irreligious nature of the drama or the various aspects of immorality and criminality associated with the stage, but in the last resort their hostility was traditional and fundamental, based upon time-honoured scriptural claims which had been employed against the theatre throughout its history. By this token, acting and play-going were, like cards and dancing, strictly irreconcilable with Christian teaching. The man who could combine theatre-going with an honourable life, declared the Congregationalist minister John Campbell in his discourses on *General Amusements* (1839), was the exception; the truly devout Christian 'will not and cannot be an attendant on such exhibitions'.[39]

The chief object of the clerical campaign against the theatre was to deter people from going to the play. This drive acquired added urgency in the Victorian period in the light of the rapid growth of a huge industrial proletariat which had little or no contact with Christian teaching but was subject to all the attractions of an expanding entertainment industry. This uneducated and irreligious mass was the object of grave concern to Victorian churchmen, and the bitterness of the theatrical debate owed a great deal to clerical fears that the stage's influence rivalled and even outmatched religion's in the battle for hearts and minds. The sense of competition between the actor and the clergyman was therefore very real – and not without justification, for, as we shall see, the growing respectability of theatrical amusements was to signal the decline of the traditional moral order and the old vision of Christianity upon which it was based.

However, this vision died hard in the nineteenth century. The argument that acting was incompatible with sincerity and earnestness of purpose continued to exert a strong influence right up to the late

Victorian years. It was fundamental to the Quaker viewpoint, which held that 'the pretence of actors to pleasure or pain' was 'contrary to Christian simplicity'.[40] But it was implicit in the doctrines of other denominations, accounting for the common clerical assumption that actors risked damaging their personal character by regularly assuming fictitious ones.[41] Even the acting of virtuous sentiments, by this token, was 'more likely than anything else to prevent their becoming part of an individual's real character.'[42] The *Saturday Review* asserted that this view explained the inferiority of the stage to music, for 'the immense body of respectable persons who cannot afford to stand ill with the clergy' took care to eschew theatricals for fear that they would lead to 'levity, and flightiness, and eccentricity, and talkativeness, and extravagance . . . and an incapacity to settle down with sobriety in the good old family house'.[43]

Before the 1870s the moral and religious ban on the theatre had a profound impact. It meant for people of all classes that play-going, associating with actors, and above all taking to the stage as a career, were actions hedged with guilt and deep heart-searching. Thomas Wright and Christopher Thomson, literate artisans of the mid-century years, both recalled the enormous pressures exerted upon the working man to shun theatrical amusements and devote his spare time instead to self-education.[44] For those who came from a strict religious background, the decision to attend a theatre could be agonising. The early Victorian playwright and critic John Westland Marston (1819-90), the son of a former Dissenting minister, vividly recalled how he extorted 'reluctant permission' from his conscience to visit his first play at the age of fifteen:

> I can still recall the boyish sophistry which prompted me to choose Sadler's Wells Theatre for my first visit. It was a small theatre and it was situated in a suburb – facts which, as they were likely to diminish my pleasure, seemed in the same degree to make my transgression a slight one. I might have gone to Covent Garden, I reasoned, and, at that renowned theatre, have revelled in the best acting of the day, whereas I self-denyingly contented myself with Sadler's Wells.[45]

Marston added that in fact the content of contemporary melodrama was so heavily moralistic, that had his father seen such a play, he would 'heartily have applauded it and recanted at once his unqualified enmity to the theatre'.[46]

Many who desired dramatic amusement, however, never entered

a theatre itself. Instead they absolved their consciences by attending semi-theatrical entertainment in non-theatrical surroundings. The largest and most famous of these venues was the Crystal Palace at Sydenham, which was accessible by rail from 1856 and offered a whole range of leisure facilities from concerts to pleasure gardens. 'There are many worthy people', complained the comedian J.L. Toole, 'who try and persuade themselves that it is not in the least wrong to see *The Steeple-Chase* at the Crystal Palace, but who would feel quite wicked if they came to see the same play at a London theatre'.[47] Exhibition rooms and lecture halls also provided a suitable substitute for the theatre. One of the most popular in London was the Gallery of Illustration in Regent Street, where Thomas German Reed and his wife Priscilla Horton were celebrated for their 'drawing room' entertainments and brief musical comedies in the years 1857 to 1873. Here the evening's performance was acted in 'parts' rather than 'acts' so as not to offend the theatrical abstainers in the audience; the whole impression was that 'you were attending a meeting and nothing in any way resembling a theatre.'[48] Yet another favourite resort of the non-theatrical public was the Egyptian Hall, where Albert Smith's one-man shows drew large audiences between 1852 and 1859. Smith's performances were really dramatised lectures, and consisted of readings, dialogues and anecdotes, enlivened with painted scenic backdrops and lantern slides. 'Penny readings' for the working man and the overtly histrionic public readings of his own works by Dickens in the years 1858-70 no doubt exercised a similar appeal to theatrical abstainers. Included in this category should also be amateur theatricals, whether in public halls or in middle-class and upper-class homes, for these clearly owed much of their appeal, certainly before the 1870s, to their non-association with the professional stage. Few participants in these proceedings would have dreamt of acting in a real theatre. Indeed, this went for some professional performers in the semi-theatrical line as well. The comedian George Grossmith expressed reluctance to accept an invitation to appear in the new Gilbert and Sullivan piece of 1877 on the grounds that were he to fail in the venture, the Young Men's Christian Association would never re-engage his services: 'because I have appeared on the stage . . . my reputation as comic singer to religious communities will be lost for ever.'[49]

In fact, the ways in which Victorians indulged in theatricals without sinning were infinitely variable. Many seem so tortuous and perverse that they would be laughable were it not evident that for contemporaries they were the expression of very genuine social pressures. Henry

Mayhew, for instance, found an exhibitor of mechanical figures who told him that his shows were particularly popular in Hoxton and Brixton, 'where they are severe for religion', because his figures were 'moral, and their children can see them without sinning'.[50] In middle-class and upper-class households, it was often the practice to take children to the opera only when there was no accompanying ballet. Many people, from all classes, who were regular theatre-goers would nevertheless have been horrified at the prospect of sons and daughters associating with actors or going on stage. Again, some entertainment was more acceptable than others. Westland Marston's father was a zealous champion of Greek tragedy and encouraged his son to recite and perform parts in Greek, but it did not alter his antipathy for the professional theatre. It was certainly no accident that the breakthrough in undergraduate theatre at Oxford, which had hitherto been conducted on a private, college basis, was achieved with a classical Greek drama, namely Frank Benson's production of the *Agamemnon* in 1880.[51]

Clergymen had to take particular care how they associated with the drama. Not all by any means shunned the theatre entirely. Some even wrote for it, such as the Rev. Henry Hart Milman, Dean of St Paul's, or the Rev. James White, who wrote several tragedies for Phelps at Sadler's Wells; and some were related to it by marriage or friendship: the actress Adelaide Neilson, who made her London début in 1865, married the son of a Northamptonshire clergyman, while celebrated performers such as Macready and Helen Faucit could number several clerics among their friends. But no churchman could afford to be too public in his association with the stage. One admirer of Helen Faucit, the Rev. John Moultrie of Rugby, permitted the actress to recite to his family, but would not attend her theatrical performances.[52] Charles Kingsley abandoned the idea of converting his *Saint's Tragedy* into a play on the advice of friends who thought it would injure his standing as a clergyman,[53] and Lewis Carroll, a great lover of theatricals, was sorely disconcerted by the Church's ban when he came to contemplate taking holy orders.[54] However, some clergymen evidently could not resist going to the play, though where this might be tolerated and permissible in the laxer atmosphere of London, it could rarely be done with impunity in the country. The Rev. Kilvert made several visits to the Christmas pantomimes in the West End in the early 1870s, but in his Radnorshire parish he took care to confine his theatrical interest to 'penny readings'.[55]

Actors themselves found it difficult to ignore the prevailing climate of opinion. Many had taken to a stage career only at the cost of alienating friends and family, and the common practice of adopting a stage name was very largely a response to the outraged sensibilities of parents and relatives. Henry Irving, who made his début in 1856, did so in the knowledge that it meant severing all ties with his mother, who was particularly religious; his family subsequently refused to attend his wedding. The profession did not hesitate to repudiate the more illogical religious persecution of the stage – the closure of the theatres on Ash Wednesday was considered especially unreasonable[56] – but such persistent pressures inevitably put actors on the defensive. This had serious repercussions for the drama as it induced an artistic conservatism in actors and managers which grew rather than diminished over the period as a whole, encouraged by the threat to the regular theatre from the 1850s of the more 'vulgar' music-halls. It meant increasingly that actors were loath to take up plays or parts which might prove damaging to their moral reputation. It resulted in the ironic situation in which performers paid closer scrutiny to the content of the drama than the censor himself on occasions. The actor-manager Wilson Barrett warned H.A. Jones to beware of 'the tendency to coarseness' in his new play *A Clerical Error* in 1879: 'How could a lady finish an act with such a speech as Muriel's "Neither in earth nor in heaven nor in hell"? They would howl at it in London.'[57] The actor's obsessive fear of being 'hissed' by audiences condemned the late Victorian 'new drama' to slow acceptance. Hardy's dramatised version of *Tess* never materialised owing to the timidity of London managers; one prominent actor told the author that he could never play such a dubious role as Angel Clare as his public reputation stood to lose were he to act ' anything but a heroic character without spot'.[58]

Thus the archetypal actor of the 1860s, 1870s and 1880s eschewed brilliance and inspiration in favour of 'safe', dignified playing which would not offend. During these years Charles Lamb's explanation of the 1820s of why the comedy of manners was extinct on the contemporary stage – 'We screw everything up to [the moral test] ' – applied with equal force to the theatre of the Kendals and the Bancrofts. 'We have no such middle emotions as dramatic interests left', lamented Lamb.[59] The source of the Victorian actor's growing respectability was also the root of his artistic weakness. In striving to combat the moral bogey which burdened his professional image, there was to be no room for the actor to develop an independent artistic ethic. Indeed, the preoccupation with respectability ensured that habits of moral self-criticism died hard within the theatre. The mid-Victorian and late

Victorian theatrical establishment repeatedly issued statements which betrayed their anxiety to expunge the 'bohemian' image of the early nineteenth-century actor. The growing popularity after 1850 of music-hall and burlesque was seen not only as a commercial threat by 'legitimate' theatre managements, but also as a moral threat which, once it had taken hold of the regular stage, risked a lowering of standards and the consequent loss of professional dignity and refinement. Thus attention was quickly drawn to theatrical practices, such as the admission of gentlemen behind the scenes, which had once been customary but now were liable to give the stage a bad name.[60] The *Theatre*, under the editorship of the influential critic Clement Scott in the years 1877-90, was particularly prominent in educating actors in their social responsibilities. It was a curse in disguise, the magazine argued, for actors to believe that they alone among artists were exempt from the normal demands of conventional behaviour. If the profession was to be responsible, its members had to be responsible. Henceforth, it declared the most responsible man was the best actor, the 'truest, purest, worthiest woman will be the best actress'.[61] The general willingness of the profession to accept these socio-moral strictures ultimately transformed it, with far-reaching consequences for the future of English drama.

But the eventual acceptance of the theatre's respectability owed as much to a changing climate of opinion among society at large as to the efforts of actors themselves. By the 1860s the earnest drive towards individual self-improvement was being overtaken by the notion of recreation for its own sake.[62] A cheap, mass-circulation press was rapidly coming into being; by the 1880s more than half the books being taken out of public libraries were of fiction. The expansion of cheap rail facilities was now enabling people to move more freely from country to town, from the provinces to the capital, from the interior to the seaside. Leisure entertainment sprouted in the wake of this bustling, pleasure-seeking public, provided not least by the theatres which from the mid-sixties experienced a new building boom.[63] Old attitudes of mind naturally came under unprecedented assault. Traditional religious beliefs faltered in their headlong rush of certainty. In his authoritative study of the Victorian Church, Owen Chadwick sees the growth of 'unbelief' as the hallmark of the years 1860-1900:

> The difference after 1860, and especially after 1870, is . . . marked. Churchmen worried more. Their presentation of Christianity was affected by the existence of intelligent agnostics. They began to treat agnostics with more respect in general society. And the whole

> question of belief or unbelief was so common in public discussion as to force the minds of the educated young – more and more numerous after 1870 – to find a faith for themselves, and no longer to inherit serenely the faith of their parents. In the vigorous spring of Victorian energy all religions flourished as never before.[64]

Tennyson, England's leading poet by 1850 and a man who was always close to the spiritual centre of his age, had already, in *In Memoriam*, dealt seriously with the problems raised by the transition in contemporary values, and had finally acknowledged the devoutly inclined agnosticism of his own feelings.[65] Macaulay poured scorn on puritanism in his history and Lecky flaunted the spirit of Rationalism. George Eliot's novels showed for the first time that morality and religion were not necessarily inseparable, and the natural basis of ethics – morality without religion – became the central issue of the philosophic schools. R.H. Hutton spoke of 'a scepticism which is of God's making', and F.D. Maurice asserted that in certain circumstances denial of God was more religious than an easy faith, and that God could be found not only in the Bible but in all secular experience, even when it was irreligious.[66] Swinburne threw all convention to the wind and preached that Christianity positively fettered the development of personality, while atheism was a liberating force. Bradlaugh's final election to the Commons in 1886 (he was the first atheist to be admitted) showed that secularism had entered public life with a vengeance.

Atheism, even agnosticism, was to remain a minority view in public life, but it was true that the religious revival was in any case progressively outstripped by the explosive growth of the population. Even the religious census of 1851 had demonstrated that less than half the nation attended Sunday service, while millions received no religious instruction whatsoever. By 1881 the situation was unquestionably worse, with whole sections of the community beyond the reach of Christian influences of any kind (the rise of the Salvation Army in the 1880s suggests that in the cities official denominational groups were making little headway). Against this background a relaxation of the traditional religious ban on theatres could not be prevented indefinitely. Many clerical strictures against the stage began to seem inflexible and unreasonable. An article in the influential *Saturday Review* for 1857 deplored the 'intolerable arrogance' of religious hostility to the drama, and warned that actors and actresses could hardly be expected to become paragons of virtue while they were so ceaselessly castigated with immorality.[67] It began to be recognised that theatrical people suffered more than most from the effects of public exposure; in reality, they were no worse than their peers in other walks of life.[68] Indeed, actors had a very strong sense of duty and generosity, it was maintained as theatrical apologists went on to the attack; the founding of their own Royal Dramatic College (in 1858) was proof enough that actors were 'not a mere careless race to whom things held sacred by the better order of citizens are altogether indifferent'.[69] Thus when the Liverpool magistrates reaffirmed the closure of the theatres throughout Passion Week in 1882, there was such a storm of protest that the order was rescinded. Thereafter Good Friday and Ash Wednesday remained the only days of prohibition, and even the latter was finally abolished by the Lord Chamberlain in 1886.[70]

Faced with such inroads on their authority, the churches had to face the prospect of coming to some kind of terms with the popularity of play-going and the rising status of actors. The dissenting groups continued to fight a rearguard action against the stage – the *Methodist Times* was still talking in 1891 of the 'ugly facts' and 'terrible evils' associated with the theatre – but the Anglican Church began to show an unmistakable shift in its thinking. There were after all growing murmurs within its own ranks. After successful attempts to disestablish the Welsh and Scottish Churches, the Anglican was hard put to ward off similar attacks as well as a movement to abolish the authority of the Athanasian creed in 1871-73. Advanced churchmen were openly advising doubting clergymen to remain within the church.[71] In this sort of climate it was not surprising perhaps that younger churchmen were, by the end of the 1870s, seeking to promote reconciliation with the theatre – with a view to reforming it from within. 'The fact is', a speaker told the London Theatrical Reform Association in 1879, 'that if the theatre is to be reformed, the reform must in great measure be brought about by the influence of the Church'.[72] In the same year, accordingly, the Church and Stage Guild was formed to forge closer links between the two. In marked contrast to earlier denunciations from the pulpit, some preachers now began to stress the positive human values of the drama, insisting even that the power of the medium, which had hitherto been the excuse for hostility, was in fact the very reason why its moral impact could be so exemplary.[73] It began to be recognised, as a result of the churches' decline in influence, that the theatre had enormous potential as a moral and educational instrument. But for the 'lessons of refinement' inculcated by the 'Stage-ministry', the Sunday Lecture Society was informed in 1880, working people risked 'a state of mental and moral perdition'.[74] Such sentiments reflected the change in attitudes which was breaking down the old vision of Christianity, a vision that had been the driving-force behind anti-theatrical prejudice for so long. As one writer put it in the mid-eighties: 'the broad ground of the essential sinfulness of all pleasure is already abandoned.'[75]

The theatrical establishment, sensing it had the initiative, was not inclined to accept these unprecedented religious overtures with much grace. The tone of bodies such as the Church and Stage Guild was altogether too condescending, and the *Theatre* alternated between forthright indignation and good-humoured sarcasm in labelling it 'impertinent' and a 'fanciful incongruity' designed to introduce curates to actresses and get actors to church once a year.[76] Instances of overt religious prejudice against the stage were now quickly seized on by the theatrical press. The purchase of the Grecian theatre in 1881 by the Salvation Army, after General Booth had called it a 'den of iniquity', created a considerable furore in theatrical circles, and the stage papers, confident of the support of the indignant East Enders, kept up a sniping campaign against the Army for some years. When the Grecian reverted to a music-hall in 1884, the *Entr'acte* expressed its hope that the new proprietors would 'brush away the cobwebs of puritanical bigotry that have been accumulating there'.[77] It was a sign of the times, too, that Irving, the acknowledged leader of his profession from the early 1870s, could publicly declare that, moral or immoral, 'the theatre must always be before all things a place of amusement'; and he chided the churches for their narrow-mindedness in condemning the portrayal of evil on stage: only by showing evil against good could the theatre hope to educate audiences.[78]

But actors could not afford to be too complacent. If prejudice against the stage was on the wane, it had certainly not disappeared. There was in particular still a reluctance to attend theatres as such on the part of many provincial people. 'The Puritan dread of the theatre is still widely spread and astonishingly operative', asserted the critic and dramatist H.A. Jones in the *New Review* for July 1891, 'It is true that great crowds of raw theatre-goers half emancipated from this prejudice are coming to our plays, but they are coming timidly and fearfully, with cramped and narrow minds and quite infantile judgements in dramatic matters'.[79] Gordon Craig witnessed something of this lack of sophistication among audiences when he toured the north of England in 1894 with a Shakespearian repertoire: '*Romeo and Juliet* was always a nerve-wracker for the audience . . . They didn't like the love-making . . . when Romeo, after getting the poison from the apothecary, tells the sky that he is going back and will lie with Juliet tonight – meaning, naturally, that he will kill himself with her, they whooped as though we had somehow slipped through the fine net of the censor of plays'.[80] In fact, it remained difficult to evade the censor. Rigorous standards were still exacted by the Lord Chamberlain on all religious or scriptural references (the lines 'I have gone to heaven' and 'Now say your prayers' had to be omitted from a play in 1877, the phrase 'My God' from another in 1885), while instances of impropriety, such as the Can Can, were invariably prohibited.[81]

So long as these conditions prevailed – and the tremendous influence of a critic like Clement Scott demonstrated that most play-goers accepted such conditions – theatrical apologists had to be careful they were not directly offending the acknowledged moral order. Irving's drama addresses of the 1870s and 1880s, which sought to educate the public to a more mature appreciation of the stage and the drama, represent a cautious revaluation of ethical and cultural standards. If the church was often misguided about the stage, in Irving's opinion, he was at pains to remind his clerical listeners that 'the main stream of dramatic sentiment . . . is pure, kindly, righteous, and, in a sense, religious'.[82] He was at one with conventional opinion, both religious and secular, that the Restoration theatre had produced among the most corrupt plays in the history of the drama:[83] 'in acting nature must dominate art', Irving told his audience, but art must interpret nature 'with grace, with dignity, and with temperance'.[84] By the 1890s his tone was more solemn than ever – possibly because of renewed clerical attacks on the theatre,[85] possibly in reaction to the current fierce debate over Ibsenism. 'Not for a moment is the position to be accepted that the theatre is merely a place of amusement', Irving declared, going back some way down the path he had come up a few years earlier; for all concerned the stage was a 'serious employment, to be undertaken gravely, and of necessity to be adhered to rigidly'.[86] Here was the voice of the responsible and sober professional man, anxious to clothe his art in the suit of conventional respectability. It was testimony to the raised status of a stage career and the shift in moral attitudes over this period, but, ironically, it also reflected the profound influence of the Victorian moral ethic, characterised by John Morley as a rigidity which reduced men's judgements of others to 'thin, narrow, and superficial pronouncements upon the letter of their morality, or the precise conformity of their opinions to accepted standards of truth, religious or other'.[87] By purging the theatre of those elements which did not conform to 'accepted standards of truth', the theatrical establishment succeeded in transforming its public image and ending its social isolation; the price of this achievement, however, was the profession's failure to develop any artistic ethic which might have brought England into line with the revolutionary changes taking place in the contemporary European theatre.

3 THE ACTOR'S COMMUNITY

Almost by definition actors are a marginal social group. Subject to unusual hours of work and liable to exceptional insecurity of employment and prospects, they necessarily operate in relative isolation, observing their own exclusive rituals, jargon and even humour. This is as true of the modern theatrical profession as it ever was. But the modern actor enjoys professional and other benefits which have effectively minimised the social isolation implicit in the nature of his work. The Victorian actor had no such advantages. Indeed, as we have seen in preceding chapters, he was the object of extraordinary moral and religious disapproval and ranked as the intellectual inferior of other artists. These factors reinforced a more fundamental feature of his situation. His working conditions were characterised by extreme irregularity. The demands of a theatrical system in which 'touring' and 'strolling' were endemic and where there was a rapid turnover of plays, on a daily basis in many companies, left the actor little leisure time outside rehearsal and travelling.[1] His occupation, far more so than today, was a total way of life, excluding him from the mainstream of social contact within the community and imposing a life-style which did not easily accommodate conventional social virtues such as a stable family circle and a permanent home. Pointedly labelled 'the actor class' by contemporaries, Victorian stage folk were therefore a community apart within society. Significantly, the social composition of the theatrical profession and its traditional isolation only began to change and break up as new patterns of work emerged in the 1870s and 1880s.

The isolation of this theatrical community is amply borne out by the lives of contemporary actors and actresses. Unfortunately, modern knowledge of individual players is limited. Hitherto, the bulk of research has been conducted into only a handful of Victorian celebrities. Many performers who were equally popular and successful and, in many ways, more representative of their profession, have since been forgotten by posterity. This includes figures like William Farren (the younger), T.P. Cooke, Gustavus Vaughan Brooke, Charles Coghlan, Henry Marston, Henry Neville, Henry Leigh Murray, Hermann Vezin, J.R. Anderson, Edward Wright, Thomas Thorne, E.S. Willard, John Clayton, and Charles Warner, and, among actresses, Ellen Tree, Mrs Warner, Eleanor Bufton, Mrs Alfred Mellon, Henrietta Hodson, Amy Sedgwick, Mrs

John Wood, Carlotta and Rose Leclercq, Rose Coghlan, Ada Cavendish and Fanny Addison; and this is not to mention the numerous family partnerships which were such a characteristic feature of the Victorian stage, notably the Keeleys, the Vandenhoffs, the Honners, the Comptons, the Chippendales, the Calverts, the Wigans, the Batemans, the Sakers and the Kendals. We still know very little about these performers, especially their early careers and private life. It is not surprising, therefore, that humbler, more obscure actors are rarely known even by name. Perhaps the greatest omission lies at the local, regional level, where the position of the actor often differed considerably from the general norm.

I have tried in a small way to correct the balance by unearthing details of the off-stage lives of approximately two hundred Victorian actors and actresses who made their débuts before 1890. By no means all yield a complete history and large gaps remain, but in general I have focused upon specific areas such as their social backgrounds, their schooling, their route to a stage career, their marriages, their children, and, in the case of London players, their residential habits (see Appendix I). Clearly, such a group remains still a tiny percentage of the total profession. Implicit in their selection (with some exceptions) is the fact that they were sufficiently talented to have left some detailed trace of their existence. As players who made a lifetime's career of the stage they do not represent those whose association with the theatre was brief and transitory, and as celebrities they had little in common with colleagues whose lot was endemic unemployment, poverty and obscurity. Above all, as the theatrical élite of their day, this group was in a position to cultivate the sort of contact with the outside world which was generally denied to humbler members of the profession.

Yet, if this group provides an incomplete picture of the profession as a whole, it nevertheless is sufficiently representative to shed a meaningful light upon developments within the theatrical world during this period. After all, these celebrities were themselves once unknown and shared the lot of all newcomers to the Victorian stage. Many had experienced long years in the wilderness before making their mark. Moreover, they too were subject to the prevailing climate of disapproval and condescension which tainted the generality of actors. As the leaders of their profession, they served as the theatrical and social models which the rank and file traditionally followed, so that what was true of their hopes and ambitions was reflected in the lives of lesser theatrical fry.

Social and occupational pressures combined to produce an extremely strong sense of solidarity among the Victorian acting community. This was based first and foremost upon close family ties. In no other occupation was intermarriage quite so common. Indeed, the actor Fred Belton (1815-89) noted that an actor marrying outside the theatre was so much the exception that its occurrence might never be known by his colleagues.[2] It resulted in veritable theatrical dynasties and gave prominence to those husband-and-wife partnerships which so characterised the Victorian stage. (See Appendix II.) Many actors and actresses were thus related and it was not unusual for a performer to spend his whole career alongside brothers and sisters, uncles and aunts, and cousins, nephews and nieces. Brought up in this environment it was difficult for the children of actors not to follow in their parents' footsteps, despite the invariable parental discouragement. Edmund Kean hoped his son Charles would take up a post in the East India Company. Macready took great pains to prevent his children from attending his performances, but both his son and two daughters eventually adopted stage careers. Henry Neville, the son of the manager of the Queen's Theatre, Manchester, forfeited his father's assistance by entering the theatre instead of the army. Irving intended that his two sons become respectively a lawyer and a diplomat; both took to the stage. Even the largest families might all be engaged in the profession.[3] Henry Compton and Ben Terry had nine children on the stage, Charles Calvert had eight, while H.L. Bateman, Dion Boucicault and Robert Brough had four apiece. This remarkable continuity seems to have been maintained even at the end of the period among families which were comparative newcomers to the theatre and had closer associations with 'civilian' life. 'Nine out of every ten actors today', claimed one observer in the 1890s, 'were "intended" for the bar, the ministry, politics, journalism, art or any other calling under the sun but acting'.[4]

Solid practical considerations, beyond sheer propinquity, encouraged this pronounced 'togetherness' in the theatre. The difficult hours actors worked would have placed excessive strain upon any 'mixed' marriage. Moreover, for an actress in particular, marriage within the profession enabled her to continue her career; in most cases where she married an 'outsider' this would not have been possible owing to the demands of convention (significantly, actresses who married into civilian life above the working-class level normally retired from the stage). This careerism was equally pronounced among the lower-paid theatrical performers, for whom marriage and work were plainly traditional, not least for pressing financial reasons. Albert Smith observed that dancers, whose career prospects were probably among the poorest in the regular theatre, nevertheless opted for working married life and commonly found husbands among other theatrical employees such as stage-hands, carpenters and scene-painters. It was a course, Smith noted, strongly guided by their parents, being designed to assist both a girl's career and the family income.[5]

But it is also clear that professional couples had more opportunity to work together on the Victorian stage than is the case today. While the stock system predominated, acting was essentially a family affair. The family unit was central to almost all companies large and small; indeed, among the smallest troupes a single family might comprise, like the Crummleses, the whole company (hence the tradition among itinerants of naming the company after the family management, such as 'Richardson's', or 'Old Wild's'.) In the more permanent companies, staff and performers alike formed an extended family group, with the management (often a family itself) attending to the needs of their employees rather as they would to those of their own children. The Keans earned a particularly good reputation as employers in this tradition at the Princess's Theatre, London, being especially solicitous of performers who were 'off' through illness.[6] Provincial managements, such as the Fishers of Norwich or the Murrays of Edinburgh[7] also excelled in this respect. Indeed, in some localities, as J.K. Jerome noted, the same acting families became associated over several generations with a single circuit, and in the course of time achieved a respectability within the local community which transcended the general stigma attaching to their occupation.[8]

In fact, it is no mere accident that the traditional types of Victorian melodrama corresponded to the age range of the extended family unit: it was a natural dramatic form for companies which comprised children, parents and grandparents. The fault of this system lay in its potential for serious miscasting, for the localised character of theatre companies encouraged an extremely slow turnover of personnel, and performers were reluctant to relinquish parts and habits which had once reaped them success. But against this was the fact that the stock repertoire enabled theatrical families to stick together, often for a lifetime. Thus, despite the popular view of theatrical marriages, divorce was comparatively rare among Victorian stage folk (though, as one would expect, more common in the case of 'mixed' marriages). Many actors and actresses who married more than once, and several could account for three partners over a lifetime, simply outlived their spouses. There were of course spectacular exceptions in the case of Edmund Kean, Mrs Alfred Bunn (who eloped with Colonel Berkeley), Ben Webster (whose liaison with Madame Celeste was well known), Dion Boucicault (who rejected his second wife Agnes Robertson), and Ellen Terry and Henry Irving. But such cases acquired a notoriety out of all proportion to their significance in a profession which attracted more than its fair share of publicity and gossip. It would also be fair to say that acting is an occupation which naturally draws to it a certain proportion of individuals whose temperaments are unsuited to the restraints of conventional domestic bliss. In general, the Victorian profession could be proud of its close family ties, and as it grew increasingly sensitive to its image, it lost no time in proclaiming the virtue of those long-standing theatrical partnerships, such as the Kendals, the Wigans and the Bancrofts, which had stood the test of time and respectability. Such couples formed the backbone of the companies which they governed, genuinely fulfilling an indispensable moral as well as professional role among their colleagues.

In the last resort, the family bias of the Victorian theatre was crucial to the smooth running of the system. It provided a ready-made organisational framework for an occupation which still operated largely on a local basis without any formal controlling bodies or professional structure. Such aspects of theatrical life as recruitment and promotion were necessarily conducted from a personal and subjective standpoint. Few actor's careers were not founded upon the personal intervention of friends and relatives, and accordingly nepotism was rife. Sons and daughters of famous parents readily traded on their names to secure engagements, sometimes irrespective of talent, and as Macready discovered at the start of his career, 'the "manager's son" was of no little consideration in the limits of a green-room circle'.[9] The system bred obvious dangers, often hindering genuine talent and encouraging artistic conservatism. It encouraged restrictive practices in some companies, while in others single families acquired undue prominence. For example, when Ben Webster took over the Haymarket in 1837, he brought in his half-sister Clara and his brother John as dancers, his nephew was engaged as the 'infant prodigy', his son John was recruited as an actor, and another brother Frederick became his stage-manager. This was no more than many other managements were doing, however, and it was often unavoidable in such a socially isolated occupation. Ironically, it was a characteristic that gave the stage a striking affinity with the traditional status professions which it sought so strenuously to emulate, for these too recruited upon a largely personal basis, though from among the contemporary ruling social class; as people from professional backgrounds began to infiltrate the theatre in the last decades of the century, it was a feature which no doubt lent the stage additional appeal as a career. 'I cannot too strongly accentuate', asserted the actor

George Arliss (1868-1946; début 1887), 'the value of making and keeping friends in the theatrical business. Whatever success I have attained has been largely due to the efforts of my friends.'[10]

Despite its shortcomings, the system did not generally operate badly. Real talent did manage to emerge by its own efforts, for in the last resort it was the public not actors themselves who made or marred theatrical reputations. In fact, it is striking how few children of the famous achieved any great reputation. Moreover, if actors born into the theatre had an initial advantage over other recruits, it does not seem that this discrimination lasted beyond the first engagement. A 'civilian' aspirant could always join an amateur group in any case, and here he was immediately in a position to cultivate acquaintance with professional actors who maintained close links with the amateur theatre. The amateur John Taylor (b. 1811) used his contacts with the managers of the Bolton theatre to secure his professional début there in 1831,[11] and Henry Irving acquired his first engagement (at the Sunderland theatre in 1856) on the strength of a recommendation from William Hoskins, a Sadler's Wells actor from whom he had received private tutelage.[12]

The family structure of the theatre provided one other valuable asset. It gave Victorian actors a comforting sense of unity in the face of their uncertain status and suspect reputation. Isolated from society at large, the self-contained nature of the theatrical community enabled a genuine family life to survive on a day-to-day basis and was a source of solace and companionship in what was, for the majority, often a lonely, unsettled and harsh occupation. If the popular notion of actors was of individuals consumed by vanity and professional jealousies, as a body they could often act with great generosity. 'Benefits' to meet with cases of individual distress or misfortune were always well supported, and the London theatres were quick to come to the assistance of fellow companies left high and dry by catastrophic fires, an all too frequent occurrence.[13] 'Benefits' such as these were an example of mutual self-help among actors at its best. Without such expressions of communal solidarity, an actor's life at the lowest levels would have been less tolerable than it evidently was. Mayhew found that the 'strollers' he encountered – most of them living scarcely above subsistence level – were rarely unhappy; one confessed that his was 'a very jolly life' and he wouldn't leave it for any other.[14] Few performers were not reluctant to retire from the stage, and many continued to work into old age. This should arouse no surprise. Acting was, until the later years of this period, a life apart, and to leave it was to accept virtual exile from family and friends.

Patterns of kinship suggest that the Victorian actor lived and worked as a member of a remarkably self-contained social grouping. Residential patterns point to a similar conclusion. In London, where there was the greatest concentration of actors and actresses in the country,[15] the profession tended to congregate in distinct districts. In the eighteenth century, most actors had lived in the vicinity of their theatres. Thus the neighbourhood of Drury Lane and Covent Garden was a popular area in Garrick's day, especially Southampton Street, off the Strand, or the Soho area (Edmund Kean had started his London career in Frith Street). Alternatively, actors performing at the minor theatres south of the river, at Astley's, the Coburg or the Surrey, congregated in Lambeth and Southwark: Stangate Street and Hercules Road, and the neighbourhood of the Obelisk in Southwark, were the traditional resort of great concentrations of actors. In the first half of the nineteenth century, these areas retained their popularity, especially Southwark and Lambeth, but even before the end of the eighteenth century there were signs that two areas outside the immediate centre of the city were becoming fashionable for actors, at any rate for the more prosperous ones. These areas were Bloomsbury and Brompton. Latterly, such famous eighteenth-century players as Blanchard, Munden, Maria Foote and Sarah Siddons had moved to Bloomsbury, while Brompton had attracted Liston, Reeve, Fred Yates and Mrs Davenport. In our own period these two districts acquired even greater popularity. Bloomsbury, which was near enough to the central theatres to be convenient and yet architecturally spacious enough to accommodate pretensions of grandeur and gentility, was already by 1850 well established as the traditional haunt of writers, academics, lawyers, Jews and artists of all kinds. Macaulay had lived at 50 Great Ormond Street in the 1820s, Millais resided at 87 Gower Street, while Burne-Jones and Rossetti were to be found at Red Lion Square. As central London became increasingly less residential, the move to Bloomsbury was a natural one for the wealthier actor. He was often a close neighbour of professional colleagues. Charles Kean and T.P. Cooke lived in Woburn Square, for example, and James Wallack and John Cooper lived at close quarters to each other in Alfred Place.

But proximity was much more pronounced in Brompton, which soon became known as 'passionate Brompton' on account of the large community of actors who resided there throughout the period.[16] Unlike Bloomsbury, Brompton had all the advantages of *rus in urbe*, being only partially built up by 1845; even by 1870 the adjacent districts,

West Brompton, Fulham and Earls Court, were hardly built up at all. The largest concentration of actors in Brompton seems to have been at Brompton Square, which must have had few residents who did not belong to the theatre in some capacity. Liston, Farren, the Keeleys, the Wigans, J.B. Buckstone, and James Vining all lived at some time in their careers in this small square. Then there was Ben Webster in the Old Brompton Road, Walter Lacy in Montpelier Square, 'O.' Smith in North Terrace, and Marie Litton in Alfred Place, South Kensington. Helen Faucit and her husband lived at Onslow Square, and Charles Mathews and Madame Vestris were at Brompton Park before moving to North End, Fulham, where Mrs Nisbet had resided before them. With the popularity of Brompton, other adjacent neighbourhoods found favour in the eyes of actors who could afford them. Thus Edward Wright could be found in Chelsea, Edward Sothern in Kensington, Henry Compton in Knightsbridge and Albert Smith in Fulham, in the same road as the Mathews. Apart from these prominent actors, there were clearly many others living in the Brompton area whose details are no longer known; this 'host of smaller theatrical fry', as one observer called them, could be seen making their way from Brompton in late afternoon into the city centre, 'to the intense delight of the omnibus drivers, who . . . invariably called the attention of the occupants of the box-seat to their presence'.[17]

For actors at the 'minors' south of the river, the vicinity of these theatres continued to be a popular place of abode, despite a profound deterioration in the social tone of the district, mainly due to the expansion of Waterloo Station and its railway complex in the 1840s. Many poorer actors and actresses who worked at the central London theatres also favoured this area as it combined cheapness with convenience, being but a short walk away from their place of work over Waterloo Bridge. In general, the rank and file of the profession were compelled to move further and further from their theatres in the course of the period, owing to rising prices of accommodation and a decrease in its availability in the centre. These actors could not afford fashionable Brompton or Chelsea, and so the trend was to suburbs like Brixton and Clapham in the south, or to Whitechapel, Bethnal Green and Shoreditch in the east, where terraced housing was the standard rather than the detached villa. Owing to the lack of evidence available for rank-and-file members of the profession, there is no means of telling whether large concentrations of stage folk built up in these areas. As the theatre became less isolated in the last decades of the century, the tendency would be for these 'ghettoes' to break up, but what little pointers there are seem to suggest that actors were still congregating in the same areas even in the 1880s. We know, for example, that quite a number of actors at this date resided in the vicinity of Kennington Oval and Kennington Park, that others were gathered at the north end of Clapham Road, and still more in a concentration in streets off Brixton Road.[18]

The pattern of accommodation for the 1870s and 1880s among well-to-do actors and actresses shows that, while the move to the suburbs was continuing, the emphasis was still strikingly in favour of 'togetherness'; incidentally, owing to the *Dramatic and Musical Directory*, started in 1883, we are able to ascertain for the first time the addresses of more than simply a handful of the leading performers of the day. The traditional haunts have held their ground well, Bloomsbury in particular, an indication perhaps of a return to city-centre living at this date as the fashion for flats in town, especially for the single man or woman, grew apace. Bloomsbury was crowded with theatrical people in the 1880s, notably Johnston Forbes-Robertson, the Kendals, Ada Cavendish, Alma Talmayne, Harry Paulton, Charles Vandenhoff, Lawrence Corrie, Florence Worth, H.J. Byron, Eleanor Bufton, Robert Brough, and the Chippendales, with a handful of newcomers to the profession like George Arliss, Robert Courtneidge, and Ben Webster, the grandson of the great Ben Webster of the Haymarket.

In Brompton there was still a large theatrical community at this date, but the trend seems to have been increasingly in the direction of adjacent suburbs. Chelsea, for instance, now had a sizeable collection of stage folk, most of them living in adjacent streets off the upper end of the King's Road (e.g. Ellen Terry, Carlotta Leclercq, Mrs Alfred Mellon, and Charles Charrington and his wife Janet Achurch). Belgravia and Pimlico also showed signs of theatrical occupation (Charles Mathews, for example, was residing at 59 Belgrave Road in 1875, having moved from Fulham, while Beerbohm Tree was a close neighbour in Wilton Street in the 1880s).

If there is any new pattern after 1860, it is towards settlement in suburbs still further from the centre of London, and in two main areas in particular: Hammersmith in the west and Regent's Park in the north. In Hammersmith there were an impressive number of actors and actresses living in the same streets, notably in Bridge View (just above Hammersmith Bridge) and in Hammersmith Grove. As we do not always know the house number, it is quite possible that some of these actors were sharing lodgings, since it was a standard arrangement for theatrical folk. Nevertheless, the proportional density of such residents in so small an area remains striking. The same is true of Regent's Park and St John's Wood. In the former district, the eastern side of the Park was heavily occupied by actors and actresses by 1890, especially along the length of Albany Street and, at its northern end, in Gloucester Avenue and Gloucester Crescent. On the western side of the Park the streets off Park Road and Wellington Road were the haven of some of the top actors and actresses of the day, in accordance with the residential fashionableness of the St John's Wood district at this time. Charles Fechter had had a house in Marlborough Place in 1864, and by the end of our period his cue had been followed up by such leading figures as Wilson Barrett, actor-manager of the Princess's 1881-6 (North Bank), Thomas Thorne, the comedian, the actress Florence St John (Wellington Road), E.S. Willard, Barrett's leading man (Blenheim Road), the actor Charles Warner (Marlborough Hill), and the actor-manager Charles Wyndham (Finchley Road).

Of course, many leading players were not necessarily trying to 'stick together', but were simply following general residential trends. One of these, encouraged by improved transport facilities, was the retreat of the well-to-do to the outlying suburbs as the inner areas were gradually built up (reflecting the tremendous prestige of the detached villa in its own grounds). Thus by the 1880s actors and their families could be found as far from the West End as Barnes (Edward Terry, Louis Calvert), Chiswick (Edward Compton, Charles Coghlan), Surbiton (John Sleeper Clarke), Dulwich (George Conquest), and New Cross (Fred Leslie). A simultaneous trend was the reverse of this process, a movement back to the centre of town as apartments became fashionable. For busy people like actor-managers, who did not have the time to get in and out from distant suburbs during the week, this fashion was clearly convenient. Thus we find the Bancrofts in Cavendish Square in the mid-eighties (though they had never moved far from the centre, having previously been at Berkeley Square), Henry Irving in rooms at Grafton Street (having separated from his wife finally in 1872: they had been living in West Brompton), Boucicault in the Strand, and Fred Leslie and Nellie Farren, favourites in burlesque at the Gaiety after 1885, both in flats in Tavistock Chambers, New Oxford Street.

The pattern displayed by the residential movements of actors is revealing. It suggests first of all that over the period as a whole there was a physical form to the community spirit of the profession, with enclaves of actors taking root in specific areas of London. This is particularly striking in districts such as Brompton where the detached or semi-detached villa was the standard form of residence, since choice of accommodation often depended upon availability rather than preference. It is probably less surprising in an area such as Bloomsbury where lodgings were the norm and landlords were no doubt accustomed to dealing with artists of all kinds. In both cases, however, accommodation was probably bought and sold or rented almost exclusively among actors and their friends, and so particular areas became the traditional resort of the profession. Families preferred to remain within easy reach of each other, even when the children had grown up and were themselves earning: the Terrys, for instance, lived for years in Stanhope Street, Regent's Park, but then moved to West Brompton in 1882 to be nearer their daughters Ellen (then living in Longridge Road, off the Warwick Road), Kate (in Campden Hill after her marriage in 1867, thence to the Cromwell Road in the 1890s) and Florence (in Campden House Road, Kensington).[19] Finally, London is a good illustration of the residential 'community' of Victorian actors. In provincial towns, where anti-theatrical feelings could often be more deep-seated than in the cities, it is less surprising to find actors isolated in separate theatrical 'digs' and apartments. London, altogether larger and more unpredictable in its social attitudes, nevertheless bred similar habits of 'togetherness' in the theatrical community. It is a striking testimony to the actor's extreme social isolation for most of this period. 'It was not a distaste for society which kept the actors of bygone days at home', explained the actress Mrs Calvert in later years. 'It was because they were seldom asked to go anywhere else'.[20]

The abnormal hours which actors had to work necessarily threw them together in their spare time. This was an added reason for living in the same neighbourhoods, and clearly a good deal of 'calling' on one another went on. It also encouraged the rise of theatrical clubs and other professional haunts. The Garrick Club, founded in 1831, is probably the most well-known actors' club, but in fact by the 1850s it was fast losing its exclusively theatrical identity and becoming the resort of many influential figures from the literary, military and professional establishment. From the actor's point of view a major defect of the Garrick was its lack of late-night facilities, and the Fielding Club was established in 1852 to provide dining facilities after the evening's performance. By this date less exclusive establishments were already the habitual resort of literary and theatrical folk, notably the 'supper-and-song' houses of the West End such as Evans's, Willis's Rooms and the Cider Cellars. By the 1860s actors and writers were frequently resorting to the same clubs. There was the Urban, founded in 1858 and itself the offspring of the famous 'Friday Knights': the chief event in its calendar was the annual Shakespeare Commemoration Dinner. The Arundel was another popular resort of actors, critics and their friends (the *Daily Telegraph* critic, E.L. Blanchard, frequently mentions visits to the Arundel with theatrical companions in his diaries). The Arundel had grown out of the Savage Club (whose members were known as 'Savages') and was alleged to include every 'journalist, artist, or actor of repute' among its number.[21] The strong theatrical links of the club were reflected in its charity performances, notably at the Lyceum in aid of the Lancashire Cotton Famine Fund (1862), an occasion attended by the Royal Family.

But clubs were naturally exclusive and tended to be the resort of the more prosperous theatrical performers and their friends. Rank and file actors had to make do with less exalted haunts such as bars and taverns. Naturally, public houses in the vicinity of theatres had invariable theatrical associations, not least because they provided the most convenient venue for conducting theatrical business. The Wrekin tavern, in Broad Court, Drury Lane, was a distinguished example, being a long-standing haunt of actors, authors and artists and it was run by ex-actors in the early Victorian period;[22] it provided premises for lesser theatrical clubs such as the Mulberry Club, whose members had to produce papers on Shakespeare, and later the Rationals, to which most of the performers in the Drury Lane and Covent Garden companies belonged. In the 1870s and 1880s, theatrical clubs were becoming indistinguishable from other professional men's clubs, but the theatrical 'pub' remained conspicuous. In London at this date the Bodega Bar in Bedford Street was a particular resort of stage people, 'a cheese surrounded by actors', as one regular recalled it, on account of the free cheese and biscuits available to its customers.[23] Another establishment popular with actors was the Marble Hall in the Strand run by the Gatti brothers, who were associated with music-halls in the 1860s and 1870s. This was the place 'Where the actor out of collar, Often raises half a dollar', a descriptive ditty which aptly summarises the impecunious character of the acting fraternity, many of whom no doubt resorted to the Marble Hall for the easy credit and cheap meals which it afforded.[24]

Early and mid-Victorian impressions of actors as a 'race apart' must have been strongly reinforced by the histrionic individuals who so often represented the contemporary theatrical profession. These were performers whose off-stage manner and appearance was overtly theatrical, giving them an air of flamboyance or eccentricity which was quite at odds with the prevailing sobriety and gentility of contemporary manners.

Colourful dress was an important ingredient in the make-up of the 'theatrical' type. The younger Charles Mathews (1803-78), for instance, took considerable pains to cultivate the manner and appearance of the town 'swell', with

> his tall hat curled up at the brim; his high black stock with his collar turned down over it; his frock-coat fitting like his skin; his wristbands turned over his cuffs, and his pink coral links; his primrose kids, his gaiter-bottomed trousers, and his patent-leather boots![25]

The actor's notorious extravagance, matched only perhaps by that of his wife, the actress Madame Vestris,[26] no doubt further enhanced the romantic image which his dress gave out. Another actor, H.J. Montague (1843?-78), had a reputation for sporting heavily braided black jackets, gay waistcoats, and an unorthodox line in trousers.[27] The two foremost actors of the post-1850 generation, Squire Bancroft and Henry Irving, both excelled in the art of dramatic self-advertisement off-stage. The writer Henry Labouchere likened Irving to Disraeli on this score, both men adopting poses calculated to draw attention to themselves.[28] Irving's particular affectation was for long hair, a 'wide-awake' and a fur-collared overcoat (this latter fast becoming the hallmark of the successful impresario long before Diaghalev made it fashionable). Bancroft could likewise be easily singled out by his swagger-stick, top-hat and eyeglass.

The fashion for flamboyance set by such leaders of the profession as Irving and Bancroft encouraged theatrical affectations among lesser fry – though in many cases eccentricity probably owed as much to the pinch of circumstance as to romantic design. George Arliss found that some late Victorian actors deliberately sported long hair to denote their serious artistic intentions;[29] and the character-actor G.B. Soane-Roby (début 1873) observed that even down-at-heel stock actors in the provinces were inclined to assume 'a swaggering air of importance' in front of other people.[30]

Itinerant stock actors often presented the most bizarre appearance off-stage as they tended to favour attire which indiscriminately mixed second-hand bargains with stage costume. Here is Robert Courtneidge's description of some of his colleagues in a stock company of the late 1870s:

> There was a lavish display of coloured handkerchiefs, serving as they did the double purpose of always being useful for old men and character parts . . . With each man there were isolated specimens of coats, trousers, flowered waistcoats and overcoats fondly cherished,

> breathing of large possessions, if one made allowance for the fit, the occasional stain, or the change in fashion . . . As with the men, some portions of the women's dresses – a leghorn hat with ostrich feathers – a stylish cloak – a velvet skirt – would not have been out of place in Bond Street, but they mingled indifferently with cheap materials and stage jewellery.[31]

Charles Brookfield's companions in Charles Kelly's touring company of 1879-80 were equally flamboyant:

> Our 'leading man' wore a frock-coat and a battered straw-hat, and travelled in carpet-slippers; another of my new friends donned a green embroidered smoking-cap with a yellow tassel, another a purple knitted Tam-o'-Shanter . . . At stations where we stopped . . . they became appallingly playful; they would hurl old jests at the porters, and pelt passing passengers with a shower of stale pleasantries from last year's Nuneaton pantomime.[32]

High spirits was another 'actorish' quality acknowledged by the Victorians. Several players (most notably J.L. Toole and E.A. Sothern) were inveterate practical jokers off-stage, a propensity which the playwright J.R. Planché considered to spring from the sheer *gaité de coeur* so common among actors.[33] Indeed, so carefree were stage folk supposed to be that their genuine misfortunes often went uncredited, according to *Punch.*[34] Robert Courtneidge thought the actor was 'addicted to conviviality', and he admitted that nearly half of his own weekly wages as a stock actor in the 1870s and 1880s went on drink.[35]

Was drinking a serious professional problem? It is hard to tell, particularly as it was the sort of charge which aroused all the defences of the profession and its friends. Some celebrities were undoubtedly prone to over-indulgence, and a few were probably virtual alcoholics: Edmund Kean, George Cooke, Gustavus Vaughan Brooke, and Fred Robson were just a few whose reputations foundered on the 'demon drink'. In some quarters of the profession, moreover, it was evidently a theatrical maxim that a tipple beforehand enhanced an actor's performance.[36] But drinking, though heavy among actors, was not a distinctively theatrical problem. In general, it was probably to be found in the theatre where it was found elsewhere, namely among the poorest and the most unfortunate – and it seems to have been more common in the early Victorian theatre than later.[37] As time went on, it was a habit which the theatrical establishment increasingly frowned upon, and as a result it became less conspicuously associated with actors. 'Corin' went to great pains to point out that 'the actresses I have met who were slaves to drink seldom kept an engagement for long in a decent theatre';[38] and Courtneidge solemnly declared that, 'Much might be forgiven to one whose life was precarious, and whose pleasures, apart from his work, were but few'.[39] It might be added that drinking was an important element in an actor's work in the days before proper theatrical agencies existed, since the tavern was often the most convenient place to conduct theatrical business or solicit support for forthcoming productions. Where an actor had to publicise his own 'benefit' performance, he stood to pay out considerable sums on refreshment for prospective supporters with little hope of such hospitality being reciprocated. This was the reverse side to stories of 'sponging actors'!

There is no doubt that the actor of the first half of the nineteenth century was, in the popular imagination, a readily identifiable type, just as the sailor of Smollett's day had been. Early Victorian novels plainly suggest this, for few theatrical figures in the works of Dickens, Albert Smith and other contemporary authors are not extravagantly histrionic.[40] As we have shown, such figures were not merely the product of the novelist's imagination but had their counterparts in the contemporary theatre, certainly well into the second half of the century (in the provincial theatre this type of actor survived long into the twentieth century). Between roughly 1830 and 1860 the stereotype of the actor was still the eccentric poseur. 'A sort of "staginess" was in vogue', recalled Percy Fitzgerald, 'of which the comedian could not divest himself, or which he thought necessary to his dignity.'[41]

It is worth speculating how far this eccentricity was what modern sociologists call 'role-playing'. That is to say, were early Victorian actors consciously responding to the 'deviant' status allotted them by society, or was such behaviour the spontaneous reaction of naturally histrionic individuals? The distinction is necessarily a narrow one, but there is some significance in the fact that actors appeared at their most distinctive at a time when the stage was so poorly esteemed; it is plausible to assume that while their status was so uncertain, they found compensation in falling back upon their particular histrionic skills to assert the special nature of their personality and occupation. Moreover, such behaviour was not without its commercial advantages, for in the days before sophisticated publicity the actor was well aware that, in the provinces in particular, he was his own best advertisement.[42] Like the Crummleses, many actors were well aware of the curiosity they aroused in each new locality they visited, and there is every reason to suppose that they accordingly played up to the image people expected of them. However, as all marginal social groups discover, unorthodoxy is a doubled-edged weapon, so that while the actor's extravagant behaviour gave comfort to his sense of professional dignity, it still further enhanced his isolation from conventional society where manners and appearance were predominantly sober and genteel.

But if the actor of this era was a social oddity, he was generally a lovable one; and though his private character might be held in poor esteem, nevertheless he could not be ignored and his life and career were the source of active interest and endless fascination among contemporaries. 'There is no class of society', affirmed Dickens in Hazlitt's words at the first anniversary of the General Theatrical Fund in 1846, 'whom so many people regard with affection as actors.'[43] Theirs was the popularity of a popular theatre, and at the local level the individual actor, whatever the stigma against his profession, received a degree of personal adulation unmatched except perhaps by public figures in political life. The critic G.H. Lewes recalled Macready's farewell 'benefit' in 1851 as attracting 'an audience such as the walls of Drury [Lane] have not enclosed for many a long year'; when the actor made his first appearance on stage on this occasion, the spectators leapt to their feet, 'waving hats and handkerchiefs, stamping, shouting, yelling their friendship . . . loosening a tempest of tumultuous feeling such as made applause an ovation'.[44] This was a special occasion admittedly, but such receptions were common for audience favourites. Many actors who had no great reputation in London might be veritable 'stars' on the provincial circuits, and their salaries proved the point. Gustavus Vaughan Brooke, the Irish actor hailed as the new hope of the stage in 1848, came back to a rapturous welcome in England after an American tour in 1853: wherever he appeared he was feted with civic receptions and presentations, and on one occasion his four-horse carriage with its two scarlet outriders was uncoupled and drawn along by the enthusiastic crowds which greeted him. Another Irish actor, Barry Sullivan (1821-91), received similar treatment. He was especially popular in Lancashire and Ireland (his Hamlet was legendary in Dublin) to the end of his career; in 1848 the leading citizens of Manchester made a special presentation to him in recognition of his talents and character, and as late as 1874 he was so popular an attraction in the city that the civic authorities were obliged to issue new traffic regulations for the vicinity of the Queen's Theatre during the fortnight of his engagement there.[45]

It was in the light of examples such as these that G.H. Lewes could conclude that of all artists the actor received the greatest approbation in his lifetime, and he did not share the regret of those who sorrowed that the actor's fame rested on his name alone.[46] Indeed, so powerful was the actor in the contemporary theatre that he quite eclipsed all other colleagues, notably the dramatist. Hazlitt had made the point in the 1820s that people invariably expected actors to be as brilliant off-stage as they were on;[47] and Albert Smith considered that one reason why playwrights were so persistently underrated lay in the confusion popularly made between the actor and his stage role, with the result that people imagined comedians off-stage to be 'perpetually pouring forth sallies of the brightest humour and jocularity'.[48]

The Midlands and the north of England seem to have held their favourite performers in particular affection. In the early years of our period famous travelling showmen such as 'Old Wild' had large and devoted followings in the north: 'Wild's' funeral at Huddersfield in 1838 drew hundreds of mourners and, according to 'Trim', his death was the talk of the country at the time.[49] 'Strollers' were always in trouble with the licensing laws, but it is clear from 'Trim's' account that the local magistrate turned a sympathetic blind eye to infringements so long as they aroused no public complaint.[50] This identification of actors with local communities went a step further with stock companies which had long associations with particular regional circuits. Members of these troupes

> took an interest in the towns, and the towns took an interest in them, and came to their benefits. They returned again and again to the same lodgings . . . They were not unknown vagabonds wandering houseless from place to place; they were citizens and townsmen, living among their friends and relations.[51]

It must be remembered that in the industrial Midlands and north, the actor and the showman offered at this date almost the only source of 'amusement' outside the saloon. In remote country localities, like northern Scotland, the visit of the players could be an event of some importance in the year and 'their performance [was] announced by the town crier as there were no newspapers'.[52] Moreover, theatrical entertainment was the most thoroughgoing means of escaping for a while the harsh and dehumanising reality of daily working life. Only in the theatre, Ruskin declared, could one know, 'for an hour or two, that golden light, and song, and human skill and grace, are better than smoke-blackness, and shrieks of iron and fire, and monstrous powers of constrained elements.'[53] The journeyman engineer Thomas Wright felt that any man who, like himself, worked twelve hours a day, was entitled to some amusement in his spare time, and the most popular resort of 'pleasure-seeking workmen' in his day was the theatre.[54]

As the repository of a generalised mood of escapism, the theatre of the 1830s, 1840s and 1850s cannot be underrated. It played an important role in the early-Victorian romantic imagination, being part of a trend which found expression in the novels of Scott, in the Oxford Movement, in Pugin and the Pre-Raphaelites, in Ruskin, and in parts of the poetry of Tennyson. It is also significant that emotion in much contemporary fiction is conveyed in stage gestures, reflecting the great symbolic impact of actors and acting upon audiences.[55] For those who could ignore the ban on theatres and enjoy the play, the actor was for a brief space the living embodiment of an ideal world of courage, love, honour, loyalty and virtue triumphant. What Hazlitt had said of John Kemble in 1817 was equally pertinent to the actor in general: 'We see in him a stately hieroglyphic of humanity; a living monument of departed greatness; a sombre comment on the rise and fall of kings.'[56] Emotions which were normally repressed to a lesser or greater degree evidently found in the theatre a means of release. Certainly early Victorian audiences, both high and low, seem to have had few inhibitions, rising on occasion to the most clamorous heights of enthusiasm and excitement and sinking equally intensely to the depths of sorrow. Confronted with melodramatic tragedy on stage both men and women were capable of openly weeping (Macaulay, for example, was so moved by the dramatic representation of distressing scenes that he became a reluctant playgoer[57]), and many spectators clearly underwent profound emotional experiences during performances.[58] 'The awful truth and recentness of the events', wrote Lady Frederick Cavendish as late as 1873 after witnessing Ristori in *Marie Antoinette* at Drury Lane, 'made it almost intolerably painful and pathetic to a degree that set many crying, me to a frightful extent'.[59] 'From the moment when I passed out of the street into the theatre, I felt myself to be in an enchanted country', St John Ervine fondly recalled,[60] and indeed in a striking manner even the most sophisticated playgoers seemed to lose some of their critical faculties as they submitted to the glow of the footlights. Dickens, for example, thought Browning's popular play *A Blot on the 'Scutcheon* (1843) – a poetic but melodramatic piece – was 'lovely, true, deeply affecting, full of the best emotion' and 'full of genius'.[61] Conventional sensibilities were also often laid aside to a striking degree once the curtain had risen. Despite the censor, improprieties did slip through the net from time to time, but raised fewer eyebrows once the novelty had passed than would have been the case in similar instances in real life. Hence the fascination exercised by acts such as the sensational Menken 'nude spectacle',[62] the can-can on the burlesque stage (though invariably banned by the Lord Chamberlain for many years[63]), and male impersonations by actresses,[64] all of them expressing conduct which would have offended private morality outside the theatre. So there was another side to the censorious Victorian playgoer, that of the enchanted spectator who for an evening could forget the cares of the real world and leave his self-righteousness at the door. Theodor Fontane, a young German visitor to England in the 1840s and 1850s, best expressed this bewitchment exerted by the stage when he recalled Charles Kean's production of *The Winter's Tale* (August 1856):

> Nothing marred the charm of this lovely pastoral . . . One sees an ideal world and one believes in it. One believes in it because the human heart needs this belief . . . O Shakespeare, O Kean, O Miss Charlotte Leclerq, what have you done? You have preached me a better sermon than any clergyman could and the impression cannot be obliterated by the thought that Miss Charlotte may possibly have three illegitimate children and twice as many lovers.[65]

In short, it is the child-like awe with which popular Victorian audiences beheld the actor on stage that is so striking. The attributes of a theatrical performance which most impressed the majority of spectators – broad actions and crude emotions, unsophisticated characterisation and visual splendours – were those which were readily intelligible to a child; intellectual subtleties were generally lost upon them. When writers recalled the special magic evoked by the theatre, it is significant that they often expressed it most vividly through the eyes of children.[66] 'There are few more pleasant things in life', wrote Albert Smith, 'in this matter-of-fact conventional world of ours, than taking a child for the first time to a pantomime'.[67] It seems that the stage enshrined for its audiences a concept of unspoilt purity which contrasted forcibly with the bewildering changes taking place in the real world of industrial expansion and shifting values. It accounts in part for the fierce reactions with which any intrusion of 'real life' on stage was greeted; and it explains the strongly held belief, often unconscious, that theatrical entertainment was only above censure if it was suitable for the whole family (the recognition that the theatre could cater for selective audiences only gained ground at the end of this period[68]).

Thus, paradoxical in so many of their beliefs, early Victorians were also paradoxical in their view of the actor. While the stage was still largely outlawed both as a career and as a form of leisure, the actor was at the same time often a popular local hero and the embodiment of cherished ideals; socially isolated as a body, actors were nevertheless often respected and admired individuals in the local community. The struggle between these two opposing sets of belief reached its height during the early Victorian era, reflecting a transition period in both the theatre's development and the social attitudes of society at large. The two were inextricably inter-related, with the professional actor emerging not in some theatrical vacuum but as a result of the interplay between shifting forces in the theatre and outside. In the 1850s the social position of the actor was still little different from that in 1800; by the 1880s it had changed dramatically. It is time to see what this change entailed and how it happened.

4 THE DECLINE OF THE ACTOR'S COMMUNITY

The major characteristics of the early Victorian stage world persisted to the end of the nineteenth century and beyond. In particular, family ties and the family structure continued to play an important part in theatrical undertakings; children of actors continued invariably to follow their parents into the profession. Such elements did not suddenly disappear and were not likely to so long as the essential nature of the actor's work and skills remained unchanged.

But by 1880 there were abundant signs that the traditional actor's community was undergoing decisive changes. The gulf which had so conspicuously separated theatre people from the rest of society was now perceptibly narrowing. The seeds of this development were discernible much earlier. In chapter 3 we saw how some actors were already infiltrating the literary and professional world through their membership of prominent London clubs in the 1850s and 1860s. This trend continued, so that by the 1880s the distinctively theatrical club was a rarity. London contained several clubs frequented by actors at this date, notably the Garrick, the Junior Garrick, the Greenroom and the Beefsteak, but only the Greenroom was exclusive to actors: the rest comprised members from all walks of professional life. Club membership was therefore an important development for it at once put the theatrical leadership in close touch with the social establishment, and there is no doubt that this influenced the growing respectability of the stage as a profession.[1] T.H.S. Escott considered that the club had put actors on intimate terms with men whom thirty years earlier they would hardly have spoken to.[2] Neither was this a one-way development. As managements enhanced the comfort of their theatres in the 1870s, providing facilities for smoking and drinking,[3] several West End houses came to rival the clubs as places of relaxation for the professional man (who could safely bring his wife as well).[4]

We also saw in chapter 3 that residential habits confirmed the social isolation of actors, but that this isolation was getting weaker among the leading members of the profession. Indeed, the tendency for the more prosperous performers to move to grander districts away from their humbler colleagues in south and east London suggests that the theatre had its own class divisions and responded to the normal social influences which segregated certain localities from others. By the time the wealthiest actors were moving to areas like St John's Wood or taking city-centre apartments, they were influenced more by general residential habits among the fashionable than by any tradition of professional solidarity. In the working-class suburbs of the East End, Lambeth and Southwark there is every sign that rank-and-file actors continued into the 1890s to observe a marked residential solidarity, but the well-to-do of the north and west were rapidly infiltrating smart society and losing their traditional distinctiveness in the process.[5] It was one reflection of important changes taking place in the social composition of the theatrical profession.

The censuses for the period 1841-91 quite clearly show that acting was an expanding occupation. The total number of actors and actresses in England and Wales increased nearly seven-fold between these dates (see Appendix III). Until Macready's retirement in 1851, recruitment to the stage was high, but it displayed a decisive drop during the 1850s when, significantly, the theatre was barren of outstanding classical actors. But numbers began to shoot up dramatically in the 1860s, resulting in a remarkable 60 per cent increase in the decade 1881-91 alone. Over the period as a whole the average rate of growth works out at around 44 per cent, indicating a flourishing occupation which was expanding proportionately faster than the general population. It was also growing faster than the traditional status professions, a trend which was shared with other emergent professions, not least in the arts.[6]

The census figures are in many ways an unsatisfactory guide, but they do show that a stage career was increasing in popularity between 1830 and 1890. This is particularly striking in the case of female recruitment. Before 1871 the numbers of actresses in England and Wales fell far short of the total actor population. In 1861 there were well under 900 actresses on the regular stage, according to the census; over the next decade, however, this figure nearly doubled, and by 1881 actresses were beginning to outnumber actors for the first time (see Appendix III). Plainly, such a remarkable growth rate cannot be explained by the natural expansion of theatrical families. It must suggest that women, like men, were beginning to defy the traditional ban upon a stage career and enter the theatre from outside in substantial numbers.

If we study the social origins of actors and actresses who made their stage débuts between 1800 and 1890, this suggestion is lent added weight. In the case of actors,[7] Tables 1 and 2 in Appendix I, which refer to two successive generations of actors who were prominent in our own period, indicate that a high proportion of recruits to the stage before 1860 were born into the profession and trained for a theatrical career as a matter of course; many made their regular débuts in their teens, some had appeared at an even earlier age.

Many others, who were not born into the profession, nevertheless had connections with the theatre which would have predisposed them to a stage career and weakened any potential family opposition to the prospect. Ben Webster of the Haymarket, for instance, was the son of a dancing-master, and his step-mother had put him on the Bath stage as a dancer at an early age; Henry Compton was the collateral descendant of the eighteenth-century Scottish actor-manager David Ross (1728-90), and his grandmother, from whom he took his stage name of Compton, was an actress on the Bedford circuit; Edward Elton was the son of a schoolmaster interested in the stage; Alfred Wigan's father was for a time secretary of the Dramatic Authors' Society; and Thomas German Reed was the son of a Haymarket musician. Acquaintance with the literary and journalistic worlds – such as schoolmasters' sons would have had – also seems to have been a predisposing factor. Samuel Phelps and Albert Smith both gravitated to a stage career through journalism, while Henry Craven, who was initially a publisher's clerk, subsequently became Bulwer Lytton's amanuensis. Printing, an allied trade, also saw several actors emerge from its ranks, notably Davidge, Tyrone Power, Leman Rede and Douglas Jerrold (1803-57). In some cases family misfortune, particularly the premature death of a father, put pressure upon a son to take up a livelihood at an early age and one which did not require an expensive formal training. In such circumstances the stage, like the armed forces, offered an easy solution, and this no doubt influenced the choice of such actors as T.P. Cooke who saw war service against Napoleon – Robert Honner, who was apprenticed to the ballet-master Leclercq at the age of eight, John Coleman and Frederick Belton.[8] The baronet Sir William Don,[9] who had to sell all his property to his creditors when he left the Army in 1845, was another surprising addition to the ranks of actors escaping the pressures of reduced family circumstances. These cases serve to confirm the complaint of the early Victorian theatre establishment that too many people resorted to the stage as a final resource on the grounds that anybody could act.

Actors of these two earlier generations who came from 'civilian' backgrounds do, surprisingly, outnumber the theatre-born actors in the group under scrutiny. Owing to the small size of this group, this picture is almost certainly not representative of the theatre's membership as a whole at this time. Again, we should exercise caution in the knowledge that our list includes largely the most prominent actors of their day; it is very probable that among the proportionately greater number of rank-and-file actors who remain obscure at all levels of the profession, there was a much higher incidence of family continuity in the theatrical tradition.[10] Still, it is significant that among the élite the family tradition of acting is often fragmented and rarely older than a generation or two. Many of the theatrical dynasties of the Victorian stage were comparative newcomers, having started their association with the stage well into the nineteenth century.

In general, the origins of 'civilian' recruits between 1800 and 1860 are solidly lower-class rather than middle or working-class. We are dealing with families engaged in occupations wholly characteristic of the urban *petite bourgeoisie*: the fathers are tradesmen, drapers, craftsmen, watchmakers, outfitters, tallow and wine-merchants, customs surveyors and publicans. As a class they ranked among the higher-skilled wage-earners and would probably have had the benefit of at least a rudimentary education. Unless particular circumstances dictated otherwise, they would have been strongly opposed, both on social and religious grounds, to the prospect of their children entering upon a stage career – hence the conspicuous proportion of actors in this group who alienated their families and had recourse to stage names. Perched between the working class on the one hand and the middle class on the other, families at this level had pronounced social ambitions. It is no surprise, therefore, that actors of these generations were generally literate and had started adult life following in their fathers' businesses as apprentices in skilled trades such as printing and engraving, or as trainees in socially ambitious occupations like the law, medicine, banking, publishing, stock-broking, architecture and the Church.[11]

Significantly, theatrical families of these generations were often influenced by similar social ambitions for their children. Conscious of the social and financial insecurity of a stage career, they too intended their sons for other trades and professions. Thus William Macready was destined for the Bar and Charles Kean for the East India Company; William Chippendale was first apprenticed as a printer and auctioneer, William Oxberry the younger was trained as a surgeon; Charles Mathews, initially intended for the Church, and Edward Saker both trained as architects; George Vining spent six years as a bank clerk and Samuel Emery was successively clerk to a stockbroker and apprentice to a goldsmith.

Where there are not special circumstances, it is impossible to know exactly why civilians at this social level chose to take up a stage career, almost invariably in defiance of their families' wishes. If, as is now thought, the period 1780 to 1830 witnessed the growth of new audiences in the theatre, as reflected in the upsurge of suburban playhouses,[12] this may have also had repercussions upon the social composition of the profession. What is more certain is that this composition did not radically change between 1830 and 1860. From time to time we can find 'civilian' recruits coming to the stage from well-to-do commercial families (e.g. Edward Sothern) or from middle-class professional backgrounds (e.g. Henry Marston, Albert Smith and Montague Williams), but they remained the exception. Indeed, for the educated man a stage career was probably less appealing after 1830 than it had been during the heyday of the Kembles and Edmund Kean, when salaries had been more equable and the less crowded repertoire had afforded the actor a more leisurely and 'gentlemanly' life-style.[13] From the 1820s, it was generally agreed by contemporaries, 'legitimate' drama had been in decline and actors' salaries had been generally depressed on account of the excessive rates paid to 'star' performers. Macready told the Select Committee on Dramatic Literature (1832) that there was less acting talent then available than fifteen years before, and he concluded that the stage was 'so very unrequiting a profession' that no one in his right mind would want to take it up.[14] With his retirement in 1851, the stage was left without any outstanding British classical actor for some twenty years; theatre-building came to a virtual standstill and the Evangelical revival put the stage more than ever at the mercy of religious antagonism. The theatre thus gave every impression of a declining occupation in the 1850s: as the census showed, this was its worst decade for recruitment in the whole century.

Between 1860 and 1890 the social character of the profession took on a new appearance. As theatre-building revived in the late 1860s and new audiences began entering the theatre, so also recruitment increased dramatically. In the group in Table 3 of Appendix I we can see that the revival of the stage's popularity as a career contained two new and important elements. In the first place, there was a remarkable upsurge in the proportion of 'civilian' newcomers taking to the stage, quite eclipsing the proportion of theatre-bred recruits. Secondly, there were unmistakable signs that these 'civilians' were now coming from superior social backgrounds to those of the preceding generation.

The new actors were almost all of solidly middle-class origin, and a few were conspicuously upper-class. Their families represented a broad cross-section of the Victorian professional world, both old and new.

Military men and the sons of military men were now being attracted to the theatre. It was not unusual for these actors to have spent several years in active service as commissioned officers before joining the stage; it meant that they reached the profession at a relatively late age, some of them in their late twenties: this was a striking contrast with the youthfulness of earlier generations of recruits. Charles Kelly was 28 by the time he had finished serving with the 66th Regiment and made his professional début in Hull in 1867. W.H. Pennington had fought in the Crimea (he was subsequently popular in military melodramas) and worked in the Civil Service before embarking as an actor. Military service in the Empire was now common to this generation and several actors had initially campaigned with the British Army in India. Clavering Power had spent eleven years in service in India (he was also 28 when he took to the stage), and Edward Mott, educated at Eton and Sandhurst, had served with the 19th Regiment there. After 1860 the Army built up a strong tradition of amateur theatricals and this no doubt acquainted officers with the stage. The Windsor Strollers, founded in 1860, was the most celebrated military amateur group (it was modelled upon and preserved strong links with the Canterbury Old Stagers, which had formed in 1842), but it had a host of imitators throughout the Empire wherever the Army was stationed: the Simla Amateur Dramatic Club was started in 1876, and was followed by the creation of groups in Hong Kong, South Africa and the West Indies.

The legal profession was also well represented among the new breed of actors. Lawyers had always had conspicuous links with the stage: they joined amateur groups (like the Windsor Strollers) and actors' clubs, and seem in some cases to have been particularly sympathetic to the actor's cause in the courts. One of the most eminent Victorian barristers, 'Serjeant' Ballantine, was especially popular with actors, and according to the actor-barrister Montague Williams, there was scarcely a theatrical law-suit in which he was not engaged on one side or the other.[15] The Bancrofts took a great pride in the eminent circle of lawyers and judges whom they knew, an attitude which had its origin in the recent days when the visit of the assize courts to a locality had been a favourite time for actors to perform.[16]

Whereas before 1860 the stage had received a significant proportion of newcomers who had been initially destined to raise their family's social status through a career in the law, after 1860 recruits to the stage were themselves the sons of legal men, some of them eminent barristers, judges and solicitors. Such prominent late Victorian theatrical figures as Frank Benson, William Terris, Arthur Cecil, Ben Webster (the grandson of the famous Haymarket actor-manager) and Arthur Pinero, hailed from legal backgrounds.

But the stage had evidently benefited also from the greater social levelling of careers which had accompanied the rise of new middle-class professions in the course of the mid-Victorian era. Thus there were now men entering the theatre who were the sons of civil servants, civil engineers, journalists, writers, lecturers, educationists and artists. Two outstanding romantic actors of the 1890s came from this new professional background. Johnston Forbes-Robertson, who made his début in 1874, was the son of an art critic and journalist, and had himself studied art for a time. Lewis Waller, who took to the stage in 1883, was the son of a civil engineer, was well educated and was intended for a business career in the City.

One further example suffices to illustrate the gradual change in social attitudes to the stage which was taking place after 1860 and enabling a social transformation within the profession. For the first time there were signs that even clergymen's sons were turning to a theatrical career. This had occurred on occasions in the past, but it had been insignificant; after 1860 several actors making their professional débuts were the sons of socially eminent churchmen. Harold Bellew, a noted performer of high comedy, was the son of the distinguished mid-Victorian preacher, the Rev. J.C.M. Bellew, who was described as 'undoubtedly the foremost elocutionist' of his day.[17] Charles Brookfield's father became an Inspector of Schools and in 1860 was appointed honorary chaplain to the Queen; his wife was the daughter of the baronet Sir Charles Elton and a niece of Henry Hallam, and he was evidently a clergyman who was well connected with the highest social and literary circles of the day. Charles Brookfield was intended for the Bar, but joined the stage in 1879 after the offer of an engagement in the touring company of Charles Kelly, another churchman's son. (Kelly was then married to Ellen Terry.) Charles Hawtrey's father was another well-connected clergyman, being a housemaster at Eton. The worldliness of these clerical families probably eased the path of sons intent on a stage career (indeed, their education and intended callings differed little from those of other professional sons), but it was nevertheless a significant departure in the light of the long-standing gulf between Church and Stage.

If the theatre's leaders had in the past frequently complained of the low educational standards of actors, it had less cause to do so after 1860. Not that many leading actors before this date had been totally illiterate, for those whose schooling we know about appear to have acquired a reasonable education under the rudimentary system that prevailed in their day (see Tables 4 and 5 of Appendix I); but it was rare for an actor to have received a public-school training before 1860, because his family either could not afford it or did not aspire to it.[18] After 1860 a growing proportion of actors had been to public school or to the more expensive day-schools such as King's College, London. Some indeed had gone on to higher education at universities like Oxford and Cambridge (the standard sequel to a public-school career by this date) or increasingly fashionable institutions abroad, notably in Germany (see Table 6 of Appendix I). It was no accident that Oxford undergraduate theatre flourished for the first time in the 1880s.

This influx of well-to-do, well-educated newcomers into the theatre had a significance out of all proportion to their numbers – which, even by 1890, probably represented a tiny percentage of the total profession.[19] Their social credentials ensured that they acquired a prominent position among their colleagues with the minimum of training and experience. As men with an intimate acquaintance of the professional world outside the theatre, they no longer felt the need to assert the distinctive character of their occupation; they therefore projected a more conventional appearance and manner when off the stage (as photographs illustrate), a style which had its effects upon histrionic method as well, suggesting yet again that acting techniques developed not in some professional vacuum but in accordance with the changing social role of the actor. The critic Percy Fitzgerald summed up the new breed of actor as 'a gentlemanly, well-dressed man . . . as little anxious to obtrude his profession as an officer or barrister'.[20] The representative actor of the 1870s and 1880s was a man like William Kendal (1843-1917). He resided in Harley Street, the heart of professional London, and was described as a 'safe' and dignified performer rather than brilliant or compulsive; 'in appearance, manner, method', wrote one contemporary, 'he is essentially agreeable, and if we miss the brilliant, erratic fire of genius, we can at least enjoy the genial play of quiet, well-bred humour, and an intelligent realisation of the author's ideal'.[21] It was the secret of Kendal's popularity and respected position, and it was the model desired by his profession.

The public-school actor gave the stage's supporters the opportunity they had always sought to assert the theatre's professional and artistic claims. At a celebration to mark the hundredth performance of Irving's production of *The Merchant of Venice* at the Lyceum in 1880 Lord Houghton told a distinguished gathering that the 'traditions of good breeding and high conduct' had now spread to the acting profession as a whole, enabling 'families of condition' to allow their sons on the stage.[22] The theatre was now as 'liberal' as any other profession, argued its friends: 'It may indeed disdain to reckon up the number of persons connected with noble families enrolled in its ranks, but it may at the same time point to them as a homage to its attraction and its dignity.'[23] Moreover, actors were now people of artistic tastes, and *The World* newspaper took great delight in its gossip columns in detailing the artistic 'confusion and neglect of order' which characterised Irving's study.[24] Henry James concluded in 1880:

> The number of stage-struck persons who are to be met with in the London world is remarkable, and the number of prosperous actors who are but lately escaped amateurs is equally striking. The older actors regard the invasion of this class with melancholy disapproval, and declare that the profession is going to the dogs. By amateurs we mean young men 'of the world' (for of the other sex, naturally, there is much less question) not of theatrical stock, who have gone upon the stage after being educated for something very different, and who have managed to achieve success without going through the old-fashioned processes.[25]

The emergence of the 'gentleman' actor had far-reaching effects upon the traditional character of the Victorian theatre. For it was accompanied by a transformation in the familiar pattern of the actor's working life. There were strong signs by the 1870s that theatrical undertakings were becoming increasingly centralised. With the enormous popularity of Robertson's plays in London, the 'long run' quickly became established practice and the traditionally varied theatrical bill was superseded by the one-piece nightly programme; in addition, national tours by city-based companies accelerated the decline of the provincial stock system.[26]

These developments effectively transformed the traditional social basis of the profession. The new touring companies rendered the popular craft foundation of the theatre obsolete, leaving the stage without its traditional training grounds; this in turn enhanced the claims of the 'amateur dramatic club', which was increasingly the preserve of the middle-class professional man. This meant that whereas in the past the profession had drawn upon the pool of talent normally thrown up by the host of itinerant troupes and minor companies which worked the provincial circuits, it was now looking to a relatively small nucleus of newcomers whose social exclusiveness was more marked than their knowledge of the stage. The trend was further reinforced by the growing dominance of 'polite' drama, where the initiative lay with the educated actor, by the deferment of practical stage experience until the late teens or early twenties, and by the tendency of leading managements to give priority to the well-to-do amateur recruit. In the long run this made it increasingly difficult for the working-class or lower-class aspirant to enter the theatre.[27]

The single nightly performance and the long run also revolutionised working conditions in the theatre. Here too the initiative passed to the middle-class actor. It meant that for the first time actors were relieved of the traditional burden of daily rehearsal and study which had characterised the old system. With plays now in performance for weeks on end and revivals a standard practice, actors in established theatre companies had unprecedented spare time on their hands. The growing acceptance of the seasonal contract also reduced the financial precariousness of acting and raised the actor's professional dignity by making him primarily a salaried employee instead of a weekly wage-earner. The well-to-do recruit had the means in any case to tide him over his lowly paid beginnings on the stage.[28] Such developments were of immediate appeal to the self-conscious professional man who had hitherto shunned the stage as a career. Alive to the fact that he could now gain entry to the theatre without undergoing the 'vulgar' apprenticeship of the stock circuit, he was also now afforded sufficient leisure to maintain the sort of social life to which he had been accustomed before joining the stage. In short, an acting career by the 1880s offered the middle-class recruit the prospect, if he made a success, of a relatively secure and independent livelihood without the necessity of too specialised a training over and above his own education. In this light, the theatre neared the definition of a 'liberal' profession.

As the barriers between the stage and society gradually began to come down in the decades up to 1890, the familiar communal solidarity of the profession showed signs of breaking up. The self-conscious theatricality of earlier generations of actors, suggesting their sense of unity, now gave way to an equally self-conscious but potentially divisive exercise in social grooming. Actors and actresses who could afford it eagerly set about the serious business of emulating the tastes and trappings of the genteel audiences and educated recruits who now invaded the theatre. They moved to smart addresses, began employing servants, owning carriages, week-ending on the coast and holidaying abroad, and finally took their retirement in fashionable resorts such as Hove, St Leonards, Worthing and Hastings.[29]

For performers who had grown up under the harsh conditions of the early Victorian stage, such dramatic promotion to the heights of gentility and affluence was bound to encourage a certain snobbery. Few theatrical celebrities omitted from their memoirs – produced prolifically in the 1880s and 1890s – the mention of the famous and influential with whom they had come in contact in the course of their careers. The Bancrofts were particularly proud of their well-to-do connections, devoting a whole chapter of their *Recollections* (1909) to the eminent legal figures they had known, and pointing in their earlier autobiography to the wide circle of friends they had gathered in the world of literature and art.[30] The Bancrofts, like the Wigans, were no doubt shrewdly aware that in raising the profession's respectability they were also boosting their own social standing; indeed, it was no accident that the sensational stage début of Lilly Langtry, a noted society beauty and intimate of the Prince of Wales, should have taken place under the auspices of the Bancroft management at the Haymarket.

But then the Bancrofts and Wigans typified the changing social tone which had overtaken the theatre between 1860 and 1880. They were spectacular examples of the 'rags to riches' glamour which had always been part of the stage's appeal. The women in particular had both come of very humble theatrical stock (Mrs Wigan was the daughter of a showman); by the late 1860s they were the acknowledged models of theatrical respectability and were prominent social personalities in London. Both resided at fashionable addresses (the Wigans in Chelsea, the Bancrofts at Berkeley Square, then Cavendish Square) and both moved in markedly upper-class circles (the Bancrofts took holidays abroad in fashionable Swiss resorts where they were sometimes paid more attention than royalty).[31]

Such unprecedented affluence and respectability created sharp social divisions among actors. This had always been a potential danger within a profession which was acutely sensitive to its social status. Theatres had always observed a strict hierarchy among their employees, which was reflected in the larger establishments by the allocation of separate greenrooms to 'stars' and rank-and-file players.[32] There was also a struggle for social status implicit in the distinction drawn between the 'legitimate' stage and other levels, between the regular theatre and the more spasmodic itinerant forms.[33] Successful players had often tended to regard themselves as a cut above their colleagues: Macready went so far as to stipulate that for his farewell benefit in 1851, the actors and actresses of the Drury Lane company should be excluded from the front of the house along with drunks and prostitutes.[34] Perhaps only Macready could have showed such arrogance to his fellow artists, but there was a natural division between a man of his breeding and the uneducated majority of his profession. Charles Kean had a similar background and his Eton schooling put him on a social level which set him apart even from such prominent colleagues as Phelps, whose more commonplace appearance and suburban milieu was the object of some condescension.[35]

Indeed, the handful of actors' sons – Macready, Charles Kean, Edmund Yates (who became a journalist), William Oxberry the younger and Charles Mathews the younger – who had been educated at public schools[36] suggests that performers who had the means to do so before 1860 actively sought to secure a more stable social status and to escape the uncertain reputation of their occupation.[37] However, in general these potentially divisive factors were subordinated to the prevailing unity of an occupational group faced with a hostile environment. Where they demanded assertion, they could be sublimated in the hierarchical structure of the profession or in those instances of professional rivalry and intrigue which occurred between actors and their colleagues from time to time. Thus, although lip-service might be paid to theatrical distinctions such as 'legitimate' and 'illegitimate', in practice it did not prevent actors passing between the patents and the 'minors' or performing now in classical tragedy and now in melodrama or burletta. In short, the versatility of the stock repertoire ensured a large measure of cohesion in a group made up of widely differing talents and education and drawn from a variety of social backgrounds.

Under the changed circumstances of the 1870s and 1880s, divisions which had once been primarily theatrical now became social in character. With the decline of the varied programme, theatrical fare became standardised and theatres began to specialise: classical and 'superior' drama at the Lyceum, 'drawing-room' drama at the Prince of Wales and then the Haymarket, society melodrama at the Princess's, musical comedy at the Savoy and burlesque at the Gaiety. It rendered obsolete the old mobility between theatres at different levels of the profession. Over and above this, however, there were signs that the West End theatre was cutting itself off from the rest of the profession, a trend mirrored in the superior affluence of its audiences. Managements anxious to accelerate the gradual return of genteel society to the theatre did not scruple at showing preferential treatment to the well-to-do amateurs now knocking at their doors. Assisting well-connected men and women to realise their theatrical ambitions was good for business, beneficial to the status of the stage and advanced a manager's own social ambitions.[38] Thus the West End companies became something of a closed shop to those sections of the profession which had traditionally graduated from the provinces and the suburban 'minors'. The East End actor accordingly saw less and less of his West End colleague; by 1880 the two were already living and working in largely different worlds within the same profession, or as one contemporary put it in somewhat dramatic terms, the one was now inured to a life of struggle and hardship, while the other was 'by nature, by cultivation, by gifts, and by intercourse with a higher grade of humanity, signalised as bearing a manner more refined and reliable.'[39]

This trend did not pass without comment. The preferential treatment of well-to-do amateurs aroused widespread resentment and dismay within the profession, especially among the old guard who expressed concern at the effects upon acting standards.[40] As we shall see, these fears were well founded. But the process of class restriction had been an integral part in the rise of a professional stage. In giving priority to the middle-class actor, the theatrical establishment remained consistent to its persistent plea in this period for better-educated members: it had always believed that in this course lay the solution to chronic problems such as poor standards and a disreputable image. Hence, in part, the short-lived success of repeated attempts to set up training schools or a national theatre. In the short term the establishment was right, for the development of a socially exclusive membership was exactly the basis upon which the accepted 'liberal' professions operated. Ironically, therefore, the actor acquired professional standing in a manner wholly different from other occupations which were emerging as professions at roughly the same time, for these had urged their claims on the basis of occupational specialisation. It was a fact which testified once again to the unique character of the actor's occupation.

5 THE POSITION OF THE ACTRESS

> Doesn't one have to be (a strange girl) to want to go and exhibit one's self to a loathsome crowd, on a platform, with trumpets and a big drum, for money – to parade one's body and one's soul?
> (Henry James, *The Tragic Muse*, 1890, I, 153)

In 1830 the history of the professional actress on the English stage was less than two hundred years old. Yet in that time her impact had been striking, affecting not only the development of English drama, but also achieving a position that was unique to her sex. For in no other trade or profession were women treated on such favourable terms in relation to their male colleagues. By the eighteenth century, actresses could earn the same pay and enjoy the same conditions as actors, in some cases more and better. This was because acting relied on talent rather than training, and because women were simply indispensable to its practice and development. Acting was therefore unique among women's occupations of the nineteenth century until the notion of female careers began to gain acceptance.

It was a distinction with positive disadvantages for most of our period. The first English actresses were necessarily drawn from among women whose social origins were humble, if not disreputable, since only such women were likely to view the unconventional nature of their actions with comparative indifference. Serious and distinguished actresses did emerge (many were the wives of actors) but it is plain that audiences generally regarded most actresses as little better than public prostitutes (significantly, the custom for gentleman visitors to go behind the scenes during performances began under the Restoration[1]). For traditional opponents of the stage the actress therefore presented a new and more substantial object of attack. Moralists could now exploit to the full their familiar claims that theatres bred vice and profanity, and it is perhaps significant that by the eighteenth century the tradition of church and academic drama, prevalent under the Elizabethans, had died out.

Until the latter part of the eighteenth century such social disapproval had made comparatively little impact upon the profession itself, largely because it was tempered in a more libertarian age by a degree of official toleration. Playgoing was still fashionable and prominent actresses gained entrée into the salons of aristocratic society. But by 1830 both these conditions had disappeared. The simultaneous growth of middle-class values of gentility and the sterner morality of the Dissenting chapel set the traditional reputation of the actress at odds with official notions of propriety. And so, despite the care with which Victorian actresses guarded their reputation, the professional actress in the nineteenth century had a formidable struggle to overcome her historical image and live down the social ban laid upon her occupation. In many quarters it was particularly the question of women on the stage which discouraged the social acceptance of acting as a career. The actress's position has therefore a peculiar significance in the history of the theatre's development as a profession in this period. 'The objection to the theatre which most good people make', declared the *Saturday Review*, 'is, that actors and actresses are not virtuous characters, or rather, although modesty and prudery may forbid them saying so plainly, they do not much care about the men, but they think that the women are bad.'[2]

Public attitudes to the Victorian actress can only be understood in the context of the accepted position of Victorian women. While the conventional role of women had changed little since the seventeenth and eighteenth centuries, there emerged during the early Victorian years, under the imagined threat of forces working to undermine that role, a stricter and narrower ideal of womanhood. It was an ideal lent added strength both by the force of law and the almost reverential tone in which the subject was discussed. Victorian marriage laws, to take just one example, were based on the assumption that middle-class women were expected to live up to a far more rigid code of conduct, especially in matters of propriety, than men.[3] It was an outlook which drew its strength from the biological and religious basis upon which the position of women had always been placed, a position reaffirmed in the 1830s and 1840s.[4] On these grounds it was argued that women were naturally inferior to men, and occupied a socially inferior position accordingly. Acceptance of this fact was the only recourse open to a woman of true Christian humility.

The social inferiority of women confined them largely to a domestic existence, a state which was rationalised by investing it with an idealised, almost mystical, virtue. Thus the most admired qualities of Victorian womanhood were modesty, devotion, tenderness, self-effacement, and quietness of manner. They were qualities essential to the exclusive female role of wife and mother. A woman's true vocation was not to seek an independent economic position for herself, but to support her husband and rear his children. It was a philosophy increasingly suited to the leisurely life-style of middle-class women who, from the 1850s and 1860s, began to set aside domestic chores and turn to the business of gentility.[5] The nature of middle-class female education was correspondingly narrow and restrictive. A smattering of artistic pursuits – literature, music, possibly painting and sculpture, but *not* drama or theatricals – was deemed sufficient to prepare a girl for her role in life, not as an artist in any of these fields (a horrifying prospect for respectable parents), but as a social ornament fit 'to sympathise in her husband's pleasures, and in those of his best friends'.[6]

The position of the professional actress ran directly counter to the prevailing view of womanhood. In the first place the actress was a working woman. This automatically set her at odds with the official notion that a woman's 'true profession' was marriage, an assumption which reflected its middle-class and upper-class origin only too patently. On this score, the actress's craft was seen not as art, but as just another branch of working-class life, and contemporary theatrical conditions cannot have done much to discourage this view. This was the real stigma against the actress, the *Saturday Review* explained in 1859, not her morality, for 'if they were not actresses, they would belong to the large class of female operatives whom, for want of a better name, we may call "grisettes" '.[7] The strong tradition of careerism in the theatre, whereby actresses commonly married fellow professionals and continued to act while wives and mothers, further enhanced this view, for work *before* marriage did not become properly respectable for middle-class women much before the 1880s and 1890s, while the dichotomy between marriage *and* work persisted at least until the First World War.[8] In the early Victorian and mid-Victorian era women who were compelled to earn their own living almost invariably lost whatever social standing they had had, as the case of governesses[9] and teachers illustrated. After 1861 women teachers outnumbered men, a factor which was responsible for the persistently low status of the teaching profession in the nineteenth century. Only authorship, a self-employed occupation which could be safely undertaken within the confines of marriage and motherhood, was exempt from this rule – though many female writers preferred to remain anonymous. Middle-class girls therefore joined the stage at the risk of ostracism by family and friends. As one young actress complained:

[My family] think a woman has no right to be ambitious except in

> her own little domestic sphere. How inconsistent people are. If I were to marry some man I cared nothing about, everyone would call on me and visit me, but because I choose to do what I feel I can do and what I like, I am cut by my friends, and my own sisters dare not ask me to their houses.[10]

But the fact that actresses were working women does not fully explain the particular horror with which genteel society viewed the prospect of its daughters taking up a stage career. It is clear that the nature of the actress's calling had peculiar connotations altogether more sinister than the normal run of women's work. In the first place, acting on the professional stage necessarily incurred public exposure of an extreme kind. It therefore came into direct conflict with the implicitly private nature of genteel womanhood. Physical work alone, under any circumstances, was considered sufficient to degrade femininity, and hence the stigma against the mass of labouring women. But the tools of the actress's trade were her own body and emotions, attributes which she deliberately and regularly exposed to public gaze and public comment. 'I would never marry an artiste of any grade', asserts a character in Geraldine Jewsbury's novel *The Half-Sisters* (1848), for a woman 'who makes her mind public, or exhibits herself in any way, no matter how it may be dignified by the title of art, seems to me little better than a woman of a nameless class'.[11] Such a view was representative of prevailing opinion at this date, for demonstrativeness in any form was exactly what the education of every middle-class Victorian girl was designed to repress. Accordingly, theatricals were rare in middle-class households for most of this period; when they did take place, amateur productions could call on few women to participate, so that female roles were usually filled by men or professional actresses specially hired for the event. In any case, few women in 'polite' society would have been capable of acting, even for fun, so fundamentally did their upbringing clash with the requirements of this public art.[12] 'All they [educated women] are taught for their own particular role,' perceived Macready, 'goes to extinguish the materials out of which an actress is formed – acquaintance with passions – the feelings common to all, and indulged and expressed with comparative freedom in a poorer condition of life, but subjugated, restrained, and concealed by high-bred persons.'[13]

Significantly, when middle-class women began to take to the stage in larger numbers at the end of this period, it coincided with the development of a restrained and muted acting style which, to its critics, appeared to have lost a dimension of expression.

The woman who went on the stage was therefore likely to lose her moral as well as her social standing. 'A large portion of the public', complained one stage journal in 1846, 'is inoculated with the disease that in the Actress, woman loses self-respect.'[14] This verdict appeared to be unaffected by even the most virtuous stage roles. If an actress was capable of performing in a 'pert, flippant manner', then it went without saying that 'she loses much of her native modesty', but was it any better that she '*act* the best and holiest feelings of her nature . . .?'[15]

It was but a small step from seeing the actress as a threat to the accepted ideal of femininity to seeing her as an ally of the most outrageous moral deviants. Her public exposure automatically linked her in the popular imagination with that other class of public women, prostitutes. Historically, as we have seen, this association had had its precedents, not without justification. But even without historical example, the common syndrome was at work which had always equated unconventional female conduct with sexual licence. It was a cross which all radical feminists had to bear, not least during the Victorian era. Though few Victorian actresses could be described as radicals in this sense, the unorthodox nature of their calling was sufficient in itself to bestow a symbolic validity upon their reputation as sexual libertarians.

Thus even the most commonplace aspects of the actress's professional accoutrements could acquire a dubious significance. Stage costume, for example, aroused inordinate interest. By modern standards everyday fashions for Victorian women were extremely conservative. Colours were normally sombre and dress lengths remained firmly at floor level throughout the period 1830-90 (crinolines gave a hint of ankle and calf, but had a short-lived career from the mid-1850s to the mid-1860s). By contrast, stage attire could often be considerably less decorous and formal. Pantomimes, burlesques, extravaganzas and ballets commonly dressed women in costume whose revealing nature almost invariably caused a stir. Dancers in particular wore dresses and petticoats which were often diaphanous and reached just below knee-level, no doubt revealing more as the actress leapt and pirouetted.[16] It is plain that many Victorian spectators considered such attire little short of nudity, with the result that ballet was a little understood art and dancers a much maligned class of performers. 'Who has not seen', thundered Dr Michael Ryan in his survey of London prostitution (1839),

> actresses appear in tight flesh-made dresses as white as marble, and fitting so tightly that the shape of their bodies could not be more apparent, had they come forward on the stage in a state of nature . . . The attitude and personal exposure of these females are most disgusting to every really modest mind, and more suited to an improper house than to a public exhibition.[17]

The obtrusive emotional tone of these remarks in an ostensibly scientific work is a familiar feature of Victorian enquiries into sexual matters. It suggests perhaps that the development of social attitudes to social problems in the Victorian period had outstripped the development of personal attitudes and introspective feelings in general.[18] At any rate, where actresses appeared to draw attention to their sexuality on stage, comment was rarely dispassionate. Epithets such as 'degrading', 'disgusting' and 'offensive to decency' were commonplace in reviews of dancing performances, and it is significant that the theatrical establishment itself was prone to dissociate the ballet from its own undertakings.[19] Dancers of course appeared on the dramatic stage in many entertainments, but even at the Italian Opera, where ballet was fashionable up to about 1850, and taken seriously, ballerinas of high repute could be accused of displaying their charms 'a little too openly'.[20] Ballet was not to come into its own again until the 1890s and there was some truth in the verdict of one of its later champions, that it had been too often regarded 'rather as an orgie than as an art'.[21]

If dancers' costume appeared risqué to contemporaries, they also jibbed at the 'revealing' nature of tights and breeches. Actresses in 'breeches parts' had first appeared in the eighteenth century, and they were popularised again, by Madame Vestris in particular, in the 1820s. But this form of female stage attire could still cause a sensation well into the nineteenth century. Fanny Kemble considered the male impersonations of the French actress Mademoiselle Déjazet at the St James's theatre in the 1840s (she acted young boys as well as Voltaire, Rousseau, Napoleon and Henry IV) as even more indecent than the performances of dancers, on the grounds that 'their revelations of their limbs and shapes are partial and momentary, while hers were abiding and entire throughout the whole of her performance, which she acted in tight-fitting knee-breeches and silk stockings.'[22] In 1855 Madame Celeste provoked further public outrage against the conduct of actresses when she appeared as the first English Harlequin. But perhaps the fiercest uproar occurred when the American actress Adah Isaacs Menken appeared at Astley's in 1864 in the title-role of *Mazeppa*. Clad in flesh-coloured tights with the 'little end of a dimity nothing fastened to her waist', Menken achieved overnight success as the act scandalised critics and audiences alike, and led to a host of imitators in what was rapidly labelled 'the nude spectacle'.[23]

It is perhaps significant that it was chiefly foreign performers who figure so prominently in such incidents. Few English actresses would have dared to risk their reputations in this manner. Indeed, serious actresses might even shun Shakespeare where the plot demanded male disguise, as in the roles of Rosalind and Viola.[24] For instance, Mrs Kendal refused to act in Shakespeare, according to Gordon Craig, 'because he was not reliably respectable'.[25] When a serious tragedienne specialised in masculine roles, as did Charlotte Cushman, she had to weather many years of critical distaste before final acceptance.[26]

Such guarded reaction to actresses in male disguise or in masculine roles strikingly indicates how far from coming to terms with the reality of an actress's occupation was the mainstream of contemporary opinion. Even within the theatre the subject was treated with a caution which acknowledged that audiences were accustomed to associating ladylikeness with virtue. 'There is nothing in all nature', asserted Irving in a public lecture of 1878, 'purer than a Rosalind or an Imogen, and, if rightly treated, these characters are all the more striking from their appearance in male attire; but the slightest departure from the most modest taste, the faintest shade of meretricious, not to say indecorous, dressing is fatal'.[27] Such remarks suggest that it was the 'revealing' nature of male disguise as much as the inherent loss of modesty involved in women imitating male mannerisms, which tended to disconcert audiences.[28] Male impersonation would offend where the act appeared to draw attention to the actress's womanhood, as opposed to her duality of identity, and in some way degraded it. Thus disapproval of 'principal boys' in pantomime grew as costumes became more scanty.[29]

If theatrical costume encouraged the view that actresses were women of easy virtue, facial cosmetics took the parallel a stage further. In general, Victorian women used make-up sparingly and with discretion. Prostitutes, on the other hand, were conspicuous for flouting this convention, hence the common description of them as 'painted women'.[30] Restoration actresses had commonly flouted convention by wearing both costume and make-up off-stage, but it was a strict rule among self-respecting Victorian actresses never to follow suit.[31] Yet women wearing make-up were readily categorised as actresses in tones of disparagement which reflected the traditional association made with prostitutes. Thus Constance Rothschild, on first seeing the Austrian Empress in Vienna in 1873, confided to her diary: 'She was rouged up to her eyes, and when she stood in front of us and began to talk she looked like an actress – or rather, like a painted doll'.[32]

The association of actress and prostitute died hard in the Victorian popular imagination. The actor Robert Courtneidge recalled that when he took to the stage in the 1880s novels and memoirs frequently connected the two occupations.[33] And in late Victorian police courts the term 'actress' was widely used as a euphemism for 'tart', a practice no doubt inspired by its usage among offenders themselves. As the music-hall manager J.B. Howard commented: 'If the profession ever did have a bad name it was largely, I believe, because when any girl of ambiguous calling got into trouble she invariably described herself as an actress.'[34]

The real extent of prostitution among Victorian actresses is impossible to determine reliably. As we have seen, historical precedents and the 'unnatural' image of the actress were likely to give credence to rumours of sexual licence. Theatrical neighbourhoods, at least until the mid-nineteenth century, were almost invariably set among squalid city slums where vice and crime were rampant. For instance, Drury Lane and Covent Garden, the heart of the West End theatre, were in the midst of notorious 'rookeries' which few policemen even dared enter. Most authorities on the subject of prostitution were agreed that the theatre was a major cause, but their evidence centred largely upon theatrical audiences (where soliciting undoubtedly took place in the first half of the century) and upon the corrupting effect of theatrical entertainment.[35] In any case the emotional tone of these enquiries does not encourage great confidence in their conclusions. There seems little hard evidence that actresses were actively engaged in prostitution. There are indications that prostitutes succeeded in infiltrating some of the lowest theatres and music-halls,[36] and indeed the manager of the Alhambra admitted that some of his performers had been found to be plying their trade from the stage – though he was careful to add that such instances were rare and would incur instant dismissal for the actress concerned.[37] Music-hall managements did not always give the best impression, however, for it was well-known that gentlemen visitors were habitually admitted behind the scenes at these establishments, and there was a tendency to engage single girls in preference to married ones as an added attraction to the young 'swells' in the audience.[38] All the same, the consensus of opinion among police witnesses at the Select Committee hearings of 1866 to review theatrical licensing was that allegations of immorality were greatly exaggerated so far as theatres and music-halls were concerned. Lurid rumours of 'private rooms' in theatres (the rebuilt Lyceum was said to be connected to a brothel by an underground tunnel) were without foundation, according to the police, and though there was some evidence of soliciting in the 'halls', it was conducted discreetly and on a small scale, and rarely involved actresses themselves.[39]

It is probable that Victorians, who were prone to pass harsh judgement on moral failings, misconstrued the cases of young dancers and actresses who got involved with wealthy or unscrupulous admirers and then found themselves in trouble. This must have been a fairly common situation, for Pisanus Fraxi, the collector of pornographic material, claimed that most of the girls found in the illegal abortion clinics of late Victorian London were 'ballet girls or women in some way connected with the theatre'.[40] It is likely, too, that stage life, which encouraged a far greater freedom of conduct between men and women than was normally acceptable in society, was easily misinterpreted. Instances of players of both sexes sharing accommodation, a common practice on tour designed to reduce expenses, could thus be seen in a rather less innocent light. Bernard Shaw put the problem in a nutshell when he explained that

> the range of an actress's experience and the development of her sympathies depend on a latitude in her social relations, which, though perfectly consistent with a much higher degree of self-respect than is at all common among ordinary respectable ladies, involves a good deal of knowledge which is forbidden to 'pure' women.[41]

The extent to which the actress was the target of the moralist showed how little her vocation was understood by contemporaries in this respect.

It is difficult to escape the conclusion that actresses were judged by harsher standards than most other Victorian women. This, again, was the price of public exposure, for a woman as much in the public eye as the actress could expect her life, on stage and off, to be subjected to the most searching scrutiny. Under these circumstances, the smallest personal 'aberrations' could acquire a disproportionate significance. It did not help that Victorian audiences often found it difficult to distinguish between illusion and reality on the stage, for this gave a credibility to an actress's performance which was taken as an accurate measure of her real personality. Hence the 'immodesty' of dancing contributed to the low reputation of dancers, and accordingly scandal dogged the careers of performers whose acts appeared to cross the bounds laid down as acceptable for the conventional female stereotype. No actress who had been associated with 'sensational' performances could escape without the charge that her private life was highly suspect. Celeste, Vestris, Menken, Langtry, as well as prima ballerinas like Fanny Ellsler, Cerrito and Taglioni, all were accredited with a murky past and a host of lovers. Inevitably, such an attitude severely limited the scope and development of drama itself. 'Unheroic' heroines automatically drew critical censure. But even in the most innocuous roles the rules of 'good taste' limited an actress's freedom of interpretation. Thus Mrs Nisbet's portrayal of Helen in *The Hunchback*, a favourite melodramatic role among serious actresses, drew the following comments from the critic Westland Marston:

> The forwardness of this young lady [Helen] has been pushed by some actresses so far, and with so much deliberation, as to be somewhat distasteful. The reader, now and then, may have seen a Helen whom any bachelor of taste would have tolerated as a romp, and avoided as a wife. With Mrs. Nisbet, however, there was . . . such a just perception of the point to which she might go, and still be womanly, that nothing was too set in intention, or great [sic] too bold in manner.[42]

The secret of Helen Faucit's success was that she excelled in roles which best realised the conventional ideal of womanhood. 'People saw in her not only a great actress', wrote her husband and biographer, 'they felt themselves in the presence of one who was in herself the ideal woman of whom poets had written.'[43] In 1879 *Blackwood's Magazine* had defined the great actress as one who is able to 'feel more deeply and to think more nobly than ordinary mortals'.[44] Faucit's approach to the Shakespearian heroines suggests that she had taken this lesson to heart; these roles appealed to her, not as a challenge to her talent, but because they represented 'all that gives a woman her brightest charm, her most beneficent influence'.[45] Female literary critics especially emphasised the abstract virtues exemplified by Shakespearian heroines. Imogen, a shining model of conjugal fidelity and devotion, came in for particular praise. Mrs Jameson considered that her character 'unites the greatest number of those qualities which we imagine to constitute excellence in women'.[46] And if Imogen was the perfect heroine, Lady Macbeth was the most exemplary villainess. Helen Faucit had found the character 'so young and yet so wicked' that she had always dreaded performing it.[47] But Mrs Jameson insisted that even Lady Macbeth had some lesson to teach women. By showing 'how far the energy which resides in the mind may be degraded and perverted', the character illustrated the importance of 'humility and self-government'.[48] Moreover, a mitigating factor in her ruthless ambition was that 'she is ambitious less for herself than for her husband'; this revealed at least a 'touch of womanhood.'[49]

The pressure to conform to the heroic ideal in drama applied to actors as well as actresses, but men on the stage, as in real life, could safely go further than a woman beyond the accepted but undefined limits of good taste in gesture, intonation and characterisation. The Victorian actress therefore had to guard her reputation with great care, both on and off the stage. But the nineteenth century saw great changes in the position of women, and these did not occur without affecting the status of the actress. From the 1850s there were the first signs that women were being emancipated from their exclusively domestic role. The plight of the single girl inspired societies and journals which sought to provide more female jobs at the middle-class level. Standards of female education were also rising at the same time, for between 1840 and 1870 some ten girls' public schools opened, with another seventy being established in the following twenty years.[50] In 1860 Florence Nightingale opened a training school for nurses, and by the 1870s it was clear that women were taking part in public life in growing numbers as authors and editors (255), as doctors, surgeons, dentists and chemists (2,993), as teachers and governesses (55,246), as school mistresses (38,734), as artists (1,834), and as musicians (7,075).[51] In fact, between 1851 and 1871 the numbers of women working in commerce, public administration, medicine and education, rose from 95,000 to 138,000, an increase of 44.9 per cent over twenty years.[52]

Although the theatre was one of the few occupations in which women had long had equal opportunities with men, it did not go untouched by the growing demand for women's careers. In the first place, it removed the acting profession from that position of dubious distinction whereby it had been the only occupation besides prostitution where a woman could earn a substantial living by her own efforts. The debate over the morality of actresses became less emotive and more objective. The *Saturday Review*, while admitting that the stage was 'a scene of temptation', nevertheless took pains to emphasise that there was not 'any great and unusual proclivity to fall' under such conditions. Actresses, like women in other walks of life, could be divided into the good, the bad and the indifferent. 'We do not think', concluded the *Review*, 'that this picture . . . is one which is worse than that which would fairly represent any body of women in a place of public resort.'[53] Another writer saw the stage as a far better means of livelihood for a woman than either governessing or domestic service, for it was the only position where she was 'perfectly independent of man, and where, by her talent and conduct, she obtained the favour of the public.'[54]

In the second place, recruitment into the theatre benefited directly from the growth in women's jobs. Between 1861 and 1891 the number of actresses in England and Wales rose remarkably from an estimated 891 to 3,696. In 1851 their numbers were roughly half those of actors; by 1881 they had comfortably outstripped actors, maintaining a numerical superiority which has continued to the present day (see Appendix III). In part, the enormous expansion of the entertainment industry in the late nineteenth century accounts for this dramatic growth rate. The demand for female performers in particular was encouraged by the spread of music-halls, where the singing and dancing acts especially suited actresses,[55] and by the increasing popularity of burlesque and musical comedy. Theatres like the Gaiety and the Savoy were famous for their chorus-lines, which gave opportunities to female performers on a far greater scale than before. And despite the low opinion in which burlesque was held in established theatrical circles, it was capable of attracting recruits to the Savoy in the person of the daughters 'of poor clergymen, doctors, and retired military men, while others belonged to the middle class.'[56]

This was just one indication that the social composition of the actress's profession was undergoing a gradual change in the late Victorian period. Traditionally, actresses had always been born into the theatre or had come of humble origins, the exceptions usually being women whose respectable families had fallen on hard times.[57] This tradition remained largely unbroken until almost the last quarter of the nineteenth century. For example, a good two-thirds of the actresses who appear in the accompanying tables (see Appendix I, Tables 7-9) as having made their débuts before 1860 could claim a theatrical parentage or upbringing – and these performers were mostly at the top of the profession. There must have been many rank-and-file actresses of stage stock whose numbers render such an estimate a conservative one for the profession as a whole. Such a clear-cut pattern yet again confirms the marked social isolation of Victorian actresses.[58]

After 1860 there are still large numbers, certainly a majority, of actresses who have entered the profession as a matter of course. Many are the daughters of large theatrical families which had established themselves in the years 1830-60. But for the first time there is tangible evidence that the stage is attracting a growing proportion of women from different social backgrounds. Some are the daughters of writers, journalists, and artists, others of doctors, businessmen, military men and even clergymen. The average actress is now correspondingly older when she makes her stage début. As a careers guide for middle-class women put it, 'the stage is, socially speaking, becoming easier of entry for girls.'[59]

The demand for entertainment from all classes in society was not entirely responsible for this development. Dramatic taste was also changing, as was the style of theatrical life. The fashion for 'polite' drama, initiated by the success of Robertson's plays at the Prince of Wales in the late 1860s, demanded a quieter style of acting which, it was thought, educated ladies could best fulfil.[60] The hard, squalid grind of apprenticeship, epitomised by the provincial stock system, had always been a source of discouragement and repugnance to the well-bred actress. This experience no longer seemed necessary. In addition, the growth of touring companies, many of them catering for the influx of educated actors and actresses, and long runs, created a milieu of relative leisure and respectability to which middle-class women were accustomed.[61] It enabled the professional establishment and 'smart society' to mingle on equal terms for the first time, and the example set by 'society' actresses such as Lilly Langtry (début 1881) and Mrs Patrick Campbell (début 1888) served to glamorise a stage career in the eyes of women of all classes.[62] But actresses were acquiring an intellectual as well as a social respectability. Admittedly, by 1890 this development was in its infancy and concerned a very select (and critically unpopular) minority of the profession, but the association of actresses such as Janet Achurch and Elizabeth Robins with Ibsen (*A Doll's House* and *Pillars of Society* were both performed in London for the first time in 1889) foreshadowed the 'new drama' movement of the 1890s and early 1900s. This in turn was partly responsible for RADA (founded in 1904), which perhaps more than any other theatrical institution encouraged middle-class women in large numbers to join the stage and further transformed the social image of the profession.[63]

We must conclude that up to 1890 the status of the actress had improved less impressively than the actor's. This was because the notion of the career-actress was still not wholly acceptable in middle-class circles at this date.[64] The movement to emancipate women had begun, but its impact was generally slow to affect social attitudes. The rise in women's employment belied the fact that it was areas already familiar to women, such as teaching and governessing, which were attracting the highest number of recruits; traditional male preserves showed greater reluctance to accept women, especially in the professions (doctoring could claim only 21 women among its ranks by 1880). But, to a greater extent than the actor, the actress remained the victim of the perennial puritanism of English culture. It is significant in this respect that Victorian feminists showed almost no concern for the theatre.[65] No doubt this was partly because actresses were already established on an equal footing with actors. But the reason was also ethical, for few feminists were not concerned about the effects of emancipation upon the essential nature of women: their cause was primarily the single girl and her occupational opportunities, not the position of wives and mothers.[66] At heart they remained orthodox middle-class moralists, and as such they could not condone the threat to traditional womanhood which a stage career appeared to pose.

6 WORKING CONDITIONS

If by 1890 the actor's social status had visibly risen, what impact did this have upon his working conditions? Here the picture is much less clear-cut. In the first place, the existing evidence about such central issues as welfare, incomes, and the rate of employment is scanty and subject to widespread local variation. As a result there are serious problems of interpretation on a national scale. Secondly, there exists the over-riding difficulty of definition. The great variety of theatrical activity which prevailed throughout the period raises the question: who qualified as actors and who did not? Contemporaries themselves could not agree as to a satisfactory definition. The theatrical establishment tended to favour what they called the 'regular' profession to the exclusion of more casual groups such as 'strollers' and showmen; judging by their conservative estimate of the numbers of actors in the country, the census commissioners appear to have followed this definition as well. But the lower levels of the theatre were quite plainly a consistent source of recruitment into the 'regular' profession, and at least until the 1870s they continued to have a noticeable impact upon theatrical conditions. In this respect, it would seem undesirable to overlook them.

One conclusion is inescapable in this period as a whole: professional status did not bring the actor professional security. He remained a casual labourer in an unregulated and extremely precarious market. Unemployment in particular was always high, for over-crowding was a chronic problem in the theatre which seems to have got worse as the period advanced. Leman Thomas Rede, the author of a stage guide first published in 1827 and reissued in 1836, estimated that in the latter year there were some forty to fifty provincial theatre companies of varying sizes and conditions in the British Isles, excluding the mass of casual 'strolling' troupes.[1] In London there were in 1836 twenty-one theatres in operation and another six which were in occasional use.[2] Rede put the number of actors and actresses 'who thoroughly know their business' at 3,000, though he admitted that seven times that number probably regarded themselves as members of the theatrical profession.[3] The more cautious census commissioners, on the other hand, gave an estimate in 1841 of 1,563 actors and actresses in Great Britain, almost exactly half Rede's figure.[4] Owing to the vagueness of the terms of reference in both cases, we have no means of explaining the wide discrepancy between these two estimates. I am inclined to think that the census figure errs on the side of conservatism, not least because the classification of actors as 'Other Educated Persons' in the 1841 report must have excluded many legitimate performers who did not measure up to this designation. If we take Rede's figure of 3,000 actors and actresses, then, and divide it by the total number of theatre companies (some 70 regular concerns), it can quickly be appreciated that even in the 1830s the stage was greatly overcrowded, for the average number of members in a theatre company at this date was probably between 20 and 30.[5]

But numbers alone, which are open to wide interpretation in any case, do not tell the whole story. Overcrowding was clearly worse in some areas than others, for the profession was not equally distributed throughout the kingdom. By far the great majority of players operated in England, and over a third of the total membership was to be found in the London area at any one time.[6] This automatically concentrated the demand for theatrical employment upon a smaller number of companies. The superior theatrical prestige of London meant that demand invariably outweighed supply there, despite the boom in theatre-building which characterised the 1820s and 1830s. Moreover, until 1843 the restrictive effects of the patent system only made matters worse, for most aspirants to a stage career were naturally keen to reach the heights of 'legitimate' drama. It was reckoned that only about one per cent of the profession ever gained entry to the patent companies.[7] The abolition of the system enabled a higher proportion of actors to appear in spoken drama, but it did not ease the situation in the long run since it preceded a long period in which theatre-building came to a virtual standstill and heralded a decade in which recruitment shot up by a remarkable 60 per cent.[8]

A second factor encouraging high unemployment in the profession was the slow turnover traditional in companies. In the provinces the localised nature of theatrical undertakings played a large part in this, but the superior attraction of the more prestigious London companies made this factor particularly acute in the capital, thereby worsening overcrowding still further. In the heyday of the patent theatres, a place in the companies of Covent Garden or Drury Lane was a much-prized achievement and few actors and actresses relinquished their position once it had been gained. The famous Regency actor William Dowton (1764-1851) had been thirty-six years at Drury Lane until his retirement in 1836. This was exceptional, but prominent early Victorian performers such as Frances Kelly, T.P. Cooke, Drinkwater Meadows, George Bennett and John Cooper could witness to some twenty to thirty years' service in the patent companies. With the removal of their privileged position, the patents lost much of their exclusiveness in this respect, but it was a trait which became equally marked in other reputable London companies, such as Charles Kean's at the Princess's (1851-9), Phelps's at Sadler's Wells (1843-62), Ben Webster's at the Haymarket (1837-53) and then the Adelphi (1844-74), and J.B. Buckstone's at the Haymarket (1853-77). These theatres contained many actors and actresses, of secondary importance rather than 'star' status, who became firm audience favourites almost through sheer permanence: notable among these were W.H. Chippendale (at the Haymarket 1853-79), Richard Smith, known as 'O.' Smith (at the Adelphi 1828-55), the comedian Edward Wright (at the Adelphi for some twenty years), Henry Marston and his wife (they had a long association with Sadler's Wells under Phelps), and, most remarkable of all, Henry Howe, who stayed at the Haymarket for an astonishing forty years from 1837, surviving the long managements of both Webster and Buckstone.

In the last thirty years of the period there is no sign that this 'stay-put' mentality diminished among actors. Indeed, the practice of long runs and the trend towards dramatic specialisation positively encouraged it. The Gaiety 'quartette' (Kate Vaughan, Nellie Farren, Edward Terry and E.W. Royce) were a permanent fixture at this theatre throughout the 1870s and 1880s;[9] Thomas Thorne was a long-standing favourite at the Vaudeville, while George Grossmith was almost entirely associated with Gilbert and Sullivan's management, first at the Opera Comique, then at the Savoy. Irving's Lyceum was a byword for impenetrability among contemporary actors: some of its members devoted almost a whole career to his service, notably Ellen Terry, who stayed for twenty-three years, John Archer, an actor of supporting roles who stayed from 1875 to Irving's death in 1905, and even a leading player of the calibre of John Martin-Harvey, who remained for eighteen years.[10]

If long attachments were the norm for even moderately successful players, we can assume that it was an example which tended to be followed by the rank and file as well. It was a practice which goes a long way to explain the artistic conservatism of most Victorian managements.[11] In many cases actors clearly felt a deep loyalty to the managements they served; some companies even transferred *en masse* when their managers moved to new theatres (e.g. the company at the Prince of Wales largely accompanied the Bancrofts to the Haymarket in

1880). But it was a loyalty no doubt compounded with a certain degree of self-interest, especially in the reputable companies, reflecting above all the extreme precariousness of theatrical employment. If unemployment was high in the 1830s and 1840s, it showed little sign of decreasing after 1860. Recruitment in this era soared to record levels as the popularity of a stage career grew. It was accompanied by a revival of theatre-building on a large scale (taking the total in London to some 45 licensed theatres by 1890), but the fresh opportunities for employment which this provided were outweighed by simultaneous developments such as the decline of the stock circuit, the class restrictions operated by leading managements, the drastic reduction in the annual turnover of productions (in their twenty years of management the Bancrofts produced only thirty-one plays), and the growing specialisation of dramatic taste. In short, the openings available to actors and actresses were fewer than ever before, a situation reflected by the theatrical agencies which by the 1870s had so many 'tried professionals' on their books that they were of little help to the newcomer.[12] It was no accident that demands for proper training schools and for a national theatre had become a major preoccupation of the profession by 1890, nor was it surprising that resentment ran so high against the West End managements: both testified to the crisis in opportunities in an increasingly over-crowded profession.[13]

Overcrowding among actors inevitably brought with it exploitation to a lesser or greater degree. It naturally gave managements highly arbitrary powers over their employees. In particular, actors had no protection against the indiscriminate use of unskilled labour. It was standard practice for theatres to hire their 'extras' on a temporary basis from casual labour rather than from among the professional rank and file,[14] and it was not uncommon for even supporting parts to be given to eager amateurs who were prepared to give their services cheap to appear in a 'star' bill.[15] 'Supers' at the Lyceum in 1879 were paid one shilling per performance, a wage which not only denoted the prestige of Irving's productions but presupposed that these 'actors' had regular jobs outside the theatre;[16] and the Savoy choruses were customarily drawn from among stage-struck London tradesmen and others.[17] Without this reserve of cheap labour, the lavishness of Victorian productions with their scores of 'extras' would not have been possible.[18]

But it was on the fringes of the regular theatre that opportunities for managerial exploitation were greatest. In an occupation where professional ethics were still largely unformulated, anybody with the necessary capital could set up a theatrical company and hire a troupe of actors. If a venture failed, it was invariably the performers who had to pay for the losses, while if it succeeded, it was usually the manager who pocketed the profits. The frequency with which companies were left high and dry by unscrupulous operators is borne out by many theatrical reminiscences of the period. But actors were so dependent upon such enterprises for their precarious livelihood that it was not uncommon, according to J.K. Jerome, for individuals to seek engagements with managers whose reputation for swindling was well-known.[19] The idea that any legal redress against such misfortunes was obtainable was inconceivable at this level of the profession, for not only was the cost prohibitive for most actors, but managers tended to 'black' any performer who had once brought a successful suit against his employer.[20]

Jerome's conclusion was that actors were the worst treated of theatrical staff. Admittedly, his evidence related largely to provincial conditions, but the impression remains that the actor's welfare did not generally rank high upon a management's list of priorities. In particular, the physical conditions in which actors worked were often appalling, and they got no better as theatres began to improve the comfort of their audiences. Indeed, contemporary novelists who depicted the gulf between the glamorous façade which the stage presented and the grim reality behind the scenes were not always guilty of imaginative dramatisation.[21] Like the slum districts in which they had emerged, theatres were notorious for their dirt, damp, dinginess and draughts. Covent Garden, despite its prominence, was primitive backstage, and remained so even after the ornate alterations had been made to its auditorium in 1837. Helen Faucit confided to her diary after a performance of *The Tempest* on 26 January 1839 that she had positively 'shivered through Miranda. I thought there would have been nothing but a lump of ice left on the stage at the end of the play'.[22] Conditions at this theatre were little better even by 1890. In 1892 the Superintending Architect of Metropolitan Buildings reported that there was insufficient lighting and ventilation behind the scenes, and that nine dressing-rooms as well as the whole corps de ballet (some one hundred persons in all) had the use of a single lavatory.[23]

Many provincial theatres were probably in an even worse state. 'Corin' reported unwholesome conditions in the provinces in the mid-1880s.[24] *The Porcupine* newspaper attacked the Liverpool Amphitheatre and Theatre Royal in 1860 for dressing-rooms which were 'the veriest dogholes', for its dangerously inadequate lighting, and for its 'noisome smells': 'That the musicians – whose wretched fate it is to sit in the orchestras – are ever free from colds and rheumatism speaks wonders for the acclimatising powers of human nature.'[25] If it was uncomfortable for the musicians, it must have been doubly so for the actors. Members of the acting profession generally had a reputation for longevity, but in fact a high proportion of performers died comparatively young, frequently from consumption and other pulmonary diseases. Such ailments were by no means peculiar to theatrical people in Victorian times, but their incidence in the acting profession could probably be directly related to the unhealthy conditions – especially the alternation of draughts and stuffiness – which characterised theatres.[26] The almost universal use of gas lighting in theatres by 1850 did not improve the atmosphere in buildings which were notoriously under-ventilated (many people refused to attend theatres on the evening after a matinée or at the end of a week as a result), and gas footlights were a terrible ordeal for actors unaccustomed to them, for the flickering worried their eyes and the combustion and heat affected their throats.[27] Such conditions did not predispose to a healthy constitution and many middle-class newcomers to the stage after 1860 must have found them disconcerting. As one mid-Victorian novelist put it, a stage career had robbed her heroine of 'that blooming complexion which is given to most young ladies who are enabled to go to bed early and breathe plenty of fresh air. Her face was pale to a fault.'[28]

Gas lights also increased the risk of fire, for there was no adequate protection for stage or costumes against naked jets. Dancers were peculiarly at risk owing to the highly inflammable nature of their long diaphanous dresses and petticoats. Ben Webster's half-sister Clara was burnt to death in an accident at Drury Lane in 1844, and the medical journal *The Lancet* deplored in 1868 the frequency of such accidents among ballet-girls.[29] Fire took a heavy toll of theatre buildings in this period, destroying ten London houses between 1830 and 1865, another ten between 1866 and 1892, and inflicting heavy damage upon numerous other occasions.

Managements were not always to blame for the low standards in backstage working conditions. In some cases progressive or conscientious lessees were hampered in their efforts by the reluctance of theatre owners to spend money on improvements.[30] But by and large the story here conforms to the pattern set in other areas of actors' conditions. Labour throughout the Victorian period was cheap in the theatre, and managements, many of them more concerned to make a profit than set high theatrical standards, were not prepared to invest money in areas where there was no incentive to do so. In an over-crowded occupation most actors were in no position to bargain with their employers, and instances of exploitation seem to have been largely accepted by the rank and file as a fact of theatrical life. The theatrical establishment, both actors and managers, were in any case not convinced that working conditions *per se* lay at the root of the theatre's tarnished image. They were much more concerned to maintain the exclusiveness of dramatic entertainment against the incursions of more 'vulgar' forms of amusement in the hope that this would attract better-educated actors and audiences alike. Significantly, the rise of the professional player resulted not so much from improvements behind the scenes as in front of the curtain.[31]

Were actors then no 'better off' in 1890 than they had been in 1830? The broad answer is that they *were* 'better off' by 1890, but only within certain limits. For here again we are faced with the intractable problems posed by the wide variation in actors' conditions over the period as a whole. The fluctuating nature of the theatrical market meant that a rise in the standard of living of certain sections of the profession was quite compatible over the same period with ups and downs or even real deterioration in others. Equally, an aggregate betterment among a growing number of actors was not incompatible with a worsening situation among an actually rising number of their colleagues. Indeed, as one surveys the evidence both at the end of this period and after it, of high unemployment in the profession, of the continuing decline of itinerant companies, of bad conditions both backstage of theatres and in some of the new touring companies, of restricted opportunities in the West End, and above all of the unchanging bargaining position between managements and their performers, the more one feels bound to exercise the utmost caution in making any straightforward conclusion about advances in the Victorian actor's standard of living. Ultimately, one must insist upon closer attention to local circumstances and the individual case.

The question of incomes highlights this need for caution. For any assessment of real wages among actors is hampered by the degree to which imponderable factors, usually neglected in broad generalisations, affected the individual case. The great variation in the size and affluence of different theatre companies would determine, for instance, the degree to which actors had to subsidise and assist their own employers. Then there would be factors such as the individual's particular terms of engagement and the character of the venture, for incomes could be seriously affected depending on the reliability of the management, the locality which was visited, the length and success of the run, the share of the guest-stars, if any, and the size of the cast, and whether payment was on a nightly, weekly or 'sharing' basis or was subject to individual 'benefit' nights. Over and above these specific occupational considerations would be additional factors common to all wage-earners: the cost of living (variable between town and country), travelling expenses, the regularity of work, the number of breadwinners in the family, and the frequency of ill-health (a serious setback for actors whose contracts throughout this period specified that there would be no payment during illness[32]).

In the presence of so many variables, we plainly cannot generalise about the 'average' actor's living standards. We can only talk meaningfully in terms of actors at different levels of the profession. For our purposes they fall roughly into three separate income groups: 'star' performers, resident members of established companies, and the casual or 'irregular' body of players at the lower levels of the theatre. Let us take a look at each of these groups in turn.

There is no doubt that for the fortunate few who reached the top of the acting profession and were acknowledged as 'stars', the rewards could be very great, both financially and socially, throughout the Victorian period. Indeed, in no other contemporary trade or profession was there quite the same blend of 'rags' and 'riches' as was to be found in the theatre, nor the sort of opportunities which could enable the talented individual to move so easily (sometimes literally overnight) from one to the other. While this 'openness' did not recommend acting as a career of reputable standing, it was no doubt the key to its popular appeal. For in a society which continued to lay emphasis upon a strictly hierarchical order of caste and class, remaining deeply conscious even under an increasingly industrial way of life of pre-industrial conditions, the stage was one of the few occupations which offered potential fame and fortune even to the humblest men. Women too, for, as we have seen, acting was unique for most of this period in being the only occupation – apart from prostitution – in which a woman could make a substantial living singlehanded.

By the 1830s 'star' salaries had been increasing for some years and showed every sign of rising higher. In the Kemble era leading performers had been paid well but not exorbitantly, so that the earning capacity of all leading members of a resident company showed no conspicuous disparities. The norm for 'stars' at this date appears to have been £15 to £20 a week in the patent theatres (though of course special engagements would have brought in considerably more from time to time), with subordinate actors and actresses earning around £8 to £10 plus the fruits of possible 'benefit' nights.[33] From about 1815, however, 'star' salaries began to show a dramatic upward movement quite out of proportion to other theatrical earnings. Celebrities like Mrs Jordan, Edmund Kean, Charles Young and John Liston were by the 1820s earning more in one night than their predecessors had gained in a week only ten years before.[34] This trend continued into the 1830s and 1840s under the stimulus of intense competition between the patents and the 'minors' in London. Thus a popular performer like Tyrone Power, who excelled in Irish stage parts, could be contracted for as much as £150 a week at the Haymarket in 1834, and as an unrivalled classical tragedian (after Edmund Kean's death in 1833) Macready was capable of earning £100 a week. Lesser celebrities were by the 1830s commonly earning around £50 to £60 a week.[35] 'Stars' had never before generally received such a high level of incomes, and it was popularly reported by contemporaries that Ellen Tree earned more than the American President, that Macready was paid better than the Prime Minister, and that William Farren earned twice as much as the Home Secretary.[36]

Of course, such high earnings were not necessarily maintained throughout the theatrical season nor during a 'star's' entire career. Indeed, owing to the fluctuations of his popularity and widely differing terms of engagement, it is extremely difficult to estimate the sort of income which a celebrity received on average. In particular two factors – touring and management – could seriously affect his earning power for better or worse. In general touring was the more beneficial and it was standard practice for leading actors and actresses throughout the period to recoup their losses or increase their earning capacity through provincial or foreign tours on a freelance basis. By starring in specially arranged benefit performances around the provincial circuits or by taking a share of the theatre's weekly takings on longer visits, celebrities could often earn more than was possible in a London season. Certain provincial favourites such as G.V. Brooke, Charles Dillon and Barry Sullivan undoubtedly earned far more outside the capital. Sullivan, who was popular as a tragedian in the provinces throughout his career, was still capable of earning £300 to £400 a week on a 'sharing' basis as late as the 1870s; Edward Sothern, who was constantly in demand in the parts of Lord Dundreary and Garrick, and the comedian J.L. Toole were equally well-paid in the provinces at this date.[37] On foreign tours (chiefly to America, but also to Australia after 1850) the rewards were higher still, as the dearth of native talent in these countries gave English actors a virtual monopoly of the market.[38] Madame Celeste realised some £40,000 from a transatlantic tour in the years 1834-8, Ellen Tree £12,000 between 1836 and 1839, while G.V. Brooke returned to England in 1853 £20,000 the richer and Barry Sullivan reaped £8,000 in America in 1858 alone.

Management, which almost all celebrities attempted sooner or later, was a more hazardous venture. It was responsible for bankrupting many players both famous and obscure.[39] By modern standards, theatre management was reasonably cheap throughout the period: even in the 1880s a moderately-sized London theatre could be rented at £50 a week for a fairly long lease, labour was inexpensive as there was no minimum wage, entertainment tax and surtax were unknown, income tax was low (8d in the pound), 'star' producers had not yet arisen and publicity costs were minimal. There were risks but they arose largely from the unpredictable nature of the theatrical market. Management was probably at its most precarious in the early Victorian era when intense competition for a small potential audience encouraged lavish productions, soaring 'star' salaries and an extension of the theatrical season alongside low if not diminishing seat prices.[40] Thus Covent Garden and Drury Lane consistently ran at a loss in the 1830s and 1840s, and 'legitimate' drama, though popular with a fanatical minority, was relatively poor box-office.[41] Charles Kean, who was earning an average salary of over £5,000 a year by the 1840s, was obliged to live off his savings during an unprofitable period of management at the Princess's in the 1850s. All the same, his enduring 'star' status ensured an average annual income over his whole career from 1835 of over £4,000, so he was personally by no means ever 'badly off'.[42]

By the 1870s and 1880s a larger potential market, higher prices, long runs and revivals, and the trend towards dramatic specialisation guaranteed more stable custom and reduced costs, so that successful managements tended to be especially profitable. Some actor-managers in the commercial theatre undoubtedly made vast personal fortunes in this era. Thus George Conquest left £64,000 at his death, W.H. Kendal £66,000, J.L. Toole nearly £80,000, and Bancroft over £174,000, chiefly as a result of successful periods of London management in the 1870s and 1880s. By contrast, Irving's more traditional style of lavish management at the Lyceum was far less profitable and was only possible because he kept wages relatively low.[43]

'Star' incomes remained high up to 1890: Toole was grossing £100 a week at the Gaiety in the 1870s, Fred Leslie even more in the 1880s, and even a classical actress like Ellen Terry could draw £200 a week on touring engagements with the Lyceum company. But the 'star' system had stabilised somewhat since the heady days before 1850 as a proportionately smaller number of performers now ranked as celebrities. This was to have important effects upon lesser theatrical incomes.

By and large, therefore, 'stars' who remained at the top had a high standard of living, and after 1860 they were probably staying at the top longer as dramatic taste became more standardised.[44] Their life-style bore witness to their absorption into upper-class levels of society and their intimacy with the influential from all walks of the Establishment confounded the otherwise low status of actors in general. By all the evidence Macready was never a very wealthy man (according to his diaries, he was earning less at the end of his career than he had been in the 1830s), but he could afford several residences and his acquaintance with the literary, professional and aristocratic leaders of his day demonstrated his high personal standing.[45] G.H. Lewes concluded: 'Although his sensitiveness suffered from many of the external conditions of the player's life, his own acceptance by the world was a constant rebuke to his exaggerated claims.'[46]

By definition 'star' performers comprised a very small minority of the acting profession and the gulf in living standards which separated them from lesser colleagues was a large one in the Victorian period. But the scale and size of 'star' incomes was one important determinant of general wage levels among subordinate actors. For these latter the years of high 'star' salaries, between roughly 1820 and 1850, meant a drop in their own incomes. Thus a wage of £10 to £12 at the patents in the Kemble era had fallen to between £5 and £8 by the 1830s.[47] Among the lowest paid company members this reduction must have entailed considerable difficulties, and some performers no doubt supplemented their incomes with spare time jobs in order to maintain their former standard of living.[48] Among talented 'leads' of less than 'star' status, the fall in incomes encouraged transfers to the 'minors' where they were able to salve their pride and increase their wages by becoming large fish in small pools. Notable examples of this trend were Liston, Abbott, Keeley, T.P. Cooke and John Cooper.[49] However, this practice carried the depressive effects of the 'star' system into a wider range of theatres, further congesting the profession at its lower levels.

In the provinces the general scale of wages was lower than in London, though probably not very different from wage levels at the suburban 'minors'. Leman Rede illustrated that wages on the stock circuits in the late 1820s averaged between 18*s* and £2.[50] We do not know, however, how he calculated these figures. Did they for instance take into account time spent out of work and seasonal variations (summer takings in theatres were generally lower than winter ones)? His list does show, though, the wide range of local variation. At one end of the scale, the average might dwindle to as little as 15*s* a week, which meant that some actors were earning very much less than this amount; at the other, on the more reputable circuits, an average of £6 (Dublin Theatre Royal) and £7 (Edinburgh Theatre Royal) could be expected. Nominally, this put actors at these theatres among the highest paid skilled workers in the country, for in the industrial and commercial sector few skilled craftsmen were earning as much as £2 a week even in the 1860s.[51] But in real terms these theatrical wages would have been worth very much less owing to the precariousness of employment. Rede reckoned that leading favourites at the principal provincial theatres could command salaries up to £500 a year,[52] but again such an income might be far from regular and could prove shortlived. However, in many ways company actors in the provinces might well be 'better off' than their metropolitan counterparts on account of the variations in the cost of living between town and country. In London rents were universally high, the standard of cheap accommodation was invariably poor, and most actors in this period were obliged to reside further and further away from their place of work, entailing great inconvenience and (when transport came) additional travelling expenses.[53] In the provinces, by contrast, the cost of living was cheaper, accommodation proportionately better, and the actor could live near his theatre in a very much smaller community.

Yet despite these differences it is significant that ambitious provincial actors tended to regard themselves as 'worse off' than their London colleagues. Their resentment of the patent system for restricting openings in London for 'legitimate' engagements reflected their common belief that the provincial theatre was no more than a necessary period of apprenticeship prior to a London career. Edward Elton explained to the Select Committee on Dramatic Literature in 1832 that despite the fact that he had been a leading provincial player for eight years, his income had never been adequate to support himself and his family (he insisted that the highest paid circuit actors earned about 3 guineas a week), and for this reason he had transferred to the London 'minors' and risked prosecution by playing in 'legitimate' drama.[54] The point here is that income was not the only factor by which actors measured their standard of living, certainly not if they were lucky enough to find regular work. In such an intensely competitive occupation prestige and opportunity could be equally important considerations which might – and did – compensate for (in Elton's case) the risk of breaking the law[55] or even a temporary sacrifice of income. It explains again the long-standing loyalty of performers to certain highly reputable managements and their acceptance of relatively low salaries for many years.[56]

Another crucial factor determining actors' living standards in this early era – and common to most skilled occupations[57] – was the degree to which they had to subsidise management. This took many forms. In particular, it was standard practice for performers to provide their own necessities, such as costumes, 'props' and make-up. This could be a costly business. Leman Rede warned the stage aspirant that items such as hats, ruffs, wigs, collars, boots, shoes, sandals, stockings, fleshings, pantaloons, breeches, buckles, swords, belts and ornaments, were rarely provided by managements, and even these were only basic necessities quite separate from the more specific requirements of a particular character or line of 'business'.[58] Actresses were probably at an even greater disadvantage in this respect as dresses were never provided and were an expensive item. Without a certain amount of ingenuity and improvisation in the way of adapting costumes for different purposes (which players had to do in their spare time), the expenses involved could be crippling. (Some items could not be improvised, such as wigs, which, according to Rede, could cost between £1 and £3 each, and tights, at 30*s* a pair). In practice, few actors could provide themselves with a comprehensive kit of necessities and probably made do with a basic minimum – one reason why standards of presentation were so universally low in the early Victorian theatre. But managers continued for many years, especially in the provinces, to expect this form of subsidy from their employees, and it was a long-standing theatrical maxim that ownership of a good set of 'props' was half-way to securing an engagement.[59] Henry Irving, for example, finally took to the professional stage in 1856 only when he had acquired the means to equip himself with the requisite 'props'.[60]

But there were other areas too which strikingly reflect the hold which management had over their employees. Some companies expected their actors to carry out their own publicity by fly-posting the town;[61] others provided such poor facilities that play scripts had to be shared among the cast and parts copied up by supporting performers in what little spare time was available outside rehearsal. Nearly all touring companies, both on the old stock circuits and later, expected actors to provide their own accommodation in the localities visited. In practice, this may not have been a great inconvenience since theatrical towns regularly visited by companies usually contained 'digs' set aside for actors (the *Dramatic Directory* from 1883 specifically listed theatrical lodgings in provincial towns) and it is possible that in the stock days repeated visits to the same towns by the same group of players led to associations which helped with the problem of accommodation.[62] Still, it was one more department in which management claimed no responsibility for its actors, and it must have been additionally unsettling for newcomers. Touring companies also often made no arrangement for paying an actor's travelling expenses: this could directly affect his income and had to be taken into the reckoning when estimating average earnings. Nor were travelling expenses normally paid where an actor took up a new engagement – a costly operation if northern England, Scotland or Ireland (where jobs were easier to come by) was the destination. In the days before passenger rail transport (that is, in the 1830s), it was not uncommon for actors to walk the journey to their new place of work on the provincial circuits: 'the expense and difficulty of postage and transit obliged many a good actor to wear out his life in the provinces and drop into an obscure grave.'[63] And when rail travel came in the 1840s and 1850s, it was not always cheap.[64] Fares from London to outlying cities in the north of England or the West Country might well be more than most actors earned in a week and would have demanded reliance on precious savings or costly loans.[65] This alone must have been a big disincentive for actors to seek work far outside London.

Perhaps the most conspicuous area in which theatrical practice worked to the disadvantage of the early Victorian player lay in the benefit system. 'Benefit' performances were a vital part of an actor's income in this era, directly affecting his average annual earning capacity. Like 'tips', they were regarded essentially as a bonus to the terms of hire, and consequently served to keep down the actor's basic wage. Sillard, writing of the 1840s, pointed out that a 'benefit' could make the difference between solvency and arrears for a provincial player,[66] and it therefore dominated the run of his engagement. With the prospect of a clear half of the night's takings, or more usually one third of the receipts, an actor had an incentive to make strong efforts to guarantee the success of his 'benefit':

> First he must work his hardest all through his engagement, so as to make himself popular with the habitués of the theatre. Next, his chance customers – people who hardly knew him off the stage –

> must be allowed to pat him on the back and call him by his Christian name . . . and be generally familiar; then he must never refuse an invitation; he must deal with as many tradesmen as he possibly can . . . he must play at many benefits, so as to get constituency from the other theatres; in short, he should leave nothing undone to make himself as popular as possible both in and out of the theatre.[67]

Big profits could be made from 'benefits', especially by 'star' players (Macready grossed £906 at his farewell benefit in 1851, Ben Webster £2,000 in 1874), but equally so could disastrous losses. The performer's costs could be heavy, for in addition to set 'charges' made by the management, 'props', 'extras', publicity and the hospitality extended to prospective customers (who might never appear on the night), had all to be paid for out of his own pocket. At minor theatres or in the case of lesser known performers, benefits were always a risk, and the view persisted throughout the period that one was lucky to survive them with only a small loss.[68]

Benefits other than for cases of distress had become rare occasions in London by the 1860s, though they continued in the provinces for many years to come – just one indication of the growing gulf between these two areas of the profession in the second half of the century. They aptly reflected a period in the theatre's history when actors' salaries were generally low and the performer was in a position of extreme subserviency *vis-à-vis* both his manager and his public. The cap-in-hand solicitation demanded of the benefit performer was only a more intense instance of the desperate search for patronage which so often characterised the generality of actors as they prepared their attractions to coincide with the Assize sessions or Race Week or one of the seasonal fairs.[69] It should be remembered, too, that benefits were mainly to the advantage of leading players, for rank-and-file company members would naturally have had little drawing power.[70] However, in restraining the basic wage of 'leads', the system also operated against the rank and file whose earnings, while open to no realistic prospect of such a bonus, were nevertheless proportionately affected by it within the gradations of the salary structure. Elsewhere we have noted that benefits could on occasion render genuine assistance to the actor or actress in distress (though, again, only the well-known), but as a means of underpinning theatrical salaries they were rarely satisfactory and the profession, in London at any rate, became increasingly hostile to the system.

Best has noted that in quite a large number of occupations, particularly the better-organised trades, the 1850s and 1860s saw an improvement in conditions of earning a living over the 1830s and 1840s.[71] This improvement seems to have applied to theatrical incomes as well, but it should be stressed that the effects were by no means uniform within the profession; indeed, they indicate that in general the London actor's earning capacity was rapidly drawing yet further ahead of his provincial colleague's. This development sprang essentially from the growing centralisation taking place in the theatre as a result of continued urban expansion on an unprecedented scale (the 1851 census had shown for the first time that a majority of the population worked in towns and cities). In particular the emergence of an extensive railway network, even by 1860, facilitated travel between the main towns in the kingdom, but especially to and from London, whose claims as the theatrical capital of the land were enhanced still further. The effects of rail travel upon the local stock circuit were profound, and in the long run hastened the decline of the system, not least by facilitating the passage of the national touring companies of later years. For the provincial theatre these trends meant a contraction of activity to the larger towns and cities.[72] In London, they heralded a new era from the 1860s of theatre-building and theatre-opening, the decline of the benefit system, and the start of long runs (initiated by the success of Boucicault's *Colleen Bawn* at the Adelphi in 1860), which in turn ensured actors reasonable wages and greater regularity of work, if also fewer opportunities.

It is unclear how far these developments had advanced in the 1850s. Probably not very far. By all accounts the theatre was in the doldrums during this decade, with people blaming the dearth of talent (Macready's retirement in 1851 had left a gap on the classical stage which only foreign players like Fechter and Salvini could fill over the next twenty-odd years), the strength of dissenting feeling against the stage, and the fall in recruitment (as we have seen, it was the worst decade by far in this respect between 1841 and 1891). Perhaps because of this depression, statistical evidence is extremely scanty at this date, but it would seem likely under the circumstances that actors' living standards showed no dramatic improvements between 1840 and 1850. Marshall, writing in 1847, claimed that the drop in middling incomes, which he laid at the door of the 'star' system, was the 'one great cause why the drama has deteriorated'.[73] Byerley Thomson, in his brief chapter on 'The Histrionic Profession', reported that 'the stage is not now much favoured out of London', but he reckoned that the 'average income of a good actor is about £500.'[74] We have no means of knowing how Thomson estimated this figure. If we suppose that 'a good actor' was in work for forty weeks of the year, then his nominal earning capacity in 1857 was in the region of £12 a week. This would have put him well into the higher income bracket of the middle classes.[75] But this seems improbable at this date for all but a handful of leading players; after all, even in 1871 this was the top wage paid to 'leads' at the Haymarket, and only applied to the Kendals and W.H. Chippendale.[76] Moreover, forty weeks was an exceptional theatrical season in the 1850s (even 'stars' were lucky to find work for so long), for most moderately-sized companies still only performed between September and March.[77] We must conclude that Thomson's figure was a very liberal one, applying pre-eminently to 'leads', and 'leads' moreover who had a substantial reputation. In the provinces leading players, even at the best theatres, probably never averaged more than £200-£300 a year at this date. At the Edinburgh Theatre Royal, one of the higher companies on the circuits, the Wyndhams were paying Irving, admittedly an inexperienced player, only 30*s* a week as a juvenile 'lead'.[78] This tallies with Troubridge's findings that actors in the lesser country companies were still earning on average between 15*s* and 30*s* a week.[79]

This picture of the 1850s is strengthened by evidence for the 1860s and 1870s. Jerome, for instance, estimated that wages at the London 'minors' during these years averaged out at between 18*s* and £2 a week once travelling expenses had been deducted, while in the provinces (making allowance for variations between winter and summer) a guinea a week was reckoned high for a 'utility', 30*s* a good wage for experienced all-round 'responsibles' (out of which a costume would have to be provided), and £3 the top wage for a 'lead'.[80] On the face of it, in fact, provincial incomes showed no improvement on the levels cited by Leman Rede in the 1830s, the result of contracting audiences in the country as theatrical business became increasingly centralised on the larger cities. The provincial player was therefore 'worse off' now than he had been in Rede's day, the London actor correspondingly 'better off'. The incentives to obtain work in London grew ever greater as a result, so much so that some leading performers were prepared to take substantial cuts in salary for the privilege of appearing in the London theatre. Walter Montgomery, for example, was engaged by Fechter at the Lyceum in 1862 for two years, at £7 a week for the first year and £10 a week for the second: this compared with a previous salary of £30 a week in the provinces.[81] Yet in real terms such a move may not have been so remarkable as it is unlikely that Montgomery would have been earning £30 a week in the provinces for the length of a whole season; it is more probable his services had been hired out on a 'starring' basis for short spells. For the great attraction of the London theatre after roughly 1860 was the growing trend for seasonal contracts, encouraged by long runs, in place of weekly wages. Again, this benefit was only extended to experienced or talented players, not the rank and file – a point of some importance. Thus Irving, who had been earning £10 a week at the Vaudeville in 1870, was able to negotiate a more lucrative seasonal contract with the Bateman management at the Lyceum the following year as a result of his success in Albery's *Two Roses*: he was then on £15 for the first year, £17 for the second and £19 for the third, and was consequently able to rent a new house in West Brompton at a cost of £52 a year.[82] Contracts at this date could be quite detailed even for lesser actors. Geary quotes the case of one C.P. Flockton who was engaged by H.J. Montague at the Globe in 1871 for £5 a week in 'old men' and 'character' parts, to run for a season of not less than nine months. It was stipulated in addition that if he was required to go into the provinces, his travelling expenses would be paid and 20 per cent added to his London salary.[83] This latter clause strikingly reflects the less remunerative reputation which the provinces now held for all but the most celebrated London actors.

It must be reiterated that the extremely variable nature of these examples invokes at best a tentative assessment. But certain impressions do suggest themselves, provided we are quite sure which actors we are discussing. In the first place, it seems clear that a growing disparity was emerging by the 1860s, possibly earlier, between the living standards of provincial actors and their London colleagues. This trend was to become more marked in the remainder of the period as practices directly affecting actors' incomes which continued to be widespread in the provinces changed in the capital. Secondly, there is every reason to believe, as a result of this trend, that the general level of incomes among company actors in London was rising. This was the general consensus among witnesses before the Select Committee of 1866, even if they were not agreed exactly as to the rate and scale of this rise: Boucicault thought that incomes had doubled over the preceding fifteen years, the theatrical agent H.J. Turner estimated that they had risen by one third to a half in only a few years.[84] Again, as they do not elaborate, we cannot be sure whether this improvement touched all levels of company membership. My own feeling is that if it did, it was more marked in the reputable and long-established theatres than elsewhere; more important, it was also more marked among leading and middling players than among the rank and file. The middling player, who could offer reasonable talent and experience, had by 1860 regained the position he had lost as a result of the abuses of the 'star' system in the 1830s and 1840s. His nominal income had risen, perhaps not by very much, but he might also be working to a seasonal contract rather than a weekly one and that season might now extend from August to May. He could, in short, start to think of himself as a salaried man rather than a wage-earner. This had important consequences for the actor's professional image, and it cannot be accidental that recruitment in the 1860s shot up so dramatically.

One important development which undoubtedly affected actors' incomes at this date was the growing competition exerted by the music-halls. Since the mid-fifties music-halls had spread on a large scale throughout London and other towns and cities, and by 1866 it was estimated they outnumbered theatres by as much as five or six to one.[85] Theatre managers could not ignore this development and regarded the halls as a dangerous threat both to their own audiences and theatrical recruitment. All witnesses before the 1866 Select Committee were agreed that the halls had affected the theatre. Boucicault thought their counter-attractions explained the existing dearth of good 'legitimate' actors, and he reckoned that salaries in the halls were four or five times greater than in the theatre.[86] The manager E.T. Smith told the Committee that an actor or actress could earn as much as £20-30 a week at the halls by performing 'turns' at different establishments for about £6 a time.[87] Some actors regarded the music-halls as 'vulgar' and would not have lowered their dignity by transferring their services, but defections were inevitable in the face of such favourable earnings. Paterson noted that salaries in the 'saloons', as he called them, were not only liberal, but regularly paid (by contrast with some theatres), and this fact was a standing temptation to actors who had lost their ambition on the 'regular boards' and simply wanted 'a comfortable engagement'.[88] But many actors alternated between the theatres and the halls simply in accordance with the work they could get; during slack periods in the theatre, such as the Christmas pantomime season when actors could be out of a job for as long as eight to ten weeks, it was common for the 'regular' performer to take up engagements in the halls – no doubt replacing those music-hall artistes who were traditionally hired by the theatres at this time of year.[89] Those who advocated unrestricted competition with the halls, such as John Hollingshead (then stage manager of the Alhambra music-hall), pointed out that actors' salaries would probably double within a short period as a result;[90] H.J. Turner felt that actors' earnings had already been pushed up by the presence of the halls.[91]

The recommendation of the 1866 Committee that restrictions on theatrical entertainment in the music-halls should be lifted was never put into practice, but there can be little doubt that the rivalry of these establishments was instrumental in raising London actors' earnings throughout the 1870s and 1880s. The continuing decline of the benefit system in all but cases of distress, and the further spread of long runs, also influenced the trend. As the Bancrofts pointed out in their early memoirs, 'the acceptance of engagements for special parts and runs of plays instead of for fixed and lengthened periods' was an additional factor now favourably affecting higher salary grades within the profession.[92] For 'leading business' these developments ensured a marked rise in incomes between the 1860s and the 1880s. Irving in 1881 estimated that salaries had doubled at this level since the sixties.[93] Thus £30 a week was increasingly common for 'leads' by 1880: Irving himself had been paid this figure by the Batemans in 1873 (after his success in *The Bells*) and his own 'leads' at the Lyceum after 1878 were earning similar sums.[94] Some highly profitable managements, such as the Bancrofts' or the Gaiety theatre under Hollingshead, could afford to pay even more, and £60 and over could be grossed a week by leading players at these establishments.

It is far less certain that this rise in higher theatrical salaries from 1860 brought equal improvement to the wage-earning rank and file of theatre companies. For by 1890 the latter's earning power was proportionately so much lower than leading rates that it is seriously in question whether over the period as a whole they had accrued any real improvement. The rank and file generally had neither talent nor experience to offer and were therefore subject to the most intermittent employment. The resident 'extra' was to the end of the period a rare member of the profession and, as we have seen, it was standard practice for theatres to hire 'supers' on a casual basis for pay which was never intended as a livelihood. Where engagements were for the run of a piece, such as a pageant or pantomime, rates at this level of the profession rarely rose above 20*s* a week (which was less even than ballet dancers were earning at this date).[95] Even in the better London companies, a 'walk-on' could expect little more than a guinea a week, a minor 'speaking part' £2 to £3.[96] And this was only the nominal figure: as one guide to women's careers warned, 'an actress would do well to reckon her salary at half its nominal amount, as she is likely to be frequently out of work'.[97] Moreover, actors were still not paid for rehearsals as a matter of course – in the new touring companies a newcomer was expected to serve an apprenticeship before earning anything (which must have deterred less than middle-class aspirants) – and the tendency for engagements to last for the run of a play only, while an improvement on the past, in no way alleviated the basic insecurity of the obscure player. 'In these matters', commented the above guide, 'actors and actresses are not well used, and when they have learnt the value of united effort they will certainly combine for securing juster terms.'[98]

The position in the provincial branches of the profession adds to the need for caution in discussing the question of improvements in actors' earnings at the end of the period. At all levels, provincial company incomes compared unfavourably with the London theatre. Irving told the Royal General Theatrical Fund in 1875 that some actors were still only earning 25*s* to 30*s* in the country, with necessities to pay for.[99] Outside the larger towns and cities, practices which had helped to keep actors' wages at minimum levels still flourished in the provincial theatre of the 1870s and 1880s. In particular, long runs were still rare, apart from the Christmas pantomime. Arthur Pinero, hired as 'utility' for a guinea a week at the Theatre Royal, Edinburgh, in 1874, had to act in seven different plays as well as the farce in the course of a fortnight's visit by Mrs Scott-Siddons in September of that year.[100] The picture cannot have been very different elsewhere in the provinces in the late Victorian era.

The rank-and-file members of regular theatre companies could easily find themselves, through ill-luck, sickness or lack of talent, sinking to the level of that broad spectrum of casual and poverty-stricken labour which comprises our third and lowest income group in the Victorian theatre. This varied body of actors, which might contain at one end respectable men and women and, at the other, 'work-shy' idlers, petty criminals, and even prostitutes, were regularly the unemployed and the ill-rewarded of the theatres. We have as yet no means of telling exactly how large this depressed area of the profession was. There are good grounds for believing that it was at all times of formidable dimensions and, though changing in character, grew yet greater as the century progressed. As we have noted, unemployment throughout these years, though unmeasurable with any accuracy, was always high and probably rose higher over the whole period. It is likely that it was consistently underrated by the profession's leaders, who always showed a tendency to gauge the situation not in terms of the total profession but by reference to the proportion of 'good' – by which they meant talented, educated and respectable – actors in work at any one time.[101] They too shared the prejudice of the world (by which, ironically, they were themselves formerly judged) that many rank-and-file actors did not merit inclusion in the profession.

If we do not know the size of this under-employed and unemployed section of the profession, we have been left in little doubt as to its character. In the cities it was to be found in the sordid surroundings of the 'penny gaffs' and saloons which catered for the poorest and most wretched inhabitants of the community.[102] If an actor could get work here, he could expect low standards, bad conditions, long hours (several performances a night was usual), and a mere pittance in pay. James Grant found the wretchedness of 'gaff' performers contrasted strongly with the lordly characters they enacted on stage. He estimated that they earned about tenpence to fourteen pence a night, on average a weekly wage of five shillings; their time outside rehearsal was too scarce to take supplementary jobs. In short, these were players near the starvation level who knew 'not an individual in the world who would move a step to rescue them'.[103] Some 'penny' theatre actors revealed a pathetic sense of dignity,[104] and indeed the standard of acting could be unexpectedly high owing to the fact that many 'gaff' actors had once been on the regular boards before losing their jobs.

But for the great majority it was an occupation which put them hardly above subsistence level. Paterson described one such group as follows:

> Most of the company I saw at Gillon's were of the same class. They had no high ambition to elevate their profession or themselves – their career was not even an effort for a living; entered upon orginally from sheer vanity, it became too often all through a lifetime, but 'another way of starving'.[105]

In the countryside the 'gaff' actor had his counterpart in the mass of 'strolling' troupes, itinerant theatres, booth actors, show folk and circus people, who characterised the early Victorian provincial scene. This large body of entertainers, competing with the established stock companies for meagre local audiences, can have found only the most intermittent work and precarious rewards. Paterson reckoned that booth players led a relatively leisurely life and he records that he never earned less than 30*s* a week, a high wage even in the regular theatres at this date.[106] Certainly, the booths offered a more healthy life than the 'penny' theatres, but average earnings probably worked out over the year as hardly enough to live on. Significantly, Paterson himself abandoned his acting career after his last engagement in the booths had earned him only £3 6*s* 6*d* for three months' service: this was less than 6*s* a week on average.[107] In a four-man strolling troupe of the late 1820s described by Edward Stirling, the highest weekly wage might be as much as 25*s* or 30*s* each, but this took no account of overheads such as costumes, travelling, and so on, and the extremely sporadic nature of their custom.[108]

Under-employment was not the only risk at this level of the theatre. Deprivation produced its own depravity and dishonesty, and the cut-throat search for meagre pickings frequently took such performers outside the law and into conflict with the authorities or with each other. Few 'penny' theatres were licensed and the travelling showmen frequently turned a blind eye to the conditions under which they were permitted to perform. In the stricter muncipalities this might invite arrest and imprisonment on a technical charge of vagabondage. Rivalries between entertainers were common at peak periods such as fair-time, leading to brawls and ruffianism which further lent show people a bad name.[109] Actors at this level could be mean and ruthless, and had a reputation for drunkenness, debts, swindling and low morals. Paterson said he knew few actors who had not been ruined time and again by the theft of their 'props' and necessities.[110] His own experiences prompted a bitter judgement on the 'strolling' life:

> Who but one haunted by a restless burning desire for dramatic distinction would welcome years of poverty, privation, sickness of soul and body, a constant sense of self-imposed beggary, and an internal reproach for frequent acts of meanness not to be avoided, and even dishonesty, which may not be shunned.[111]

On all the lower rungs of the theatrical ladder life must have been little more than a struggle for survival and far removed from the exalted artistic claims vaunted by the professional establishment. Those who were unable to cope with the strains sank inexorably to suicide, intemperance or the workhouse, a common range of fates in the early Victorian era. More often, the actor was little more than a casual migrant seeking shelter for a time in the theatre before moving to other equally precarious occupations.[112] For the mass of itinerants early Victorian life saw decreasing opportunities as urban expansion, the spread of rail travel, and the exigencies of the law combined to force them out of business. The larger, more organised concerns kept going well into the later years of the century,[113] but by the 1850s the individual entertainer was fast losing his traditional customers to the established theatres, saloons and music-halls.[114]

We cannot tell what finally happened to these people. Many no doubt drifted to other occupations and many others, such as tumblers, jugglers, conjurors, contortionists, acrobats, stilt-dancers, fire-eaters, and sword-swallowers, would have been absorbed into the regular theatre and the music-halls to appear in pantomimes and spectaculars. We cannot doubt that still more joined the swelling ranks of the theatrical unemployed, but there is no means of estimating upon what sort of scale. What is incontrovertible is that many actors, probably a growing number, were always near the bread line and endured no less misery and hardship than their predecessors because their life was centred upon the playhouse as opposed to the barn, fairground or street. If the experiences of actors and others in the 1870s and 1880s is to be believed, the profession of that day – especially in the provinces – could be as prone to swindling, drunkenness, corruption, poverty and exploitation as anything seen in the less sophisticated thirties and forties.[115] Examples abounded to show the widespread exploitation that awaited innocent newcomers who put their trust in unscrupulous managers, and careers advisers made no bones of the fact that the stage novice serving his or her probation in one of the numerous touring companies could expect only 'hard work, ill quarters, and uncertain pay.'[116] As one idealistic young actress of the 1880s found to her cost, 'difficulties, anxieties and hardships' were still inseparable from a stage career, conditions poignantly summed up by one entry in her diary: 'I am wretchedly poor. Two days without dinner.'[117]

How then, finally, are we to assess the living standards of actors and actresses in this period? Social historians of the Victorian years conclude, on the one hand, that general living standards improved only marginally between the 1830s and 1860s and that thereafter there was a clear upward trend; on the other, they maintain that while there was an incontrovertible boom in the nation's gross national income between 1851 and 1881, there is little evidence to show that wage-earners as a class benefited much from it.[118] Something of this same ambivalence is apparent in the Victorian theatre. For if actors at certain levels of the profession were demonstrably 'better off' in the 1880s than they had been in the 1830s, other actors at other levels were equally clearly not so. Moreover, even where improvements were made in living standards, such progress did not necessarily rest wholly, or even mainly in a great number of cases, on such nominal increases in earnings as occurred: these could, at the lower levels, be negligible when taken with the rise in the cost of living which we know to have occurred in England roughly between the 1840s and the 1870s.[119] Equally or more important were other signs such as the rising proportion of better-paid jobs, greater leisure time, more stable work, and a more responsible attitude from managements.

It seems to me undeniable that by 1890 one group of actors in particular was considerably better off than they had been sixty or even thirty years before: this group comprised those skilled performers, demonstrably talented or experienced or both, who found regular employment and were members of predominantly reputable companies, particularly in London. This group, swelled by the ranks of middle-class recruits entering the theatre after 1860 in growing numbers, accounted for an increasing proportion of the total profession by 1890. Their real earnings were unquestionably higher than they had been in 1830, their hours were visibly shorter owing to the reduction in regular rehearsal time and in the length of the nightly bill, and their status within their companies and in society now rested upon a more assured foundation.

These improvements had important implications for the growing respectability of acting as a profession, for it was just this group which could be identified with the increasingly middle-class image of the theatre. In almost all respects, pensions apart, their conditions of work now associated them with the salaried professional man as opposed to the wage-earner. Take the question of working hours alone. In the 'stock' days actors were working on average about fifteen hours a day in terms of study, rehearsal and performing time.[120] Sometimes this involved working into the small hours of the morning, and in some cases as many as eighty to ninety major parts a year might be played.[121] This had put acting hardly above the level of the 'sweated trades', for whom fifteen hours a day was not uncommon throughout the period; it certainly made them 'worse off' than most other skilled wage-earners, for whom the norm was twelve hours a day up to the 1850s. By contrast, by the 1890s the working man was down to nine hours a day or a fifty-four hour week,[122] while actors could, during a long run, have 'days of time' on their hands.[123]

Other benefits had accrued to the established company actor as well by this date. He now paid an agent to secure him engagements, a practice which in itself was a reflection of his raised status. Following the fashion instituted by the Bancrofts at the Prince of Wales, he was now attended upon by the theatre treasurer for payment of his salary instead of queueing for it himself as had always been done in the past: a small point in itself, it again dissociated the performer from his previous wage-earning image. His company now did far more on his behalf than before, taking care of its own publicity, providing its own wardrobe and 'props', paying for his travelling expenses (on reduced block bookings now provided by the railways) while touring, and in some cases arranging his accommodation in the towns and cities which were visited. His legal status within the company had also improved. Whereas in the past the terms of contracts had invariably been a source of potential friction between actor and manager owing to their vagueness, and had thus invested management with highly arbitrary powers, by the 1870s and 1880s these ambiguities had been substantially eliminated by changing theatrical practice and the influence of a number of important test-cases in the courts. In particular, it became standard practice that, unless otherwise stated, payment was for the season only – and was payable whether an actor was working all the time or not: this ended disputes as to whether an agreement to be paid meant throughout the year or simply when the theatre was open. Other areas of uncertainty, such as absence through illness and whether an actor had the right to perform elsewhere while engaged to one theatre already, were also put on a clearer legal basis by 1890. Thus it was established as an implicit condition of a contract that an actor could not perform elsewhere, while if he was ill, it was agreed that he should not be paid (a long-standing theatrical tradition in any case) and, in certain circumstances, could have his contract revoked by the management; he was not, however, liable to damages for non-performance through illness.[124] But even in sickness the company actor was not necessarily ignored; following the traditional Victorian pattern and the examples of Drury Lane and Covent Garden (which had long had their own charitable funds), many reputable theatres started charities and sick funds for their less fortunate employees. Pensions, of course, were not paid, but some attempt was made by the profession even here to safeguard the interests of its more reputable and deserving members into old age (see chapter 7).

Some of these improvements touched actors at all levels and must be weighed in the balance when considering whether even the lowest paid performers were not 'better off' by the 1880s than they had been. Yet, if a growing proportion of actors could now rank as salaried professional people, it is no less clear that a large percentage of their colleagues, also rising in numbers, were no better off than wage-earners as a class at this date. I refer again to the large body of rank-and-file performers who by the 1890s were earning no more than 25*s* to 35*s* a week at the most (in the provinces such a category would have included more than simply the rank and file). This did not, in nominal terms, mean they were badly off. According to the statistician Baxter's 'hierarchy of labour', such a wage would have put them on a level with the most skilled working men in the late 1860s.[125] By 1890 such a wage bestowed solid working-class comfort, particularly as prices for food and clothing were falling considerably at this date.[126] But Baxter reckoned that the precariousness of employment was such, even in skilled trades, that real wages ought to be calculated at fully 20 per cent less than nominal full-time wages. How much more did this apply to the wage-earning actor. If 'good actors' were out of work in the 1880s, as they seem to have been,[127] surely most other performers were unemployed too. Could rank-and-file members under these circumstances afford to calculate their salaries by even half their nominal value, as Bulley and Whitley suggested to aspirant actresses? At this level, many actors and actresses who did not have independent means must have lived hardly above the poverty line, another factor reinforcing the ascendancy of the educated, well-to-do recruit. There therefore existed a disproportionate gap between the salaried actor and his wage-earning colleague that had its parallel outside the theatre in the contemporary tendency for the proportion of skilled jobs in society to grow at the expense of the unskilled, and for middle-class groups to benefit at the expense of wage-earners. In the theatre this was translated into the sort of social divisions we discussed in chapter 4, making it no less of an oddity among professions than it had always been. Thus even in the 1880s contemporaries were still arguing about the status of the player.

In one important respect, actors were definitely worse off than many working men by 1890: they had as yet no formal union organisation to protect their interests. This was not for lack of antagonism between management and employees in the theatre. In the 1840s newspapers like *The Theatrical Times* were virulent in their condemnation of managerial tyranny, calling on actors for 'a spirit of union' which would provide them with some form of 'protection society'.[128] Equally, the popular belief that theatre managers were tyrannical and autocratic, conveyed in the wider press and in fiction, must have had some basis in the demonstrable experiences of actors and their known complaints. Why then did no concerted demand come from actors in this period for greater protection of their interests?

I think there are several reasons. Firstly, actors were in a bad position to organise. Their small numbers and the disparate nature of the theatre, which had no formal ruling bodies or institutions, discouraged the sort of cohesion which was possible in the factory or shop.

It meant the fragmentation of allegiances amongst a host of different companies and theatres, and could produce in some cases deep loyalties to the more reputable and benevolent managements: thus those who were perhaps in the best position to take a lead in organising theatrical labour were the very actors who felt the least need or desire to do so. It must surely be of some significance in this respect that many Victorian managers were also actors at the same time. This may have helped to reduce any potential friction between actors and managements and it would have fostered the traditional 'family' spirit evident in so many theatres great and small. But it was also true that the ranks of actors were never as united as their social isolation appeared to proclaim. As we have seen in chapter 4, there was precious little solidarity at times between skilled players and their 'unskilled' colleagues, a pattern which had its parallel in other fields where trades and unions were fiercely competitive.[129]

In the second place, the theatre stands out as one of the few areas of 'sweated labour' which attracted almost no concern from the outside world in the nineteenth century. Legislation for the stage is minimal in this period; where it does occur, it relates not to actors or their conditions, but to the licensing of theatres and the welfare of audiences, and in many cases its pertinence to the stage is purely incidental and part of the wider trend towards administrative standardisation which was sweeping through local government throughout the century. In part this is explained, again, by the insignificant size of the theatrical work force compared to the huge numbers engaged in industrial labour. Possibly also the glamorous image which the theatre tended to radiate blunted the true facts of life behind the scenes in the public mind, or perhaps the social isolation of stage folk simply discouraged curiosity. But more probably there is a particularly Victorian reason for the lack of concern: this had its source in the prevailing notion that actors were 'idlers' and deserved their fate. Entertainers of any sort would hardly have been the favourite subject of those social reformers and Evangelical politicians who stood out as the champions of shorter hours and better conditions in industry. Public figures who did turn their attention to the realities of the actor's life were more often inclined to moralise than administer. The redoubtable Bessie Parkes, one of the few 'Women's Rights' campaigners of this period to suggest that actresses could be usefully organised in the fight for better female conditions of work, observed that if the stage was referred to at all, 'it is rather to "point a moral or adorn a tale", and to be held up as an example of mischief'.[130] Such a reputation did not recommend the actor to the philanthropist.

But the chief obstacle to theatrical 'combination' in this period lay in the very reason that the player achieved professional status. If conditions among actors, as among many working men at the time, were ripe for conflict in the 'hungry' thirties and forties, they were far less so after 1860. As middle-class newcomers entered the theatre in these later decades, they effected a transformation out of all proportion to their numbers. Intent upon the pursuit of professional equality and anxious accordingly to dispel the theatre's unrespectable image, the theatrical establishment became increasingly preoccupied with the outward trappings of social status at the expense of real improvements in working conditions. It was a drive which did not lend itself to political activism of the sort taking place in the workshops of the nation, indeed it produced a positive distaste for labour politics with all its proletarian associations. Hence the self-conscious preference of the profession for a genteel phraseology, for 'salaries' rather than 'wages', for 'resting' rather than 'unemployed', and for 'associations' rather than 'unions'; and hence the laborious path towards self-protection in the theatre (not fully achieved until 1929 when Equity was founded), so many years behind other occupations.[131] It was only when middle-class actors themselves began to experience some of the worst forms of theatrical exploitation, that efforts began to be made to 'organise' in the form of the Actors' Association of 1891 and the Actors' Union of 1905. Neither secured wholehearted support, however, being viewed with suspicion by many established managers and actors alike.

One other result came from the largely successful pursuit of respectability: it gave the initiative in theatrical matters even more completely to management. Despite the improved legal position of the actor, it is not difficult to detect the immense power which the late Victorian actor-manager wielded in his own domain, backed up by an unambiguous set of rules and regulations which were infringed only at the risk of heavy fines or outright dismissal. Given the fact that it was the theatre manager first and foremost who had been responsible for attracting 'polite' society back to the playhouse and raising the player's status accordingly, his dominance was perhaps predictable and he could be excused for thinking that his profession had never had it so good.

Finally, it might be asked whether the actor is a particularly political animal. In France there might be a different answer from the one in England. Certainly, the prominence of actors in France during the Revolution, and their subsequent association with (predominantly left-wing) political life to the present day, has no parallel in the English theatre. Whether there are theatrical reasons for this difference or more deep-rooted cultural ones, I cannot say. The 'conservatism' of the English theatre from 1890 right up to the 1950s has, I am sure, much to do with the manner in which the Victorian player became also a professional man. But then it is hard to escape the conclusion that the very nature of the actor's occupation, centred as it is essentially upon himself, mitigates against the ideological confrontation of the sort which inspired working men's movements. Even the 'worst off' in the Victorian profession could accept their fate with a certain resignation, blaming ill-luck, lack of talent, or simply a fickle public rather than a 'system' which bred exploitation. Given to the grandiloquent gesture, especially in the Victorian theatre, actors could have found little appeal in the dry monotony of committee meetings, with their agendas and resolutions, the very stuff of labour politics. Nor, they felt, was this necessary, for few players did not think that their day would come sooner or later.

7 ESTABLISHING A PROFESSION

In the eighteenth century there had been a large element of private patronage in the organisation of the arts. This had prevented artists from developing as distinct occupational groups, a process which could only be achieved by the growth of a wider public. Such a public was to arise as the nation became more urbanised from the middle of the eighteenth century, with the result that literacy spread, the press and other forms of literature grew in popularity, and ultimately public attitudes towards the concept of leisure and culture underwent a profound transformation. In our own period there is clear evidence that the whole field of art and amusement expanded enormously in popularity,[1] and it is under these conditions that artists of all persuasions were able to develop as professionals. As we saw in chapter 1, the rise in the status of the arts was not a uniform process; the stage in particular lagged behind the advances of other creative occupations. However, the importance of this period in English theatrical history lies in the fact that actors showed for the first time an awareness of what was required to transform their standing. If by 1890 their track record was less impressive than that of other emergent professions, nonetheless their actions suggest that they were no less eager to attain the same objectives.

In this chapter I do not propose to explore in great detail the practical efforts made by actors and managers to improve theatrical standards, an indispensable prerequisite to the stage's acceptance as a profession. Important as these efforts were, they have been treated adequately elsewhere and are now largely familiar to theatre historians. I would only stress in passing that such achievements, like many other Victorian social reforms, had implicit moral as well as technical objectives in view, and it should not be forgotten that the care with which large numbers of ordinary actors and actresses sought to maintain an irreproachable respectability in their private lives made no small contribution to the rising esteem of their calling. It might also be added that the movement to eliminate impropriety and discomfort in theatres was assisted by the total growth of public administration, both nationally and locally, in so far as an increasing amount of parliamentary legislation covering all places of public resort brought theatres within its scope as well.[2]

The main purpose of this chapter is to show how actors and others concerned with the theatre sought to assert the special claims of acting as an art-form and bring it into line with the accepted criteria of a profession. This was not always a conscious or concerted course of action in an occupation which was organised upon such a disparate basis; petty rivalries and ill-concealed snobberies between individuals, theatres and different branches of the stage served as a constant drawback to attempts to establish national bodies and a professional structure. Moreover, the actor's resentment of outside criticism of his calling made him slow to respond to movements for reform, as did the weight of theatrical tradition which had lain unchanged for centuries during the theatre's long social isolation. Such teething troubles were common to all emergent professions, but they were particularly acute in the theatre and reflected the peculiar problems which actors experienced in conforming to the demands made by the prevailing professional ethic.

In the censuses actors are first classed as professional men in 1861, along with other imperfectly defined but distinct occupational groups such as authors, artists, musicians, teachers and scientists. While this classification owed something to convenience upon the part of the census commissioners, nevertheless it bore some relation to reality. For if actors had few professional bodies or institutions to their name by the 1860s, there is no doubt that they had begun to think in professional terms by this date. This is made clear by two themes in particular which predominate in the actions and public pronouncements of theatrical leaders throughout this period. The first of these was their adherence to the principle of restrictive practice; the second was their determination to promote the actor as a responsible member of the community.

Ever since the establishment of the patent system in the mid-seventeenth century, acted drama in the English theatre had been organised on a restrictive basis. By the nineteenth century the licensing laws as they related to theatres were complicated and cumbersome, but their primary purpose was to protect the exclusiveness of the spoken drama by allowing its performance in a limited number of playhouses. From the early 1800s, however, there was a growing demand for the abolition of this sytem, which reached a peak in the 1830s, and was finally successful in the Theatres Regulations Act of 1843. The story is now a familiar one to theatre historians and would seem to show that the trend in the 1830s was towards theatrical 'free trade'.[3] In fact, however, the measure of 1843 was solidly protectionist in spirit, effectively replacing a monopoly with a system which, albeit more broadly based, was nonetheless highly restrictive.[4] Indeed, the dramatic halt to theatre-building in central London for the following two decades and more is partly explained by the rigorous conditions which continued to govern the licensing of new playhouses. Such restrictions were entirely compatible with the aims of the pressure-groups behind the campaign to end the patent monopoly, for it had never been the intention of the 'minor' proprietors to establish unrestricted theatrical competition.[5] In their eyes such a step would have had disastrous commercial disadvantages in such a small theatrical market, and, as we shall see in a moment, they were no less concerned than the patentees over declining professional standards. What the 'free traders' of the 1830s wanted, by contrast with their counterparts of the 1860s, was the continuance of restrictive practice in which they too had a share.

In other words, the struggles between the 'majors' and the 'minors' in the thirties and forties represented not only a long overdue rationalisation of the maze of theatrical licensing laws, but also the tentative first steps of an occupational group seeking to raise itself to a position of professional exclusiveness. In other emergent professions of the early nineteenth century the main impetus towards professionalisation came not from their top practitioners but from the lower branches; this was the case both in medicine and the law.[6] The same was true in the theatre. For it should not be forgotten that under the old system the patent companies effectively formed an exclusive professional élite. Although there were no formal barriers against actors from the 'illegitimate' stage entering the patent companies, in practice the royal houses of Drury Lane and Covent Garden tended to take newcomers who had served at the leading provincial patents, and they housed their own form of actors' 'nurseries'.[7] Combined with the slow turnover of employees, these factors effectively created a closed shop at the patent houses, and judging by the complaints of other actors in the 1830s, entry to these prestigious theatres was becoming increasingly difficult.[8] The decline of standards at the patents and the demands from new audiences coming into the theatre between 1780 and 1830 for more spoken drama gave the 'minors' the chance to win a share in this privileged closed shop. It heralded the beginning of the stage's growth as a profession.

By eliminating the divisive patent monopoly, and taking their place alongside the 'legitimate' houses, the 'minors' succeeded in establishing a coherent occupational group within the theatre world which was all the more powerful for its common legal identity. Prior to 1843 the legal definition of a theatre had been any building into which the public was admitted on payment to watch a stage-play. Such a loose definition had allowed for wide interpretation under the law, and had meant in effect that all stage performers, however crude, could claim to be actors; hence Macready's lament that the educated tragedian ranked no better than a rogue or vagabond.[9] In fact, this designation was only applicable to unlicensed performers who in any case were not always apprehended as such – certainly not within the Lord Chamberlain's jurisdiction – but fined instead. The 1843 Act reaffirmed fining as the penalty for unlicensed performances.[10] It could find no satisfactory definition to the term 'stage-play'[11] – a thorny problem which continued to add fuel to the battle between theatrical protectionists and free traders throughout this period – and in cases arising out of the Act subsequently magistrates continued to be unclear as to what constituted 'dramatic' entertainment and what simply entertainment.

The effect of the Act, however, was to draw a sharper distinction between the 'regular' theatre and its 'irregular' counterpart. This greatly advanced the claims of the institutionalised stage at the expense of its more casual branches. For it was understood after 1843 that a theatre had to be a permanent building and that performers on temporary stages would be liable to tougher penalties in the future. Thus in the first case to appear before the courts after the passing of the Act, the owner of a travelling theatre was fined £5 4*s* 0*d* for erecting a wooden stage in Southampton and performing tumbling, equestrianism and acted interludes without a licence from the local JPs. The prosecution argued that such entertainments should not be permitted to threaten the respectable local theatre run by Mr Abingdon, and there was talk of 'a duty to the regular profession' to penalise such showmen.[12] The Act did allow booth players to ply their trade without a licence at fairtime and on feast days, which explains why the larger travelling theatres could still be found in operation on such occasions well into the century. But, as Sam Wild was to find in Leeds, the sort of latitude which itinerants had been accustomed to under the law before 1843 was now greatly diminished.[13] Coming at a time when the growth of cheap rail travel was already eroding the popularity of the travelling shows, the Theatres Act served as a further incentive to showmen to pack up their portables and, where possible, set themselves up in residential business.

It must now be apparent that the outcome of the theatrical reform movement of the 1830s was instrumental in bestowing a new legal and psychological strength to the exclusiveness of the 'legitimate' theatre. Far from destroying the principle of restrictive practice, it had reaffirmed it. This was no accidental result. It reflected the influence of the men who were beginning to assume the theatre's leadership in the course of the 1830s and 1840s. They were the theatrical equivalent of the rising middle-class activists who in the course of the early nineteenth century sought to assert their social and political supremacy. All of them came of literate backgrounds and had been brought up in circumstances of relative comfort. But the most significant common factor was that none of them, not even those who were the sons of actors, had been trained to the stage from childhood.

Ironically, the best educated representatives were those with theatrical parents (yet another indication of the Victorian actor's sense of social insecurity): Macready had been to Rugby, Charles Kean to Eton, and Charles Mathews the younger, who took over the management of the Adelphi from his father in 1835, had been to Merchant Taylors and had initially trained as an architect. Phelps had received his education at Dr Reed's reputable classical school at Saltash (his father was a prosperous Devonport wine-merchant) and first underwent a career as a compositor and reader on a London journal; Edward Elton, a leading witness against the patents at the hearings of 1832, was the son of a schoolmaster, and was to be a conspicuous committee man as secretary to the Shakespeare Club and co-founder of the General Theatrical Fund Association in 1838. Buckstone, the reigning comic favourite at the Haymarket in the years 1833-9, had once been articled to a solicitor and was a prolific author of farces, melodramas and pantomimes; Ben Webster was highly literate too: though his father had been a humble dancing master, Webster had been well educated by the academic standards of the day, for he ran a bookshop on the side while a young actor at Drury Lane in the 1820s and subsequently penned some one hundred plays. Lastly, there was the new entrepreneurial breed of actor-manager, identified with the Surrey-side playhouses in London. At the Select Committee hearings of 1832 this group, led by Davidge of the Coburg and Osbaldiston of the Surrey, represented the most outspoken opponents of the patent interests. Davidge was the son of a merchant freeman of the City and had been educated at the respected St Paul's School. Little is known of Osbaldiston's early life, but his father was a Manchester businessman and it is likely that his knowledge of business came in useful in theatrical management.

The first point to establish about these men is that they had spent their early lives outside the narrow confines of the theatrical world. Most of them had received a 'liberal' education, or something approaching it, and had spent some time training for occupations which had links with the literary or business worlds or which, like solicitoring and architecture, had pretensions towards professional status. In other words, these men – and many more like them were to enter the theatre in the 1830s and 1840s – had some idea of the standards, both moral and professional, currently expected of respectable callings. This knowledge they took with them into the theatre, surely not without some effect.

The second point is that these men came to prominence in the theatre at a time when it appeared to be in serious decline. The evidence of witnesses before the Select Committee of 1832 revealed that play-going had lost its former fashionableness, that the size of the theatre-going audience was not keeping pace with the increase in population, that classical drama was dwindling in popularity, and that moral indignation at the unsavoury aspect of theatres and their neighbourhoods was hardening and keeping polite spectators away. Equally disturbing were signs that the provincial theatre, the traditional recruiting ground of the London stage, was experiencing a depression as a result of the adverse economic climate, especially in the manufacturing districts, and the growing opposition of religious sectarians. The London 'minors' were assuming the role of the provincial theatres, with the result that actors could expect a less pure training in 'legitimate' techniques.[14]

In some cases, no doubt, these factors were advanced by witnesses with a special case to plead, but both sides in 1832 were substantially agreed as to the symptoms of theatrical decline, however they might choose to interpret them. It suggests that the stock system in the provinces was already breaking down before 1830 and the coming railway era. For the educated theatrical leaders of the 1830s, some of whom had thrown up the prospect of a professional career for the stage, this crisis in the theatre confronted them with the harsh facts of their occupation's low standing. The flight of the fashionable from the theatre within a decade of their becoming actors must have been particularly galling. There were signs too that as the standard of life in central London deteriorated, theatrical entertainment was becoming ever more a working-class preserve – with all that that entailed for the standards of the 'Drama'. For from the 1820s onwards there is evidence of a distinct growth in working-class consciousness. The emergence of a cheap popular press in the form of penny papers was accompanied by the development of saloon entertainments, 'penny-gaffs' and other illegal theatres catering for the urban proletariat.[15] The rundown in the social tone of central London and Westminster, exemplified in the late 1830s and early 1840s by the deterioration of Lambeth and Southwark in the face of industrial and railway projects (such as the building of

Waterloo Station), drew the more prosperous sections of the community off to the suburbs, with the result that audiences at 'minors' like the Surrey and the Royal Coburg became less fashionable and more local.

I would suggest that this crisis in the theatre was the spur to the protectionist attitudes of 'legitimate' actors from the 1830s onwards. They were acutely aware that the higher drama was in danger of disappearing altogether. The patent theatres had been discredited, the stock training grounds were in decline, and the spread of less literate forms of entertainment threatened to engulf the stage in a flood of spectacle, farce and musical extravaganza. It is against this background that we must view the growing self-consciousness of 'legitimate' actors as a body and the high moral tone, as well as class bias, which characterised their actions. The efforts of the 'minors' to abolish the monopoly had been seen by the patents as a threat to the 'legitimate' stage, but the examples of Phelps at Sadler's Wells in the 1840s and of Charles Kean at the Princess's in the 1850s demonstrated that they too, as much as Macready when manager of the two royal houses, were occupied in a battle to revive the fortunes of classical drama and the conditions under which it could thrive. The underlying unity of the licensed theatres on this score only became apparent, however, when rival forms of entertainment threatened to undermine the restrictive practice which had been so carefully cultivated around the 'legitimate' stage during the course of the forties and fifties.

From about 1850 a new phenomenon arose in the Victorian entertainment world: the music-hall. These were saloons which had been granted music and dancing licences in a bid to counteract the influence on the working man of the public house, which, according to a Select Committee Report of 1854, was responsible for an appalling degree of drunkenness and depravity in society.[16] Indeed, from 1854 music-hall licences were issued on a large scale; by the mid-sixties it was estimated that such establishments out-numbered theatres by as much as five or six to one in some cities.[17] What worried the theatres was that the halls were increasingly demanding the right to perform dramatic entertainment, and that some, if not many, were infringing the law in this respect.

The fact that the music-hall case bore strong similarities to the cause of the 'minors' in the 1830s was not apparent to the theatres. In the halls actors chose to see a wholly new and dangerous threat to the survival of the 'legitimate' stage. At the Select Committee hearings of 1866, set up to review the licensing laws in relation to this issue, they were united in their condemnation of the 'tobacco and spirits' atmosphere which they saw as the chief attraction of the music-halls.[18] If such establishments became theatres as well, it was argued that only the worst standards of acting and drama would prevail, which hardly solved the current problem of finding suitable training grounds to replace the stock circuits. An actor could only learn bad habits from acting in the halls, asserted Ben Webster, 'because the audience are composed of "doubtful people" ': a comedian, for instance, would lose his style and subsequently be unable to 'take a position in high comedy or high tragedy in London'.[19] Implicit in these views lay a conviction that the demonstrably proletarian associations of the halls would foster the 'wrong' sort of actor. The playwright Tom Taylor voiced these fears when he spoke of burlesque, the staple fare of the halls, as encouraging a 'lower class of actors' in the profession.[20] Horace Wigan, actor-manager of the Olympic, concluded that for actors to perform in the halls would compromise the advance in dignity and status which they had achieved over the preceding thirty years.[21]

The Select Committee were naturally anxious to establish whether the theatrical case was based on anything more than simply distaste for unrestricted competition. What was so special about dramatic acting, it enquired, that it should not be subject to the laws of supply and demand? Theatrical witnesses were hard put to furnish a convincing reply, but their answers were characteristic of self-conscious professional men. Webster declared that 'the drama is a matter of high art' and should be granted special treatment because it required exceptional study and devotion for success. Other witnesses talked in terms of the 'interests of the pure drama' and 'intellectual entertainment'. Some advocates of free trade, notably John Hollingshead and Dion Boucicault, argued that theatrical salaries would benefit from open competition with the halls (which paid far better), but Wigan self-righteously insisted that 'actors, as a class, are not so much amenable to moneyed influences as other classes'. It was a well-bred anti-commercial gesture of which any professional practitioner would have approved.[22]

The theatres' case did not convince the Committee, which recommended that restrictions on the music-halls should be lifted. Certainly, on the evidence of contemporary theatrical activity, the claim to preferential treatment must have sounded a hollow note. The scarcity of classical acting in the London theatres of the sixties did not lend much authority to arguments on behalf of the 'higher drama'.[23] Moreover, it appeared from police evidence that the moral standards of the halls were not nearly as low as their opponents alleged. Dion Boucicault had pointed out in his evidence to the Committee that the theatre proprietors' objection to smoking and drinking was really a red herring, since the drama made intellectual demands and would not attract the sort of audiences who wished primarily to indulge in such activities (ironically, within a few years theatres were providing their own customers with refreshment facilities).[24]

What is perhaps surprising is that the recommendations of the Select Committee of 1866 were not followed up: the dramatic restrictions remained on the music-halls to 1890 and beyond. Attempts were made to resuscitate the issue from time to time in parliament, but without success. This implies that the theatres had some political weight in the second half of the century and suggests that their claims to professional standing were being taken seriously in official quarters. The revival of theatre-building on a large scale and the return of polite society to the play in the course of the seventies and eighties no doubt furnished actors with more plausible grounds on which to argue their case for special treatment. The emergence of celebrated performers as social personalities, and the influence which theatrical leaders such as Bancroft and Irving were able to exert upon their aristocratic and political acquaintances, must have gained actors certain advantages in the political sphere. Whatever the reasons – and they provide a worthy subject for further theatrical research in the nineteenth century – legitimate actors were able to preserve their exclusiveness from other entertainers in a rapidly expanding leisure industry, despite the fact that the differences between the two were not always well defined. In 1866 John Hollingshead, a lifelong advocate of free trade in theatrical matters, angrily told the Committee that actors had been protected for so long that it was useless to show them the benefits of unrestricted competition: they were 'not a class that you can discuss free trade with, because they lose their temper.'[25] And when parliament next reviewed the question of lifting restrictions on the halls in 1892, the attitude of the theatres had not changed. Irving told the Select Committee that the 'legitimate' stage had special rights to protection, for the theatre was a 'special institution, and differs in purpose, aim, scope, and method from all other classes of entertainment'. He was not averse to 'sketches', as opposed to plays, being performed in the music-halls, but he was in some difficulty to define the two. As in 1866, in 1892 actors were insistent that the dramatic stage demanded no ordinary qualifications. 'An actor', Lionel Brough told the Committee, 'is of necessity bound to be a man of more or less education, or he could not pursue his avocation.'[26]

The continuous battle between protectionists and free traders in the theatre highlights the growing self-consciousness of actors as a professional body. In their concern to preserve the survival of the 'legitimate' stage, and the superior status that this implied, they had displayed a remarkable consistency to the principle of restrictive practice. The struggle between 'majors' and 'minors' in the 1830s had temporarily obscured this adherence, but the force of the 1843 Act and the closing of ranks before the threat posed by the 'vulgar' music-halls had revealed very clearly the direction in which the theatrical establishment was travelling. In many cases, no doubt, its cause was inspired by commercial motives, but the need to argue a responsible and coherent case for keeping restrictions encouraged the development of professional attitudes and a determination to educate the public to the special claims of the theatre as a serious art-form.

The overriding weakness of the theatre's insistence upon professional exclusiveness was its lack of any coherent professional structure. Occupations which sought professional standing in the nineteenth century knew they had to establish a regular system of professional education that was supported by a recognised body of knowledge and acceptable standards of qualifications. By the 1850s doctors and lawyers were well ahead of other occupations in setting this pattern of development. By 1831 attorneys and solicitors had formed their own incorporated Law Society; by 1836 the Society was holding its first serious qualifying exams.[27] Likewise, under the Medical Act of 1858 doctors acquired a single regulatory body to govern their affairs in the shape of the General Medical Council.[28] Actors, who did not share the traditionally 'learned' image of doctors and lawyers, could claim no such advances. The pragmatic tradition of the English stage and its lack of any accepted body of principles necessarily hampered the theatre's search for a regular system of training. The failure in this period to find any satisfactory solution to this problem played a large part in the theatre's increasing dependence upon the criteria of the 'liberal' professions and the class bias which this implied.

But actors never lost sight of the need to transform their occupation along professional lines. Already by the thirties there were moves afoot to promote a corporate identity. This was greatly assisted by the growth of a specifically theatrical press. In 1830 only ten periodicals in the United Kingdom dealt with theatrical matters, and of these all but two ran for less than thirteen issues. By 1850 there were some fifty-four theatrical journals outside London alone, and in the second half of the century another 263 appeared, no doubt boosted by the emergence of dramatic reviewing a normal part of newspaper journalism.[29] Where coverage of theatrical affairs had been almost wholly uncritical or mischievous, it was now increasingly responsible, providing members of the stage with substantial comment and information on their calling as a whole. The *Era*, destined to run for a century and become the acknowledged organ of the profession, appeared in 1838; the *Dramatic and Musical Review* was to run from 1842 to 1852; the *Theatrical Times*, one of the most radical stage papers of its day, appeared weekly for three years from 1846.

It was no accident that this press emerged as the first national theatrical bodies came on the scene. These took the form of charitable fund associations, an extension of the sick funds which Drury Lane and Covent Garden had instituted in the mid-eighteenth century. In 1839 the General Theatrical Fund was established, its purpose being to grant pensions to actors, actresses and other performing members of theatre companies. In 1853 the Fund was incorporated by royal charter. The 1850s saw the growth of further theatrical charities. In 1855 the Dramatic, Equestrian, and Musical Sick Fund Association (DEMSFA) was founded, to assist members of these callings in sickness and distress. This society ran its own newspaper from 1856. In 1858 the Dramatic College was founded, and it was incorporated by royal charter the following year. This institution was intended to be both a charity and, later, a training school for aspirant actors;[30] its charitable purpose was to provide homes and maintenance for actors and actresses forced to retire through old age and infirmity.

The theatrical funds were clearly not very successful ventures, and were to be followed by numerous other charities, both national and independent, in the course of the century (for example, the Britannia Theatre Sick Fund Association, the Shakespearian Relief Fund, and, in 1882, the Actors' Benevolent Fund). They were perennially short of cash, for their chief source of income was derived from public contributions, and as often as not they were the cause of professional acrimony. The choice of beneficiaries of the funds' monies, invariably more numerous than could properly be accommodated in such a precarious occupation, did not always meet with general approval,[31] and certain fund-raising practices, notably the Crystal Palace fêtes in aid of the Royal Dramatic College, came to be regarded, like 'benefits', as unworthy of a self-respecting profession.[32] Yet the manner in which these bodies arose reflected the professional models which actors had in mind. The pattern of first establishing an unofficial association, and then conferring on it corporate status, at best by obtaining a royal charter which guaranteed maximum prestige, was one which all occupations aspiring to professional status pursued in the early nineteenth century.

Where the funds departed from conventional professional example was in not graduating to become proper regulatory bodies for the profession as a whole. However, the concern with pensions and relief which they expressed suggests that actors were increasingly aware of the need to turn their calling into a proper career which earned the same rewards as faithful service in other professions. When the General Dramatic Agency and Sick Fund (to give the DEMSFA its earliest name) was founded in May 1855, it was conceived as a conscious effort to fill a conspicuous gap in the actor's welfare; provision for relief in cases of illness or distress thus complemented the job currently carried out by the Royal General Theatrical Fund in the field of pensions. It is no less significant that the Sick Fund association was also calculated to 'root out the evils of the prevailing mode of agency', which meant in effect that dramatic agencies were henceforth to be stopped from sending unqualified actors to managements. This intention gave notice of the association's awareness of the need for some kind of professional regulation that went beyond simply charity.[33] A similar group consciousness was expressed at the establishment of the Dramatic College. The meeting at the Princess's theatre in 1858 which gathered to approve the bequest for building the College almshouses denounced as an 'injustice' the fact that actors were still one of the few occupational groups without their own charitable institutions, and the hope was expressed that the new scheme would finally put an end to the 'equivocal position in which [actors] alone are placed with respect to the rest of their countrymen'.[34]

In this respect, the theatrical fund associations served as a valuable public platform from which actors could proclaim their growing responsibility in the conduct of their own affairs. Dickens, a favourite speaker at Royal General Theatrical Fund gatherings, invariably used such occasions to stress the importance of the actor's work, both to himself and to society at large; by showing humanity 'in a thousand forms of humour and fancy', Dickens declared, the actor rendered an 'inestimable service to the community every night of his life'.[35] Irving was to expand this same theme in later years.[36]

But the theatrical fund associations were no substitute for a properly regulated professional structure. In this respect theatrical leaders showed growing concern for the calibre of recruits which the stage attracted. Most knew only too well the type of candidate they would have preferred. In 1839 J.W. Calcraft, the lessee of the reputable Dublin Theatre Royal, referred to acting as an art which required 'a rare combination of mental and physical endowments', for the successful player had to possess 'the mind and manners of a gentleman, and the attainments of a scholar.'[37] This lofty conception of the actor no doubt drew its inspiration from the model set by the accepted 'liberal' professions, but it is significant that even less idealistic commentators were preoccupied more with the social bearing of aspirants to the stage than with their talent and technical skill. The *Theatrical Times* put it quite bluntly in 1848 when it asserted that actors would only raise their social status if they became more 'presentable'; this did not mean that actors had to have gentlemanly manners, the paper went on, but it was offensive 'for a Hamlet or Macbeth to speak with a provincial accent, to leave out the letter h, and commit similar solecisms'.[38] A decade later matters had clearly not changed very much. J.W. Cole, the biographer of Charles Kean, again highlighted the need to make entry to the stage more exclusive when he admitted that there were still too many actors in the theatre who did not measure up to 'the high intellect, varied acquirements, polished bearing, and regular gentlemanlike habits' which their calling demanded.[39]

Before the 1870s, however, there was little serious support in the theatre for a regular system of professional education. Training schools of a sort had existed earlier in the century, but most were little better than elocution classes run by prominent actors or were private ventures without any solid foundation. Frances Kelly had started a school for actresses in her Dean Street theatre in the 1840s, and a Musical and Dramatic Academy had arisen in nearby Soho Square in 1848, but neither made much impression and both ended in financial difficulties. How little had been achieved in this area by the middle of the century can be gauged by the fact that when Irving sought to acquire the rudiments of his chosen calling in the early 1850s, he had to resort to private tutelage (from a member of Phelps's Sadler's Wells company) and the meagre facilities offered by the City of London Elocution Class, then run by Henry Thomas, a friend of the comedian Charles Mathews.[40] The formal establishment of the Royal Dramatic College in 1859, and its opening in 1860 by the Prince of Wales, gave promise of a more ambitious scheme; Charles Kean, Webster, Dickens and Thackeray were appointed to the board of trustees, and students were evidently enrolled as there is a record of their performances meeting with some approval.[41] But the Dramatic College was a training school in name only, for the provision of housing for pensioners seems to have been its sole achievement. Money troubles no doubt account for this, for by the 1870s the College was experiencing serious financial difficulties in the face of dwindling public support; in 1877 it had gone bankrupt, and its property was put up for sale the following year.[42]

The failure of the Dramatic College is confirmed by the growth of renewed interest in the subject of actors' training schools from the early 1870s. By this date changing theatrical conditions made the matter one of some urgency. For the coming of long runs and national touring companies was hastening the demise of what little remained of the provincial stock system. As London managements increasingly used the provincial Theatres Royal as a vehicle for 'bringing out' their latest productions prior to a run in the metropolis, provincial managers abandoned their traditional role as 'nurses' of new talent and became little more than booking agents. At the same time long runs and constant revivals drastically reduced the working experience of actors. Critics of the new system saw fresh dangers for the health of the 'legitimate' theatre, as most long runs were associated with 'society' drama, burlesque and musical comedy.[43] The call for proper professional training thus went hand in hand with a growing demand for a national theatre which would fitly house the classical drama. This was made clear in the earliest calls for better professional education after 1870. In a lecture to the Society for the Encouragement of the Fine Arts in 1871, the actor Henry Neville said that it was no wonder that actors were 'barely tolerated in society' on the same level as other artists when theatrical standards were so low; improperly trained actors and actresses, he continued, were responsible for the current vulgarity of dramatic output. Neville concluded his address with an appeal for government support for the establishment of a dramatic institute which would improve the public mind on these matters: 'We had a Sir Joshua Reynolds, a Sir Michael Costa, and a Sir Jules Benedict – why not a Sir William Macready?'[44] The following year there was a further call for some remedy to the existing lack of any professional education for the theatre when Mr Richardson Gardner advocated the founding of an actors' training school, to be called Shakespeare College.[45]

The first systematic scheme for a dramatic school appeared in 1874 on the occasion of the presentation of a site for the proposed Shakespeare Memorial Theatre. This was the brainchild of Mr Charles Flower, the mayor of Stratford, who anticipated a properly endowed acting school which would be run on the same lines as other professional training schools. Every stage aspirant would have to pass through the college, undergoing tests as to his suitability in the form of an educational examination and a short period of probation. If he passed this stage satisfactorily, he would continue his studies at the college for three or four years, ending up with a diploma which would be his passport to future engagements in the professional theatre.[46] The *Era* optimistically reported the project as a 'University of Dramatic Art' which would have its own 'libraries, class-rooms, houses for instructors, scholarships for students, and special chairs for Professors'.[47] It was hoped that the scheme could be linked to a dramatic academy in London which would not only be a training ground for young players but a national institution on the same lines as the Royal Academy, the Comédie Française or the Paris Conservatoire. Yet when the Shakespeare Memorial Theatre was finally opened in 1879, there was still no prospect that the much-discussed project would ever get off the ground. The same year Matthew Arnold issued his famous call to 'organise' the theatre,[48] and the *Theatre* magazine made renewed pleas for an 'academy of acting' which, it was predicted by one approving writer, would 'create, organise, and control a complete system of instruction.'[49] However, this venture too went the way of its predecessors, despite initial promise. In 1882, with the view to raising educational standards on stage 'by offering some obstacles to indolent incompetency', an association was formed with Lytton, Tennyson, Matthew Arnold, Henry Morley and Wilkie Collins on the committee;[50] in October of the same year this body was able to open its academy, yet within three years lack of funds had forced it to close.

The idea of a dramatic school continued to be canvassed throughout the eighties and nineties,[51] and in 1900 the *Era* was still calling for a Royal Academy of Drama.[52] No practical scheme came to fruition, however. Thus those who sought a training for the stage in the 1880s had little alternative but to accept, like Frank Benson, an elementary tutelage at the hands of reputable stage veterans such as Walter Lacy, William Creswick and Hermann Vezin,[53] or, like George Arliss, an expensive apprenticeship in one of the few good 'training' companies such as Sarah Thorne's Margate theatre (which was more of a 'finishing school' for the stage-struck members of middle-class families than a systematic training school[54]). The amateur club offered another opening for aspirant actors and was increasingly popular as a prelude to a professional career, so much so that some proposed it should form the basis of future training for the profession, serving the stage in the same way as the military schools served the army, namely under the control and support of professional management itself.[55] But again no practical scheme emerged along these lines.

Disenchantment with the failure to set up a regular system of theatrical education turned attention to other areas of concern, notably the threat to the survival of the classical repertory and other non-commercial drama. The idea of a national theatre as a permanent home for the classics aroused considerable debate between 1870 and 1890. Such a scheme had been mooted as early as the 1840s, but it was not till the 1870s that the subject was discussed in earnest. The ageing Phelps had touched off the debate when in 1876, at the Mansion House banquet in aid of literature and art, he had advocated a national theatre which would carry on the tradition of Shakespearian drama in the way that his own company at Sadler's Wells had done.[56] In the following years the columns of the *Theatre* and other theatrical papers were full of the arguments for and against the scheme.[57] The opening of the Shakespeare Memorial Theatre at Stratford, and the inauguration of annual Shakespearian festivals in the town, would seem to have fulfilled Phelps's dream, but in fact the Memorial Theatre, even under Benson, never acquired national status, remaining in a theatrical limbo in relation to the more prestigious London managements. As far as the theatrical establishment was concerned, London, with the 'very pick of the Dramatic Profession', should be the rightful home of a national theatre; so the debate continued.

Why did none of these attempts to establish a professional structure in the theatre achieve anything? The short answer is lack of money. Both the theatrical funds and the national dramatic institutions failed to find any satisfactory means of regular financial support. Without a proper endowment these bodies could not continue, for public support was precarious at the best of times. By the 1870s this lesson was beginning to be learned. The *Era*, which had consistently opposed the Royal Dramatic College scheme as 'false in principle and useless in practice', perceived that the chief error had been to build such an institution 'without the prospect of an endowment'.[58] But where was such an endowment to come from? Here there was little unity in the theatrical camp. The obvious answer seemed to be state aid of some kind, but many advocates of a national theatrical institution were either against this course on principle or felt it unrealistic in the current climate of feeling towards the stage. The playwright Tom Taylor, while agreeing with Henry Neville's plea for a dramatic institute which would relieve managers of their dependence on the box-office, judged that a government subsidy was too much to expect; he put his faith instead in a system of private subscription.[59] The *Theatre* was even more positive about the chances of state aid when it concluded in

1879 that the 'inveterate prejudice against theatrical entertainments in a large section of the community would suffice to prevent any Ministry from bringing forward such a scheme.'[60] And ten years later when William Archer came to review all the arguments in 'A Plea for an Endowed Theatre', he ruled out both state and municipal aid as practical possibilities, plumping instead for large-scale private patronage exercised through theatrical boards of trustees.[61]

But in some quarters there was hostility to the idea of state aid on the grounds that art would suffer. When the question had been debated in the late 1840s, the consensus had been that state aid would diminish the theatre's independence; the *Theatrical Times*, maintaining a strictly laissez-faire posture, argued that such interference might be tolerable in France, but was anathema to freedom-loving Englishmen.[62] This same theme reappeared in the seventies and eighties. The critic Percy Fitzgerald took the French example of a state-subsidised theatre to show that actors were worse paid under such a system, that it did not guarantee sound administration, and that original dramatic talent was deterred by state control of artistic policy. Fitzgerald suggested that a monopoly of a few good theatres would be a better scheme, endowed by the wealthy City of London which, he commented, too often wasted its money on 'the salaries of its officers and in building griffin memorials'.[63] B.W. Findon, the advocate of the amateur club as the future school for actors, was also suspicious of state control, fearing that 'a State-aided school would quickly become fossilised, and produce nothing but dramatic dummies.'[64]

Yet the truth is that much of this debate was academic, carried out not by professional actors and managers but between critics, playwrights and other intellectuals. If changes in the structure of the profession were to be achieved, the initiative and support had to come from the top London managements; as a writer in the *Saturday Review* saw it, their commercial competitiveness had to be turned into a more disinterested effort; but was it reasonable, he asked, to expect such altruism at a time of growing theatrical rivalry and rising costs?[65] Here lay the real obstacle to progress. So long as the London managements were commercially successful, they saw no reason to jeopardise their position by a costly commitment to the dubious benefits of 'Art', a commodity which patently paid few dividends. The feeling in the professional theatre was that a theatre for purely artistic ends was wildly utopian; indeed, there was 'no good reason', asserted a writer in the columns of the *Theatre* in 1879, 'why the interests of art and pocket should not be identical', for the one depended upon in the prosperity of the other.[66] If a national theatre was really needed, suggested another, then Irving's Lyceum company admirably fitted the bill.[67] Irving himself was one of the few London managers who would have supported a national theatre in principle, but he would hardly have concurred with Ruskin's condemnation of 'the idea of making money by a theatre and making it educational at the same time'; his view was rather that until the state endowed a national theatre, a manager's first duty was to make his company pay.[68] Thus the traditional conflict between the businessman and the artist, common to every theatrical era, mitigated once again against attempts to establish a central professional organisation which would foster an appreciation of the acted drama throughout the country.

Finally, it is difficult to see how professional institutions could have arisen in the theatre at this date without the more general acceptance of a solid body of dramatic theory. Before 1890 this prospect was slight. There had, of course, always been available handbooks on histrionic method. In the early nineteenth century George Grant's *The Science of Acting* (1826) and Leman Rede's *Road to the Stage* (1827) were notable examples, providing the reader with a guide to expression on the stage, but both were extremely rudimentary and unanalytical; they were in any case dispensable in a theatre which traditionally followed the style set by its most celebrated performers. Significantly, a more systematic approach to the study of histrionic method emerged only when current acting style underwent a period of transition in the second half of the century and no one performer was outstanding enough to set the predominant fashion. In *On Actors and the Art of Acting* (1875) G.H. Lewes was at pains to explain 'the very general confusion which exists in men's minds respecting naturalism and idealism in art'.[69] Lewes's work was ostensibly a collection of reviews, written while he had been drama critic for the *Leader* newspaper between 1850 and 1854, but as the title indicated it was also an analysis of contemporary conceptions of acting. Many of these, Lewes pointed out, were misguided, in particular the tendency to underrate the trained skill of the actor which was too often mistaken for genius.[70]

Lewes's contribution was a useful corrective to the uncritical appreciation of theatrical art which prevailed in his day, but it was essentially philosophical rather than technical and had little application to the professional stage. Some attempt to remedy this state of affairs was made in the 1880s. In 1877 the *Theatre* had printed a translated version of Talma's thoughts on acting, and in 1883 this was published in book form with a preface by Henry Irving, who considered that it supplied the existing lack of 'a permanent embodiment of the principles of our art'. A year before there had appeared Gustave Garcia's *The Actor's Art*. Dedicated to Irving, this work was a practical guide, containing illustrations and exercises, to the use of voice, gesture and deportment on stage. It was the result, wrote Garcia in the preface, of his conviction that acting, like singing, could be taught 'by means of a series of rules'. It was a view based on practical experience, for since 1868 Garcia had been director of the London Academy of Music and Dramatic Art; founded in 1861 by Dr Henry Wylde, this institution has initially been a school for singers, but the actress Mrs Stirling had been employed in 1867 to teach elocution as well. The desire to turn acting into a more exact science was characteristic of the late nineteenth century mentality, and reflected the trend towards specialisation which was overtaking all fields of Victorian thought and activity at this date.[71] But the derivative nature of this body of theory also suggests that it had been inspired less by a practical knowledge of the peculiar conditions of the contemporary English stage than by past historical tradition and continental example. Republication of Talma's writings and the fact that Garcia's guide was substantially modelled upon Delsarte's system showed the strong pull exercised by French influence in particular. William Archer took a new tack in 1888 in his *Masks or Faces?*, the first practical attempt to analyse current English histrionic method: on the basis of a questionnaire submitted to the leading players of the day, Archer deduced that English acting was 'inspirational' rather than 'technical', a thesis which countered the long accepted theories of the Diderot school and which, implicitly, threw doubt on the hopes of applying a more scientific approach to the training of actors.

But before 1890 such efforts to inspire a fuller debate on theatrical education were too meagre to have much influence upon the professional theatre. In any case, it is difficult to escape the conclusion that the theatrical establishment remained out of sympathy with the theorising of its more intellectual adherents, a position which was underlined both by the lukewarm reception given to the idea of an arts theatre and by the fierce critical divisions aroused by the growing debate over the 'new drama' of the Ibsen-Shaw school. Irving, a relatively intellectual actor by the standards of his day, took great pains to educate the public to the special value of the theatre, but there is no doubt that the driving force behind his campaign was primarily a desire to improve the social image of the player; reorganising the structure of his profession came a very poor second on his list of priorities. Consequently, the first proper attempt to professionalise the theatre along modern lines, in the shape of the Actors' Association of 1891, met with little enthusiasm from the establishment. No doubt, the fact that the Association had sprung up in the provinces and was the brainchild of relative newcomers to the stage partly explains this cautious welcome. But the new body, which aimed to remove 'bogus' managers, improve back-stage conditions and make contractual agreements between actors and managers more explicit and more equitable, also seemed dangerously 'political' in a calling whose leaders were traditionally managers as well as actors. Irving himself, though he subsequently accepted the presidency of the Association, initially called it 'destructive to our best traditions of comradeship and understanding';[72] and the dramatist Pinero voiced the suspicions of many established professional colleagues when he emphasised that he could not support such a 'combination' if it was designed to set actor against manager.[73] As a palliative to these fears, the Association took care not to press home its more radical proposals, such as payment for rehearsals, and it quickly made known its intention to hound the dishonest or incompetent actor as well as the unscrupulous manager.[74]

The difficulties of the Actors' Association, which was never to make much of an impression, reflected the inherent problem posed by attempts to professionalise the stage: was it an art or a business? How could a professional structure be built upon an occupation which, like a trade or industry, was divided between managers and men? To those who thought of actors as artists, an actors' union which would seek for its members 'the rights and privileges of artisans' seemed an unwelcome prospect with undignified connotations.[75] Yet if actors were to safeguard their rights, a confrontation with management at some level was inevitable, increasingly so as managers became principally businessmen rather than actors. The Actors' Association was therefore the first step on the long road to the eventual unionisation of stage performers. But it also marks a fitting end to the theatre's attempts to establish itself as a profession in this period. If some professionals interpreted the new Association as a union, its supporters were in no doubt that its aim was to 'strive in a corporate capacity for the elevation and advancement of their profession',[76] or as Lionel Brough, one of its vice-presidents, put it, 'more especially to guard what we consider our privileges'.[77] The Association showed all the hallmarks of a professional body. It was incorporated by royal charter in 1891, and was run by a ruling Council organised on a strictly hierarchical basis. As Robert Courtneidge explained, the intention was eventually to admit managers to the

Association who were not also actors, in the same way that the Institute of Journalists admitted newspaper proprietors who were not journalists. But, like other professional bodies, the Association placed the emphasis on occupational exclusiveness: members paid an annual subscription fee and had to be persons who were 'in actual employment as professional actors and actresses'.[78] More importantly, it was envisaged that the Association would also be a disciplinary body, the first of its kind in the theatre, for abuses by either actors or managers were to be reported to the committee, which would investigate such incidents at its discretion. The power to discipline its members was the ultimate prerogative of the professional association, but it could function only where that power was acknowledged. The Actors' Association was never, however, to emulate the achievement of the General Medical Council, and many of its objectives were therefore doomed to frustration. It remained unaccepted by the profession as a whole. It marked the end of formal attempts to professionalise actors; thereafter, the struggle centred upon unionisation.

8 THE ACTOR ARRIVES

Faced with the prospect of assessing what sort of change had occurred in the actor's position between 1830 and 1890, it is difficult not to conclude that we are left with something of a curiosity. It is plain, for instance, that the theatre by 1890 was a flourishing social institution patronised by all classes, not least by royalty itself. Its standards had also improved immeasurably; the best theatres in 1890 were recognisably modern and most playgoing conventions have altered little since. In this light it was undeniable that the social status of the actor had risen. In 1834 the actor William Robertson had claimed that the player was 'an undefined, unrecognised, disregarded alien' whose character could be 'traduced – without being known – by any vulgar, low-bred defamer, and his professional attainments tarnished without any consistent analysis, by all the young aspirants after literary distinction'.[1] No such judgement was possible fifty years later. Robertson's own daughter, the celebrated actress Madge Kendal, could assert in 1884 with equal conviction that there was 'at last a recognised social position for the professional player', for his calling was acknowledged as an important one and 'the society of the intelligent and cultivated actor is eagerly sought after'.[2]

For those, like Mrs Kendal, who took seriously the niceties of social convention,the qualification was an important one. For the plain fact was that, despite all its advances, the status of acting as an occupation still largely depended upon the individual actor. It did not of itself bestow professional standing. As we have seen, it could still by 1890 not live up to the strict demands of the professional ethic. It had no recognised system of professional training or self-regulation, and its standards of commercial morality were accordingly low (as the Actors' Association acknowledged). While on the Continent the theatre possessed its training schools and academies, and was, with state and municipal aid, an integral part of cultural and intellectual life, the English stage was unique among the arts in possessing none of these institutions or forms of support. Under such conditions actors could not guarantee to exclude from their ranks undesirable or incompetent practitioners. It is therefore no surprise to find that the debate over the actor's status continued to rage to the end of the period and beyond. Those who felt the stage was as honourable as any other profession could point to the knighthood which Gladstone had tentatively offered Henry Irving in 1883.[3] Others were less sure. The critic F.C. Burnand thought there was no question that an impoverished peer who took to the stage would lower his standing (though so would presumably a peer who undertook *any* career at this date), while few middle-class parents would wish to see their sons, still less their daughters, adopt a theatrical career.[4] Another critic asked: 'If we grant that the representative of the Prince of Denmark is well entitled to rank as a gentleman or even to receive the dignity of a knighthood, are we quite so sure about the personator of the Second Gravedigger?'[5]

Yet in many ways this debate, with its hair-splitting emphasis upon rank and position, was irrelevant and obsolete by the 1880s, possibly even earlier. For the late Victorians such considerations were important, but they did not alter the fact that, as Burnand acknowledged himself, actors had at last 'made it'. In a strictly theatrical sense they had 'made it' because acting was now a thoroughly distinct occupation within the stage world itself. For whereas the early Victorian player had often to serve as stage-manager, prompter, door-keeper, costumier, bill-sticker and theatrical agent as well as performer, his late Victorian counterpart could expect (in the best theatres at any rate) to leave these jobs to specialists and concentrate on his acting. And in this his chosen sphere the many technical developments which had overtaken the theatre in the course of the period to produce a strict separation between performers and spectators – the use of a stage curtain, a picture-frame proscenium, a darkened auditorium and stage spotlighting – these had taken the actor to new heights of professionalism. He was now as never before in control of his audience. Indeed, it is possible that his role will be never quite so distinct again, for some modern trends in the theatre, such as towards audience involvement and improvised performances, appear to be reversing this process. In so doing they are blurring the distinction between the world inside the theatre and that outside it and there is a risk that the actor will be devalued as a professional.[6]

But the actor had 'made it' by the 1880s in a more general sense. For as his standards had improved so the world around him had changed as well. A broad levelling process had been at work as a new ideology of culture and leisure had gained increasing strength over the period. The tremendous growth in the numbers of persons employed in the general field of 'art and amusement' between 1841 and 1891 was ample testimony to this development.[7] Nowhere was it more striking than in the case of 'men of letters'. The numbers of people making a living from literary work rose from about 200 in 1841 to some 11,000 by the end of the century; authors' numbers grew by 214 per cent in the decade 1841-51, by 219 per cent between 1851 and 1861, and even as late as 1891 there had been a 68 per cent increase in their ranks over the previous ten years.[8] In 1853 three times as many books, most of them fiction, were being published as twenty-five years earlier. This new readership was the result less of the circulating libraries (where a three volume novel could cost as much as one and a half guineas) than of the serialisation of fiction in the cheap popular press. And it was in the field of journalism that the real character and extent of the new cultural age was evident.

Thackeray's romantic picture in *Pendennis* (1849) of Fleet Street as 'the great engine' which never sleeps, with 'her ambassadors in every quarter of the world – her couriers upon every road', had by the mid-sixties some substance in reality, for by this date the press was already entering the era of the cheap mass-circulation daily. The abolition of the newspaper tax and the launching of the penny paper the *Daily Telegraph* in 1855 (it could boast the largest circulation in the world by the end of the 1860s) were followed by the appearance of a rash of popular dailies. The growth of a large periodical press was equally evident in the fifties and sixties. Here could be found remarkably high standards of journalism – which were also commercially successful – among a number of serious journals of opinion. The *Saturday Review* and the revamped *Spectator* pioneered the new line in literary weeklies, while the *Fortnightly Review*, the *Contemporary* and later the *Nineteenth Century* and the *National Review* inaugurated the popularity of the monthlies. With more popular appeal perhaps were the new shilling monthly magazines catering for a family readership with stories, miscellaneous essays and reviews. The most notable in this category were Dickens's *Household Words, Macmillan's* and Thackeray's *Cornhill*, which began publication in 1860 with an initial sale of 120,000. Much of this prolific output was in the early Victorian years heavily didactic in tone, taking an uncompromisingly moralistic, political or religious standpoint. By the end of the 1870s, however, as that late Victorian faltering of self-assurance becomes discernible, dogma and doctrine gave way to an unconcealed delight in literature and knowledge of every kind for its own sake. The age of Appreciation had dawned and the host of magazine critics and newspapermen were joined by an equally enthusiastic race of 'book-lovers, bookmen, vignettists, gossipers in libraries, adventurers among masterpieces'.[9]

Implicit in this unprecedented outpouring of the literate and the literary was the fact that a new public had arisen which veritably hungered for intellectual guidance and imaginative stimulus. But the essential character of the new market was its bustling demand for casual entertainment and packaged information. The learned diatribe and the ponderous quarto were relics of the past. 'The grand achievement of the present age', wrote J.S. Mill with characteristic prescience, 'is the *diffusion* of *superficial* knowledge'.[10] Walter Bagehot (1826-77), the most brilliant journalist of his generation, thought the rage for reviews and reviewers exemplified the transitory and fragmentary nature of modern literary output. Books appeared on every conceivable subject in every opinion and style, but all were small. 'People take their literature in morsels, as they take sandwiches on a journey'. Readers had changed and reading had now to be short, sweet and to the point if it was to interest the 'merchant in the railway, with a head full of sums, an idea that tallow is "up", a conviction that teas are "lively", and a mind reverting perpetually from the little volume which he reads to these mundane topics, to the railway, to the shares, to the buying and bargaining universe'.[11]

The rise of the journalist and man of letters had important implications for the actor. In part, of course, this was because the new craving for intellectual diversion and leisure pursuits touched the theatre as well as literature. Just as the growth of new journals and newspapers reflected the emergence of a new middlebrow readership, so the building of new theatres in the sixties and seventies heralded a new middlebrow audience. In many cases no doubt the two groups were one and the same, and certainly dramatic taste in the West End from the mid-sixties was as much inclined towards the purely amusing as was the reading matter offered up by the *Cornhill* or the *Daily Telegraph*. Above all, though, the demand for diversity which was such a striking feature of the new culture was also characteristic of modern theatrical entertainment. Theatres began to specialise in particular dramatic styles so that by the 1880s playgoers knew, for example, that if they went to the Savoy they could expect musical comedy, if to the Princess's sensation melodrama, or if to the Lyceum the finest classical tragedy. And then, over and above the theatres, city pleasure-seekers had resort to innumerable music-halls, entertainment galleries and concert-rooms. The two worlds were not mutually exclusive either; many playgoers also attended music-halls and other entertainments.

By the end of the period in fact a mass-market entertainment industry was a living reality in England. It was estimated in 1892 that there were 1,300 places of amusement in the nation's 530 towns, a total which comprised 200 theatres, 950 concert halls, galleries, public halls and gardens, and 160 music-halls. Together they created an industry employing 350,000 people. In London, as always, the figures were out of all proportion to the rest of the country. Here there were 550 places of amusement, 50 of them theatres, directly employing some 150,000 persons.[12] Given these sorts of statistics, no one could doubt, whatever his reservations as to standards and propriety, that theatrical forms of entertainment now held an unassailable position among the recreational pursuits of the population. And it was this mass market, unprecedented in theatrical history, which served to raise leading actors and actresses to the level of celebrated social personalities by the end of the seventies. Or rather, it would be truer to say – for the theatrical audience proper was never a mass one by comparison with the market the music-halls drew on – that the essential character of the new ideology of culture and leisure found easy expression in a sphere where intellectual solemnity was out of place and gossipy curiosity could find plenty to satisfy its roving eye. The lives of stage celebrities, both on and off the stage, and every trivial detail of the hitherto obscured theatrical world now became grist to the encyclopaedic attentions of the journalistic mill. 'The theatre just now is the fashion', observed Henry James, 'just as "art" is the fashion and just as literature is not . . . Plays and actors are perpetually talked about, private theatricals are incessant, and members of the dramatic profession are "received" without restriction . . . it is as if the great gate which formerly divided the theatre from the world has been lifted off its hinges'.[13]

But actors and journalists were united by more than simply a common cultural climate. Actors provided journalists with excellent copy, and it was therefore natural that the two should increasingly mix in the same society. As a growing number of members in both occupations from the 1860s came from well-educated, professional backgrounds, there was a common bond of sympathy in any case. R.E. Francillon confessed in his memoirs, published in 1914, that his ignorance of the theatre world had made him an untypical representative of the mid-Victorian generation, for it was really impossible to be a journalist, critic or novelist at this time without knowing some people on the stage.[14] This had hardly been true of an earlier generation when even drama critics, approaching their task with fastidious high-mindedness, had taken little or no trouble to acquaint themselves with performers. From the 1860s, however, actors and journalists actively sought each others' company, thronging, as we saw in chapter 3, the same clubs, supper-houses and other bohemian haunts. On each side, no doubt, there was an awareness of the benefits the other could bestow, but to a remarkable extent the two worlds of theatre and journalism coalesced in a genuine spirit of mutual enthusiasm and interest. Many critics and men of letters pursued their theatrical passions beyond mere play reviewing, and many actors, if less intellectually versatile, nevertheless sought to fulfil themselves in other roles than their stage ones.

One of the most remarkable mid-Victorian drama critics was G.H. Lewes (1817-78). Today he is chiefly known for his connections with George Eliot, but Lewes was in fact an extremely agile and wide-ranging journalist. Editor of the weekly *Leader* (where he was also drama critic 1850-54) and of the *Fortnightly*, editorial adviser to the *Cornhill* and the *Pall Mall Gazette*, he nevertheless found time to write a biography of Goethe, a number of philosophical works (he was an early English admirer of Comte), some fiction, and, under the pseudonyms of 'Slingsby Lawrence' and 'Frank Churchill', a series of pot-boiling farces and melodramas as well as his dramatic essays. He also acted professionally for a brief period, making his last appearance at Edinburgh as Shylock when he was already in his thirties and an established man of letters. Lewes clearly enjoyed the flamboyant theatrical world and its habitués, and much of his frustrated histrionic ambition went into the lively glimpses of London's bohemian life which he portrayed in his early novel *Ranthorpe* and in 'Vivian's' semi-satirical column in the *Leader*.

A less gifted but more typical theatrical journalist of the new type was John Westland Marston, whose early forays to the theatre, as we have seen, were attended with such misgivings. From the 1840s he was a recognised playwright (he attempted a blank verse tragedy with a contemporary setting in *The Patrician's Daughter*, 1842) of costume dramas and comedies, and in the 1860s served as a dramatic critic, an experience which later enabled him to write up his reflections on the performers of the Macready era and after in *Our Recent Actors* (1888). Marston too had histrionic aspirations, but he restricted himself to the amateur stage where he was, with another critic and journalist John Forster (1812-76), a prominent member of Dickens's private circle. Another leading journalist turned amateur actor was the robust Mark Lemon (1809-70), the first editor of *Punch*; despite the criticism of some colleagues that it showed lack of taste, Lemon was a keen dramatic reader and performer who became best known for his appearances as Falstaff in the north of England in 1869. It was a measure of how far things had changed in theatrical matters that Lemon's biography (by another journalist Joseph Hatton, who also ghosted the comedian

J.L. Toole's memoirs) highlighted his theatrical activities as opposed to his journalistic; indeed, the book is titled *'With a Show in the North'* – *The Reminiscences of Mark Lemon* (1871).

But then by the end of the 1870s journalists were abandoning any scruples they might have had as to the suitability of the stage and its members as a case for treatment. Books and articles full of theatrical memorabilia of every description soon constituted a minor industry in itself. Many contributions were made by actors and actresses themselves, quick to see the commercial potential of their own careers on the literary market. Even journalists had their lives chronicled for posterity if their theatrical connections were anything out of the ordinary. Thus one critic, Clement Scott, wrote a life of another, Edward Leman Blanchard, in 1891. Blanchard (1820-89) is today unknown, but in his heyday as a prolific author of pantomimes and farces and as drama critic, in the sixties and seventies, for successively the *Daily Telegraph* and the *Era*, he was a leading light in those club circles where writers, journalists and actors felt most at home. Perhaps most typical of the growing army of theatrical vignettists were Edmund Yates and Percy Hetherington Fitzgerald. Yates (1831-94), like both Lewes and Blanchard, came of a well-known theatrical family; like them too, he felt most at ease in that witty and casual bohemian company which offered such a contrast to his own settled position as a civil servant in the Post Office. This career, like Trollope's before him, did not prevent his dabbling in journalism where his talent as a gossip-columnist, under the pseudonym of 'The Lounger at the Clubs', soon became apparent. Yates had shrewdly perceived that his particular style of personal journalism, however much it might be deprecated by the serious-minded, was in tune with the temper of the new age of cultured leisure. His journal the *World*, founded in 1874, specialised in malicious social chit-chat but, despite the frequency of libel suits (or perhaps because of them), it remained the most popular society magazine of the time. It was in the *World* that Yates's articles on 'Celebrities at Home' first appeared (they were later reprinted in book form under the same title in 1877 and 1878), among which he devoted space to chatty descriptions of the domestic lifestyles of Irving, Charles Mathews and J.L. Toole. As his memoirs illustrate,[15] Yates clearly knew many actors from his membership of the chief literary clubs, notably the Fielding and the Garrick (where, in Yates's early days, the most influential member was J.R. Durrant, a wealthy Stock Exchange man who specialised in giving good investment tips to actors), and it was perhaps indicative of his popularity in the theatrical world that, on his release from prison after a successful libel case against him, he was banqueted by two hundred friends at the Criterion.

If Yates was the Comic Man of theatrical journalism, Fitzgerald (1834-1925) was the Heavy (though he did not scruple to use Yates's theatrical portraits to his own purpose when it suited him – as in *The World Behind the Scenes*). His approach was nothing if not anatomical, and there was something of the bookman and antiquarian in his writings. These were prolific and covered a host of different subjects; by his death he could claim authorship of over two hundred works, and this despite his activities as a sculptor and member of the Irish Bar. He produced many books on the theatre, notably *The World Behind the Scenes* (1881), *Music Hall Land* (1890), *The Art of Acting* (1892) and *Sir Henry Irving* (1895). Much of this work was little more than an excuse to retell theatrical anecdotes and enumerate the conventions and habits of stage people, often with an earnestly snobbish eye upon the social pretensions of the middle-class market he was catering for; he was capable, for example, of remarks such as, 'It is pleasant to think that nearly all actors of the first rank have been *dilettanti,* and have shown elegant taste in the collection of books, or pictures, or *virtu*'.[16] On the other hand, Fitzgerald's writing on theatrical subjects, however ponderous, represented an important contribution to the actor's rehabilitation in the late Victorian years. As an apologist he lacked subtlety, but he offered his readers what they wanted, a glimpse behind the scenes and an assurance that the glamour of the footlights did not end when the curtain came down.

By 1890 the enormous coverage of theatrical matters in the press and elsewhere offered ample testimony to the seriousness with which actors and acting were now treated in all quarters. The critics alone, by reprinting voluminous editions of their collected reviews, essays and other ponderings, had contributed by the end of the century a considerable body of knowledge and opinion by which the stage could be assessed and revalued. Their influence in creating a climate of opinion in which the theatre could take its rightful place in the nation's cultural life was undeniable, and Clement Scott was right to emphasise the fact. Scott himself (1841-1904) had played a major part in this development. He is discounted today as a critic because of his hysterical campaign against Ibsen and the Ibsenites, but after serving as drama critic of the *Daily Telegraph* for over a quarter of a century and editing the *Theatre* throughout the eighties and nineties, he was recognised as the doyen of English reviewers. The theatre he reigned over was respectably literate rather than distinctively literary, and Scott's own style of criticism tended to be gentlemanly and patriotic rather than discriminating; he was too often concerned to educate both actors and audiences to their responsibilities to be fully alive to the possibilities of the drama – he was, for instance, against using religion as dramatic subject-matter. But then the limitations of Scott's taste were shared by the playgoers of his day, and accordingly his work consistently appealed to them. In his *Labour, Life and Literature* (1913) Frederick Rogers described the fierce debates which took place in artisans' workshops in the seventies and eighties over the merits of Irving's radical style; the stage was as urgent a topic of conversation as politics in this world, and amateur dramatics were a popular pastime in the workingmen's clubs.[17] Critics like Scott were justified in feeling partly responsible for this remarkable display of interest in which, in a very genuine sense, the theatre had become a part of the normal cultural experience of many ordinary people.

The stage had also by 1890 regained its precarious perch among the other arts. This was a natural consequence in part of the renewed interest shown by influential intellectuals – and critics such as William Archer, Joseph Knight, G.H. Lewes, Henry Morley (who was a Professor of Literature at London University, 1865-90), and A.B. Walkley can hardly be described as anything less. Academia itself, encouraged by theatrical enthusiasts who were fast gaining a foothold at Oxbridge, began in its own fastidious way to realise it might be missing something. The scholarly William Cory, Fellow of King's, Cambridge and Assistant Master at Eton, 1845-72, confessed he had 'a constant affection for actors and actresses', but regretted there was 'no English language that seem to suit them'.[18] Some men of the theatre now had impeccable academic credentials. The novelist and dramatist Charles Reade held the Vice-Presidency of Magdalen, Oxford, a sinecure post which demanded its occupant's celibacy; the playwright Tom Taylor was a Fellow of Trinity, Cambridge; Henry Irving lectured at Oxford (where Jowett, unsuccessfully, proposed he should receive an honorary degree in 1886), Trinity, Dublin (where he *did* receive a D.Litt. in 1892), Harvard, Edinburgh and the Royal Institution. Everywhere it seemed actors were taking up the pen and assuming the guise of the writer. The best known were Boucicault, Tom Robertson and Arthur Pinero; dramatists with a craftsman's eye to the practical staging of their pieces as a result of their own experience on the boards. But many others followed in their wake, most totally unknown today. The actor-manager J.B. Buckstone was a prolific author of farces, melodramas and pantomimes; so was George Conquest, actor-manager of the Grecian (he was said to have run off over 100 plays, many adapted from the French). Edmund Falconer, an Irishman playing leading business in the provinces in the 1850s, successfully brought out his play *Heart for Heart* at the Lyceum in 1856, and five years later his drama *Peep o' Day* ran for over a year at the same theatre. Henry Thornton Craven, an actor who had formerly served as Bulwer Lytton's amanuensis, contributed to Fred Robson's fame with his acclaimed Olympic dramas *The Chimney Corner* (1861) and *Milky White* (1864). Even Charles Hawtrey, one of the greatest late Victorian actor-managers, scored his first great success in his own play *The Private Secretary* (1884), which ran for two years in London. H.J. Byron, one of the most prolific Victorian burlesque authors, had earlier started his career in like manner, making his first London appearance in 1869 in one of his own comedies. Thereafter he played almost entirely in his own pieces, which ultimately numbered nearly 150, ranging from sentimental comedy to pantomime.

But by no means all such actors restricted their literary aspirations to play-writing. Albert Smith wrote novels as well as burlesques, and contributed to *Punch*; and in fact his Egyptian Hall entertainments in the 1850s were as much literary and scientific lectures as dramatic performances. The Grossmith brothers, George and Weedon, were early initiated into the literary habit by a journalist father: together they were responsible for *The Diary of a Nobody*, which was first published in book form in 1892 having previously been serialised in *Punch*. Weedon, who, ironically, tended to specialise in Pooter-type parts on stage, exhibited at the Royal Academy, wrote a novel *A Woman with a History* (1896), and later made a great hit in his own play *The Night of the Party* (1901). George published two volumes of his reminiscences and was a remarkably versatile singer, composer, comedian and parodist, in a sense the entertainer counterpart of the intellectually agile man of letters at this date. Before joining the stage he had worked in his father's line as a police-court reporter, and this job he briefly resumed on his father's death in 1880 despite his growing fame in the Gilbert and Sullivan operettas. Lionel Brough's career was rather similar. His father and brothers were all dramatists and he had first started in journalism, working for the *Illustrated London News* and then the *Daily Telegraph*. He took to the stage seriously in 1864, but for a short spell in the 1850s he was serving both the *News* and the Mathews management at the Lyceum. The Irish actor-manager John Coleman wrote several theatrical biographies, Samuel Phelps's (1886) among them, two volumes of his own reminiscences, and a number of pot-boiling stage novelettas.

Almost every successful and self-respecting actor or actress felt obliged, or was called upon, to pronounce upon theatrical art, and as we have noted these public utterances by the profession were both a cause and effect of the actor's rising status. Irving, of course, was pre-eminent in this field, but many lesser names found themselves, like Henry Neville, delivering lectures to earnest gatherings such as the Society for the Encouragement of Fine Arts (Neville opened an acting studio in Oxford Street in 1878). Edward Terry combined a talent for low comedy (he was one of the famous 'Gaiety Quartet', 1876-84) with the respectability of a local worthy in his home locality of Barnes: he was an eminent freemason, a trustee of the Barnes Charity and a member of the Board of Guardians, credentials which no doubt enabled him to address the Church Congress at Cardiff in 1889 on the subject of theatrical amusements (he pointed out the beneficial effects of melodrama on audiences, and advised clergymen to visit theatres more often before they passed judgement on the stage).

But perhaps the most complete man of the theatre of the new type was Lewis Wingfield (1842-91). He successfully combined the roles of actor, writer, artist, and aesthete. His titled background, Eton schooling and Continental higher education placed him squarely among the cultured and well-to-do class of aspirants then entering the theatre. He played in burlesque, acted Rodrigo to Ira Aldridge's Othello at the Haymarket in 1865, and then designed for productions, notably the Lyceum *Romeo and Juliet* with Mary Anderson and Mrs Langtry's *Anthony and Cleopatra* in the 1880s. He was drama critic for the *Globe*, wrote several plays and novels, travelled to the interior of China, and exhibited at the Royal Academy. In many ways he was the first proper theatrical producer, foreshadowing the all-round role which figures like Gordon Craig and Granville-Barker were soon to play in the English theatre, as were Reinhardt, Stanislavsky and Taïrov on the Continent. And it was this break with the monopoly held by the old actor-manager which was really to bring the English stage, albeit rather briefly, back into the mainsteam of intellectual life.

Even in the 1880s a new artistic comradeship was discernible in the rarefied atmosphere of a community like Bedford Park which, with its intimate circle of painters, academics, journalists, actors and cultivated professional people living in country surroundings, was a sort of rural Bloomsbury. Here life centred on the local club, managed by the actor Captain Percival Keene between 1879 and 1881; it gave three or four productions annually for nearly a decade, and these attracted prominent writers and designers (E.W. Godwin was one) as well as the more cultured breed of actors and actresses, by 1890 figures such as Alma Murray, Winifred Emery, Cyril Maude and William Terris.[19]

The rise of the journalist, however, did not merely serve to introduce actors to intellectuals. His real benefit to the theatre lay in his down-to-earth treatment of literature as a career and a business. In this respect journalism was the reverse side of the coin on which Victorian culture, portraying the artistic figure as one with a more intense sensibility than other men and therefore detached from ordinary life, ran in direct line of descent from the Romantics through Arnold's *Culture and Anarchy* and Pater's *Renaissance* to the elegant aestheticism of the 1880s and 1890s. The two sides touched each other at several points, notably in the persons of those bookmen and bookish men who began to infiltrate the higher reaches of journalism at the end of the seventies,[20] but were never completely reconciled. Few major nineteenth century writers would have gone quite as far as Ruskin, who dismissed Fleet Street's entire output as 'so many square leagues of dirtily printed falsehood', but most of them regarded the growth of the press as a very mixed blessing indeed. However, the new journalism was demonstrably popular, prosperous and influential. If in the 1850s there were still doubts as to whether it was a fitting occupation for a gentleman, by the 1860s a steady flow of recruits from the universities was a reality. New outlets for men of letters – and increasingly women too[21] – multiplied rapidly as magazines, periodicals and publishing houses sprouted on every side in the eighties and nineties (London contained over four hundred separate publishers by the end of the century). Literature was now a commodity and the successful writer in New Grub Street had, like Gissing's Jasper Milvain, to play the market: 'when one kind of goods begins to go off slackly, he is ready with something new and appetising'.[22] Trollope, Thackeray, Dickens, Collins and Reade each accepted, and excelled at, the business of novel-writing. Reade's work epitomised the new approach. The inspiration for his novels came from an assiduous perusal of the 'hard facts' in newspaper cuttings and government blue-books, and nowhere was his market mentality better illustrated than by his readiness to carry litigation against offending publishers and piratical rivals. Amongst publishers he earned a reputation for a shrewd business sense, matched only by his bluntness of approach: 'I come to you', he wrote to one, 'as a trading author, determined to make money by my great labour'.[23] Reade was simply more successful than most. Many a dependable literary man could make a steady income, entering his study every morning 'as regularly as a barrister goes to chambers' and clearing his desk of a book review and an article here, a learned paper and an unfinished novel there. A hundred years earlier such a man would have been 'the cause of contempt for Literature itself'.[24]

That he was so no longer re-established the Theatre on the same level as Literature. The Romantic distaste for the commercial values of the stage could not now go unchallenged within artistic society. Actors and dramatists, for so long the butt of aesthetic condescension, could now be seen to have the same relationship with their public as the majority of literary men. Indeed, it is highly significant that so many of the latter tried their hand as men of the theatre; both groups knew the value of a deadline, and the rising rewards of novel-writing and journalism were matched by the growing protection and prestige of playwrights (not least by Boucicault's insistence on the author's share of the profits). If the critics sometimes expressed despair at the undistinguished literary results of this development (though the same critics were also not above tossing off their own theatrical potboilers), this did not greatly affect the theatre's undoubted commercial success and popularity. Cultural values were invested by a prevailing middlebrow standard, particularly from the 1870s. The job of conjuring away the whole problem of relative values which was so successfully undertaken by the most cultured journalists of the day (Andrew Lang, the doyen of this breed in the 1880s, was as staunch a defender of Stanley J. Weyman and Rider Haggard as he was of Homer and Milton), was carried out in the theatre with equal singlemindedness by Robertson's 'cup-and-saucer' dramas and Clement Scott's robust reviews. It was a mood reinforced by the sort of men and women now entering the theatre. Some had degrees in their pockets, many were well-to-do, and most possessed a liberal self-confidence which saw the stage, not so much as Art, but as a more exciting alternative to the Bar, accountancy, journalism or the family business. The tone of the new acting profession was set, on the one hand, by the leisurely and flirtatious apprenticeship served by the stage-struck sons and daughters of the well-heeled at Sarah Thorne's expensive training school in the Theatre Royal, Margate in the 1880s ('somebody in that company', recalled George Arliss[25]); and on the other by the muscular theatricality of the Bensonians, among whom cricket and fencing assumed as much importance as rehearsing and performing. If proof was needed that the stage was now professionally acceptable, the actor in flannels, so redolent of the gentlemanly, public-school image, provided it.

In the long run the transformation of the Victorian theatre by middle-class and middlebrow influences was to have unfortunate effects. Playgoing became increasingly expensive and exclusive, particularly in the West End where early dining and evening dress were both *de rigueur* by the 1880s. The end of the old craft basis of the stage, for so long embodied in the stock companies and their provincial circuits, was hastened, and as a result future opportunities for significant working-class participation were effectively reduced; working-class audiences and actors alike increasingly gravitated to the music-halls. The whole social tone of the theatre shifted accordingly, leaving it with the sober and genteel image it was to carry well into the twentieth century (at least until the 1950s). Such a style had a less than salutary influence upon the art of acting. This did not go unnoticed by contemporaries. Henry James called the new style 'the art of acting as little as possible', and the *Saturday Review* complained that, though well-bred actors made the stage socially acceptable, audiences were now paying for a no more 'lively display of the passions or humours of life than they can witness for nothing in their own houses'.[26] Things had hardly changed nearly fifty years later. Philip Godfrey remarked in 1933:

> The actor of today models himself into a close resemblance of the Man about Town. His conversation is of golf, motoring, bridge, cocktail-parties, and social personalities . . . The theatre is primarily a place for the expression of emotion; but the actor who spends his life restricting his emotions by acting the gentleman ends by becoming a tailor's dummy, and that, in many conspicuous cases, is what happens.[27]

The effect on play-writing was to preserve the dominance of 'society' drama which, widespread as it was up to 1914, acquired a veritable stranglehold between the wars.

It is difficult to see, however, how the theatre could have regained its fashionableness in the nineteenth century without changing its social image – and it should not be forgotten that theatrical standards rose as a result. The actor *is* the abstract of his time, animating the changing conceptions of man throughout his history, and in many ways the Victorian theatre was a microcosm of wider Victorian society, mirroring in miniature its paradoxical mixture of obstinate conservatism and self-confident openness, its vulnerability to social pretension, its capacity to flaunt convention. As a witness to the emergence of a new professional class and as a beneficiary of the spread of new concepts of leisure, the actor's world provides an admirable vantage-point from which to assess the revolution in cultural values that accompanied the growth of industrial society in nineteenth century England. And yet we should not press the actor's claims too far. It has to be admitted that his remained, and remains, a freak among professional occupations; the process of professionalising actors is not finished even today,[28] and perhaps will prove impossible so long as the essential character of acting remains unchanged. For it is a vocational livelihood by and large which operates at odds with the everyday world, appealing to its recruits not for the practical considerations which draw men to trades and professions, but out of a passion for the work itself and through that persistent social myth which makes of the stage a more glamorous calling than any other. If the actor's livery is today unobtrusive, thanks largely to the efforts of his Victorian predecessors, the real distinction remains.

NOTES

INTRODUCTION

1. See Richard Southern, *Seven Ages of the Theatre,* 1968, pp. 240-7.
2. John Philip Kemble died in 1823, Mrs Siddons in 1831. Edmund Kean, increasingly incapacitated by alcoholism by 1830, died in 1833.
3. For a list of these theatres, see Allardyce Nicoll, *A History of English Drama, 1660-1900,* vol. IV, 1970, Cambridge University Press, Appendix A, pp. 222-33.
4. There were no railways at all in the modern sense before 1825, but the success of the Liverpool-Manchester line encouraged large-scale building in the thirties; by 1848 some 5,000 miles of track had been laid. See W.J. Reader, *Victorian England,* 1974, pp. 16-17, and Geoffrey Best, *Mid-Victorian Britain, 1851-75,* 1971, pp. 68-72.
5. See chapter 8 of this book.
6. Ibsen, Shaw, Archer, Poel and Granville-Barker were the leading advocates of this new movement, but they in turn relied upon the support of hitherto unknown performers such as Janet Achurch, Elizabeth Robins and Alma Murray. Such 'intellectual' actresses would have had little scope before 1890 and their emergence was a sign of the changing times.
7. Cf. George Rowell, *The Victorian Theatre,* 1956; Allardyce Nicoll, vol. IV, and vol. V, 1967, CUP; and Richard Southern, *The Victorian Theatre: A Pictorial Survey,* 1970.
8. M.C. Bradbrook, *The Rise of the Common Player,* 1964. In recent years there have been signs that the balance is beginning to be corrected. Cf., for example, Kenneth Richards and Peter Thomson (eds.), *Nineteenth Century British Theatre,* 1971.
9. For a survey of the theatrical press in the nineteenth century, see C.J. Stratman, *Britain's Theatrical Periodicals, 1720-1967: A Bibliography,* 1972, New York Public Library.
10. No work has yet done justice to this genre. To date, a cursory mention in more general literary studies remains the standard treatment. Cf. Patricia Thomson, *The Victorian Heroine 1837-73,* 1956, pp. 73-6.

CHAPTER 1

1. Centred principally at Bath, Bristol, Norwich and York. The York circuit contained six theatres by 1805, the East Anglian circuit eleven by 1828. An Act of 1788, legalising dramatic acting in the provinces, cleared the way for the growth of the provincial circuits. For the development of indoor theatre forms, see Richard Southern, *The Georgian Playhouse*, 1948.
2. The rise of the actress can be found in Rosamond Gilder, *Enter the Actress*, 1931, chs. VII and VIII *passim*.
3. For a concise history of the patent system and English theatrical censorship, see Phyllis Hartnoll (ed.), *The Oxford Companion to the Theatre*, 1967 edn, pp. 247-50, 722.
4. Both France and Germany had a well-established tradition of state patronage of the arts. By the end of the 18th century the two countries could boast national theatres and national acting schools. In the course of the nineteenth century Germany went on to develop state and municipal theatres as well. See W.H. Bruford, *Theatre, Drama and Audience in Goethe's Germany*, 1950.
5. The aristocracy, especially younger sons, were less scrupulous in this respect. Several titled peers married successful actresses during the Regency period, but it became a rare occurrence in the Victorian era, though more popular with the Edwardians.
6. Sir Frederick Pollock (ed.), *Macready's Reminiscences and Selections from his Diaries and Letters*, 1875, pp. 26-7.
7. T.H.S. Escott judged that the English professions were valued according to their 'stability, their remunerativeness, their influence, and their recognition by the State'. *England, Its People, Polity, and Pursuits,* 1885, vol. II, p. 332.
8. The distaste for specialisation, which bestowed a certain glamour on amateurism, was particularly marked among the officer class of the Army – with disastrous results, it might be added, during the Crimean War. See W.J. Reader, *Professional Men,* 1966, p.74.
9. Ibid. p. 70.
10. Edmund Yates, *His Recollections and Experiences*, 1884, vol. I, pp. 299-300.
11. For an analysis of these aspects of the Victorian mentality, see W.E. Houghton, *The Victorian Frame of Mind*, 1957, especially ch. 3.
12. T.H.S. Escott, p. 334.
13. W.M. Thackeray, *The Newcomes* (1855), 1908, The Oxford Thackeray, Illustrated, p. 339.
14. Cf. Francis Davenant, *What Shall My Son Be? Hints to Parents on the Choice of a Profession or Trade*, 1870, p. 151.
15. For these developments, see W.J. Reader, pp. 67-8, 96-8.
16. Ibid., 208, Appendix 1, Table 1.
17. For a discussion of these developments, see in particular Raymond Williams, *Culture and Society 1780-1950*, 1963, Pelican, Part I, 'A Nineteenth Century Tradition'. Some valuable points are also raised in Arthur Pollard (ed.), *The Victorians*, 1970, Sphere History of Literature in the English Language, Vol. 6, especially chs. 1-3.
18. J.B. Schneewind (ed.), *Mill's Essays on Literature and Society*, 1965, p. 109; 'What is Poetry' first appeared in the *Monthly Repository*, 1833.
19. Ibid. p. 267 ('Bentham', in the *London and Westminster Review*, Aug., 1838).
20. P. 112.
21. This was the theme of his article 'The Amusements of the People' in *Household Words*, 30 March and 15 April 1850. See also H. Stone (ed.), *Uncollected Writings of Dickens: Household Words, 1850-59*, 1969, Vol. I, p. 343.

22. *Modern Painters*, Vol. III, 1856, Part IV, ch. 1, secs. 17, 18, in *Works*, V, pp. 32-3.
23. *Stones of Venice*, Vol. II, ch. 6 ('The Nature of Gothic'), 1899 edn, p. 165.
24. *Works of Thomas Carlyle*, Vol. II, pp. 234-6.
25. *Culture and Anarchy: An Essay in Political and Social Criticism*, 1869, pp. 15-16.
26. *Works*, Vol. VII, pp. 147-8.
27. 1904 edn, p. 239.
28. By the same token, teaching was difficult to classify, and it is perhaps significant that its status was uncertain in the nineteenth century – though the large number of women practitioners undoubtedly played a part here.
29. The Royal Academy of Arts, with Sir Joshua Reynolds as its first president, was founded in 1786. The Royal Academy of Music was established in 1822, under the direct patronage of George IV, who granted a royal charter in 1830.
30. Occupation Abstract 1841, Part 1, England and Wales, *Parl. Papers*, 1844, Vol. XXVII, p. 31.
31. *Parl. Papers*, 1863, Vol. LIII, Pt. I, p. 32.
32. Ibid. 1883, Vol. LXXX (Census Report), p. 30.
33. Ibid. By modern standards, the methodology of the nineteenth century censuses was primitive, and we should be cautious about laying too much store by comparisons between decades. As far as the status of the arts is concerned, the censuses can only be a rough guide. In general, the reports pitch the standing of artists perhaps a little too high, reflecting the demands of convenience and possibly the bias of the census commissioners themselves.
34. Walter Donaldson, *Recollections of an Actor*, 1865, p. 199. *The Theatrical Times* had complained in 1848 that the best actors did not compare with the best painters or musicians. Vol. III, pp. 433-4.
35. H. Byerley Thomson, *The Choice of a Profession*, 1857, p. 355.
36. This practice was bitterly resented by professional actors, for obvious reasons. Cf. 'Sucking Actors', *The Theatrical Times*, I, 1846, pp. 195-6.
37. 'Councils and Comedians', *Fortnightly Review*, Vol. XXXVIII, 1885, p. 371.
38. *On Actors and the Art of Acting*, 1875, ix (from the prefatory 'Epistle to Anthony Trollope').
39. J.W. Cole, *The Life and Theatrical Times of Charles Kean*, 1859, p. 15.
40. Ibid. pp. 19-20.
41. For a contemporary account of dancers, see Albert Smith, *The Natural History of the Ballet-Girl*, 1847. The best modern examination of the Victorian ballet scene is to be found in Ivor Guest, *Victorian Ballet-Girl: The Tragic Story of Clara Webster*, 1957; see also Guest's *Fanny Cerrito: The Life of a Romantic Ballerina*, 1956.
42. Rank-and-file musicians probably did not have a very high status.Like actors, they were not considered original creative artists, and they were paid directly for their services. By contrast, composers and musical virtuosi could reap high public honours. In general, however, music was an extremely popular recreation, both in the home and the concert-hall, and the status of the musician was accordingly rather higher than the actor's.
43. *Parl. Papers*, 1852-3, Vol. LXXXVIII, Pt. I, xcii.
44. Ibid. xciii.
45. Ibid. 1863, Vol. LIII, Pt. I, p. 32.
46. In educated circles, money was seen as degrading to art, artists being 'ideal creatures who should be above such vulgar trafficking as money-making'. Sophia Beale (ed.), *Recollections of a Spinster Aunt*, 1908, p. 176.
47. Cf. T.H. Escott, p. 335. The point here is that direct payment for his services put the professional man on the same footing as the tradesman. By this

token, authors, who were paid through their publishers, had a high professional status, and it is no surprise that their numbers grew so spectacularly in the course of the century.

48. Theodor Fontane, *Journeys to England in Victoria's Early Days, 1844-59,* 1939 (translated by Dorothy Harrison), p. 66.
49. Cf. A.L. Kennedy (ed.), *'My Dear Duchess': Social and Political Letters to the Duchess of Manchester, 1858-69*, 1956, pp. 154-5, 199; Henry Reeve (ed.), *The Greville Memoirs, 1818-60*, II (1885), p. 96; and Gervas Huxley, *Lady Elizabeth and the Grosvenors*, 1965, p. 67.
50. Cf. Oscar Wilde's *Dorian Gray*, 1890, and a novelette like Leonard Merrick's *The Position of Peggy Harper*, 1911.
51. *On Actors and the Art of Acting*, pp. 46-7.
52. P. 81.
53. Quoted in J.B. van Amerongen, *The Actor in Dickens*, 1926, p. 32.
54. 'Corin', *The Truth about the Stage*, 1885, p. 157.
55. *Journal of a London Playgoer*, 1866, p. 9.
56. *Footlights*, 1883, p. 173.
57. The great majority of theatrical journals and newspapers were very short-lived: see C.J. Stratman, xii-xiii. The *Era* was started in 1838 and continued right through the century, but it did not become a specifically theatrical newspaper until well into the second half.
58. Lamb was chiefly referring to Shakespearian productions of his own day, which he found so crude that he was forced to conclude 'that there is something in the nature of acting which levels all distinctions'. See his essay 'On the Tragedies of Shakespeare' in George Rowell (ed.), *Victorian Dramatic Criticism*, 1971, p. 28. For a discussion of Lamb's views on the theatre, see J.I. Ades, 'Charles Lamb, Shakespeare, and Early 19th Century Theatre', *Publication of the Modern Languages Association*, May 1970.
59. See John Bailey (ed.), *The Diary of Lady Frederick Cavendish*, 1927, p. 34; and Sophia Beale, p. 274. *Punch* took especial delight in guying the delivery of contemporary actors, Charles Kean being a favourite target. July-December 1841, Vol. I, p. 53.
60. Cf. Henry James's verdict on Irving's production of *Faust* in 1887, in George Rowell, *Victorian Dramatic Criticism*, p. 126.
61. 'The Renaissance of the Drama', *Saturday Review*, 8 December 1888, p. 677.
62. Tennyson's flirtation with the stage through Irving can be found in James O. Hoge (ed.), *The Letters of Emily Lady Tennyson*, 1974, Pennsylvania State University Press, pp. 307, 320.
63. See John Coleman, *Players and Playwrights I have Known*, 1888, Vol. I, p. 218.
64. Op. cit., p. 6.
65. The actor Henry Neville, addressing the Society for the Encouragement of the Fine Arts in 1871, deplored the current rage for 'tinsel and spangle nakedness'. *The Victoria Magazine*, August 1871, Vol. XVII, p. 362.
66. *Leaves of a Life*, 1890, Vol. I, p. 65. There was little money to be made as a playwright. Journalism and fiction were far more lucrative. The lack of copyright protection in the theatre did not help. See M.R. Booth, *English Melodrama*, 1965, pp. 48-9.
67. The practice was common in the fifties and sixties 'of always trying to speak with a full face to the front of the house, and placing the other actors with their backs more or less turned to the audience'. Sir Theodore Martin, *Helen Faucit, Lady Martin*, 1900, p. 263.
68. Macready's rivalry with Edmund Kean, whose supporters called themselves the 'Wolves', led to frequent clashes between spectators, while his later

rivalry with the American tragedian Edwin Forrest culminated in the fatal Astor Place riot of 1849.
69. Lady Pollock, *Macready As I Knew Him*, 1884, p. 74.
70. Examples of these practices abound in theatrical reminiscences of the time. 'Corin', and Peter Paterson, *Glimpses of Real Life*, 1864, cover most of them. Long-standing traditions died hard in the theatre: when George Arliss joined the stage in the late 1880s, he found that his first employers required that 'everything had to be done in the same way as it had been done for twenty years at the first production'. *On the Stage*, 1928, p. 134.
71. Cf. Thackeray's *Pendennis* (1849), and Dickens's *Pickwick Papers* (1837), *Nicholas Nickleby* (1839), *Hard Times* (1854) and *Great Expectations* (1862).
72. Vol. I, p. 73.
73. Vol. I, p. 170.
74. Elizabeth Lynn, *Realities*, 1851, p. 126.
75. Ibid. p. 129.
76. *Saturday Review*, 8 May 1858, Vol. V, p. 480.
77. Sir Frederick Pollock, Vol. I, p. 156.
78. Ibid. Vol. II, p. 12.
79. Ibid. Vol. II, p. 36.
80. Fanny rated acting the lowest of the arts as it did not originate, and was therefore uncreative. See Frances Anne Butler, *Journal*, 1835, Vol. II, pp. 82-6.
81. Cf. her letter to Mrs Jameson, 13 May 1837. See Frances Kemble, *Records of Later Life*, 1882, Vol. I, pp. 79-80.
82. H.C. Shuttleworth (ed.), *The Diary of an Actress or Realities of Stage Life*, 1885, p. 32.
83. Ibid. pp. 23-4.
84. I am indebted to Mrs Sarah Stowell of Durley, Hants., for a copy of this letter, part of a family collection of items relating to the Bradfields and the Baddeleys, another famous theatrical family.
85. 'Corin', p. 98.
86. Cf. a review of Dickens's amateur group in performance in the *Saturday Review*, 1 August 1857, Vol. IV, pp. 106-7; and a review of 'Princess Mary's Amateur Theatricals' in ibid. 6 June 1863, Vol. XV, p. 728.
87. Foreign actors and companies (notably the Comédie Française and the Saxe-Meinigen) strongly influenced improved theatrical standards of presentation in the 1870s and 1880s.
88. Sir Theodore Martin, p. 235.
89. Elvan Kintner (ed.), *The Letters of Robert Browning and Elizabeth Barrett Barrett 1845-6*, 1969, p. 22.
90. Ibid.
91. *The Dynasts*, parts first and second, 1913, xi (from the preface, 1903).
92. 'The French Play in London', *Nineteenth Century*, August 1879, Vol. VI, pp. 239-40.

CHAPTER 2

1. *I Was An Actor Once*, 1930, p. 32.
2. Newman, for example, preached the value of 'work with a mission', stressing the importance of 'fighting with yourselves' as an integral part of that work. See his *Discourses to Mixed Congregations*, 1849, p. 128.
3. II, p. 94.
4. See Ch. 6 in particular.
5. New Oxford Illustrated Dickens, 1955, p. 41.

6. *Journal of a London Playgoer*, 1866, p. 162.
7. Sir Frederick Pollock, Vol. II, p. 259.
8. Cf. the evidence of J.P. Collier, a former Licencer of Plays, before the Select Committee on Dramatic Literature (July 1832), *Parl. Papers*, 1831-2, Vol. VII, Q. 442. See also J.F. Stottlar, 'A Victorian Stage Censor: The Theory and Practice of William Bodham Donne', *Victorian Studies*, March 1970, Vol. XIII, p. 257.
9. T.H.S. Escott, Vol. II, p. 549.
10. 'For and Against the Play', *Nineteenth Century*, June 1877, Vol. I, p. 613.
11. T.H.S. Escott, Vol. II, p. 551.
12. Cf. Andrew Thomson, D.D., 'Two Discourses' (1818), republished in 1867 with a foreword by Robert S. Candlish, in *Sermons, Allon-Dykes 1866-69* (Bodleian Library); and Rev. R.E. Roberts (ed.), *Sermons on Theatrical Amusements,* 1865, notably sermon X, 20 November 1842.
13. Francis Close, D.D., *The Stage, Ancient and Modern*, 1877, p. 25.
14. Ibid. p. 27.
15. Rev. R.E. Roberts, 180, sermon IX, 31 October 1841. In a previous sermon Best had claimed that criminals had confessed to the stage's influence upon their offences. Ibid. p. 164, sermon VIII, 31 October 1840.
16. See Rev. A.J. Baxter, 'The Theatre – "A Religious Institution" ', 1865 p. 5, in *Theological Pamphlets, B-Bisset, 1864-69* (Bodleian Library).
17. *Sketches in London,* 1838, p. 163.
18. R.J. Broadbent, *Annals of the Liverpool Stage,* 1908, p. 217.
19. *Parliamentary Debates,* 1833, Vol. XX, pp. 275-6. For the background to the parliamentary debates on Bulwer's Bill of 1833, see Watson Nicholson, *The Struggle for a Free Stage in London*, 1906.
20. *Theatres, Their Uses and Abuses*, 1881, p. 14.
21. Cf. W.R. Greg, *Literary and Social Judgements*, 1869 edn, pp. 146-83, in which the works of Dumas, Eugene Sue, Georges Sand and Paul de Musset come in for strong moral criticism. Henry Irving admitted in later years that French-imported plays made 'a mock of domestic purity'. *The Stage*, 1878, p. 25 (an address to the Perry Barr Institute, Birmingham).
22. On the 'woman question', see Mrs E. Sandford, *Female Improvement,* 1836; Mrs S. Ellis, *The Women of England*, 1839; and J.S. Mill, *The Subjection of Women,* 1869. The Society for Promoting the Employment of Women was founded in the 1850s, along with the *English Women's Journal* which advertised posts for women, even in the professions.
23. Dr William Acton described seduction as 'a sport and a habit with vast numbers of men, married . . . and single, placed above the ranks of labour'. *Prostitution, Considered in its Moral, Social and Sanitary Aspects*, 1857, p. 175. The subject exercised a morbid and emotive fascination for Victorians throughout the period. See in particular Michael Ryan, *Prostitution in London,* 1839; W.R. Greg, 'Prostitution', *The Westminster Review*, 1850, Vol. LIII, pp. 448-506; and W. Logan, *The Great Social Evil,* 1871.
24. Cf. Michael Ryan, p. 5.
25. Jehangeer Nowrojee and Hirjeebhoy Merwanjee, *Journal of a Residence of Two Years and a Half in Great Britain,* 1841, p. 106. Until Macready's campaign against soliciting in the late thirties, only the Italian Opera, patronised by royalty and aristocracy, actively forbade entry to known prostitutes.
26. Acton, p. 118.
27. Ryan, p. 200; W. Logan, p. 54.
28. Acton, p. 118, and ch. IV *passim.* Henry Mayhew had reached similar conclusions; see *Westminster Review*, pp. 461-68.
29. Cf. J.K. Stottlar, p. 278.

30. 'The Abominable Opera', 16 August 1856, Vol. II, p. 352.
31. 'The Stage Drunkard', November, 1879, New Series, Vol. III, pp. 184-6.
32. Rowell, *Victorian Dramatic Criticism*, p. 207.
33. Cf. *Saturday Review*, 16 August 1856, Vol. II, p. 352.
34. *Theatre*, March, 1881, New Series, Vol. III, p. 144.
35. Methodism showed a remarkable expansion, increasing its chapels from 825 in 1801 to 11,007 in 1851. For these and other facts about the religious revival, see G. Kitson Clark, *The Making of Victorian England*, 1962, Ch. VI *passim*.
36. Cf. H. Byerley Thomson, p. 335.
37. Sir Frederick Pollock, Vol. II, p. 205.
38. See *Theatre Notebook*, XI, October 1956-July 1957, p. 46.
39. Rev. R. Ferguson and Rev. A. Morton Brown, *Life and Labours of John Campbell, D.D.*, 1868, p. 152.
40. Alfred Pease (ed.), *Diaries of Edward Pease*, 1907, p. 31.
41. *Observations on a Recent Pamphlet Entitled 'The Pulpit Justified, and the Theatre Condemned'*, by a Visitor, 1844, p. ii.
42. *An Appeal to the Women of England to Discourage the Stage*, by a Lady, 1855, p. 6.
43. 28 February 1863, Vol. XV, p. 265.
44. Christopher Thomson, *Autobiography of an Artisan*, 1847, pp. 186-7. Thomas Wright, *Some Habits and Customs of the Working Classes*, 1867, pp. 152-3.
45. *Our Recent Actors*, 1888, Vol. I, p. 5.
46. Ibid. p. 6.
47. Joseph Hatton (ed.), *Reminiscences of J.L. Toole*, 1889, Vol. II, p. 90.
48. F.C. Burnand, *Records and Reminiscences*, 1904, Vol. II, p. 333.
49. *A Society Clown*, 1888, pp. 97-8.
50. *London Labour and the London Poor*, 1861, Vol. III, p. 78.
51. See Alan MacKinnon, *The Oxford Amateurs*, 1910, p. x. Undergraduate theatricals had been banned in 1869 and the University statutes forbade students associating with actors and ropedancers. From 1884, however, as a result of the impressive effect of Benson's production, the authorities gave their blessing to public productions so long as only Shakespeare was performed.
52. Sir Theodore Martin, 1900, p. 190.
53. Ibid. p. 257.
54. S.D. Collingwood, *Life and Letters of Lewis Carroll*, 1898, p. 74.
55. William Plomer (ed.), *Kilvert's Diary: Selections from the Diary of the Reverend Francis Kilvert, 1870-1879*, 1960, Vol. I, pp. 21, 25, 29, 301; Vol. II, p. 108.
56. Cf. *The Theatrical Times*, 11 March 1848, Vol. II, pp. 82-3; and *The Stage-Manager*, 24 February 1849, No. 2, I, 12.
57. Marjorie Thomson, 'Henry Arthur Jones and Wilson Barrett: Some Correspondence 1879-1904', *Theatre Notebook*, Vol. XI, October 1956-July 1957, p. 43.
58. 1894. Florence Emily Hardy, *The Life of Thomas Hardy*, 1962, p. 265.
59. Rowell (ed.), *Victorian Dramatic Criticism*, p. 256.
60. Cf. *Theatre*, March, 1881, N.S., Vol. III, p. 183.
61. Ibid. February 1879, N.S., Vol. II, pp. 8-11.
62. Thomas Wright recalled that on their Saturday night out, 'the theatre is the most popular resort of pleasure-seeking workmen'. Op. cit., pp. 196-7.
63. For the development of urban leisure facilities between the fifties and eighties, see T.H.S. Escott, Vol. II, ch. XXIX, pp. 417-49.

64. Owen Chadwick, *The Victorian Church*, Part II, 2nd edn, 1972, p. 112.
65. Tennyson's agnosticism is discussed in Basil Willey, *More Nineteenth Century Studies*, 1956, Ch. 2, pp. 53-105.
66. Chadwick, pp. 122-3.
67. March 21, 1857, Vol. III, p. 264.
68. Ibid. 26 March 1859, Vol. VII, p. 368.
69. Ibid. 23 July 1864, Vol. XVIII, pp. 119-20.
70. R.J. Broadbent, p. 176.
71. Chadwick, pp. 136-9.
72. Arthur W. Fluck, *Theatrical Reform*, 1879, p. 10.
73. Cf. Rev. H.R. Haweis, *Shakespeare and the Stage*, 1878 (a sermon on behalf of the Shakespeare Memorial Fund). Haweis was one of the Church's 'honest doubters' and gained a reputation in the 1880s as an advanced broad churchman.
74. J. Panton Ham, *The Stage and the Drama in their relation to Society*, 1880, p. 7. J.M. Dixon felt that 'a good play' could not fail to improve a person's 'moral feelings'. *The Pulpit and the Stage*, 1879, pp. 6-7. As for actors, their longevity proved to Dixon that the stage was a moral influence: 'men and women who lived so long could not have been intemperate or fast livers'. *The Pulpit and the Stage*, 1881, p. 5.
75. W.H. Hudson, *The Church and the Stage*, 1886, p. 52.
76. Vol. III, November 1879, p. 183; and Vol. III, December 1879, p. 247.
77. Quoted in Frances Fleetwood, *Conquest: The Story of a Theatre Family*, 1953, p. 129.
78. Henry Irving, *The Stage*, p. 14.
79. Henry Arthur Jones, *Renascence of the English Drama*, 1895, pp. 94-5.
80. Edward Gordon Craig, *Index to the Story of my Days, 1872-1907*, 1957, pp. 158-9.
81. George Rowell, *The Dramatic Treatment of Women's Status, 1865-1914*, Oxford B. Litt. thesis, 1950, p. 57.
82. From an address to the Church of England Temperance Society, 31 March 1876, reported in *The Year Round*, 22 April 1876, Vol. XVI, p. 133.
83. Henry Irving, *English Actors, Their Characteristics and Methods* (a discourse delivered in the University Schools, Oxford), 1886, p. 17.
84. Ibid. p. 60.
85. In 1891 the Church once again challenged Irving's vindication of the stage, declaring its influence the most demoralising with which organised religion had had to contend. See Laurence Irving, *Henry Irving: The Actor and his World*, 1951, p. 533.
86. Ibid. p. 679.
87. *Critical Miscellanies*, 1886, Vol. I, p. 182.

CHAPTER 3

1. Henry Compton always lamented the fact that the demands of the stage left him little time to pursue his scientific hobbies. Edward and Charles Compton, *Memoir of Henry Compton*, 1879, p. 120.
2. *Random Recollections of an Old Actor*, 1880, p. 91.
3. According to Ben Webster (of Haymarket fame), actors were prone to marry young and have large families, a tendency which hindered their careers and increased their difficulties. See Margaret Webster, *The Same Only Different*, 1969, p. 28.
4. J.A. Hammerton (ed.), *The Actor's Art*, 1897, p. 196.

5. *The Natural History of the Ballet-Girl,* 1847, p. 91.
6. For example, they kept up the young Kate Terry's salary while she was 'off', though this went against current theatrical practice. Marguerite Steen, *A Pride of Terrys,* 1962, p. 65.
7. W.H. Murray (1790-1852) had a distinguished career as manager of the Edinburgh theatres (the Royal and the Adelphi) until his retirement in 1851. His second wife was an actress in his own company. For his management at Edinburgh, see J.C. Dibdin, *The Annals of the Edinburgh Stage,* 1888.
8. *On the Stage – and Off,* 1885, pp. 123-4. In some provincial areas, the end of the stock circuit era confined the actor, ironically, more than ever to the circle of his professional colleagues at a time when the barriers between stage and society were generally weakening. See, for example, G.T. Watts, *Theatrical Bristol,* 1915, p. 117.
9. Sir Frederick Pollock, vol. I, p. 68. It is interesting to speculate whether Charles Kean would have gone so far without the memory of his famous father, a point which did not escape some of his contemporaries. Cf. John Coleman, vol. I, p. 89.
10. *On the Stage,* 1928, p. 168.
11. The managers of the Bolton theatre in 1831 were Mr and Mrs Copeland. Taylor, a local lawyer, was a keen amateur and played in many professional benefits, but he retired completely from theatricals in 1841 on the grounds that 'acting on stage was detrimental to my position in society'. See J. Clegg (ed.), *Autobiography of a Lancashire Lawyer,* 1883, p. 111.
12. Laurence Irving, p. 64.
13. See St Vincent Troubridge, *The Benefit System in the British Theatre,* 1967, pp. 79-83. Society for Theatre Research.
14. *London Labour and the London Poor,* 1861 edn, vol. III, p. 141. In his first engagement, Henry Irving frequently rehearsed from ten o'clock in the morning until long after midnight, but he confessed that it was easy to remain cheerful: 'there is no restraint on a laugh or joke, no governor to stop your mouth, no petty subjection to one another, because they are equal – they work for a prize free for all'. Laurence Irving, p. 74. This 'freedom' must have seemed highly attractive to desk-bound clerks such as Irving had recently been.
15. The censuses of 1841-91 indicate that on average a good third of all actors in England and Wales worked in London; among actresses the figure rises to almost 50 per cent on average.
16. *Punch* in 1879 refers to 'Passionate Brompton' in one of its sketches: 14 June 1879, LXXVI, p. 270.
17. P.H. Fitzgerald, *The World Behind the Scenes,* 1881, p. 127. This description is in fact Edmund Yates's, and Fitzgerald had taken it from the latter's *Celebrities at Home* (first series), 1877, p. 60. Yates reckoned that in the 1850s 'you might have laid hands upon the best representatives for the complete cast of a comedy within the radius of half a mile from Brompton Square'. Ibid. pp. 59-60.
18. *The Dramatic and Musical Directory of the United Kingdom,* an annual publication after 1883, is the first comprehensive list of actors' and actresses' addresses in London, and these areas show a high proportion of 'professionals' in residence at this date.
19. See Marguerite Steen, *passim.*
20. Mrs Charles Calvert, *Sixty-Eight Years on the Stage,* 1911, p. 267.
21. Clement Scott and Cecil Howard, *The Life and Reminiscences of Edward Leman Blanchard,* 1891, vol. I, p. 183; a list of the Arundel's membership in 1868 can be found on p. 241 of Vol. I.
22. R.W. Warner, the husband of the actress Mary Huddart (joint-manager of

Sadler's Wells with Phelps from 1844), was the Wrekin's landlord in the late thirties, and he was followed by Hemming, a former actor at the Adelphi and the Haymarket.

23. J.M. East, *'Neath the Mask*, 1967, p. 48.
24. The Strand was then known as 'Prosser's Avenue', a 'prosser' being someone who persistently accepted drinks at other people's expense. The ill-paid Victorian actor was probably no stranger to this practice.
25. John Coleman, *Fifty Years of an Actor's Life*, 1904, vol. I, p. 212.
26. Regarded as one of the most fascinating actresses of her day, Vestris had a penchant for wearing stage jewellery and was invariably accompanied by fancy spaniels. See Westland Marston, vol. II, p. 149. For a concise examination of her character and career, see Rosamond Gilder, ch. XII. Her achievements as a 'producer' were considerable, however: see W.A. Armstrong, 'Madame Vestris: A Centenary Appreciation', *Theatre Notebook*, Vol. XI, October 1956-July 1957, pp. 11-18.
27. Laurence Irving, p. 159.
28. See Percy Fitzgerald, *Sir Henry Irving*, 1895, p. 86, n.I.
29. Op. cit., p. 146.
30. 'My First Experience of Hamlet', *Stage Stories of Actors and Actresses*, 1895, No. I, p.7.
31. *I Was An Actor Once*, 1930, p. 109.
32. Charles Brookfield, *Random Reminiscences*, 1902, pp. 96-7.
33. *Recollections and Reflections*, 1872, vol. II, p. 27.
34. *Punch*, 1841, vol. I, p. 48.
35. Courtneidge, 1930, p. 117.
36. Cf. 'Corin', pp. 70-1; and Mayhew's Punch-and-Judy man, who liked to drink before appearing 'because the performance will go far superior': *London Labour and the London Poor*, 1861, vol. III, p. 48.
37. Clement Scott's edition of Edward Blanchard's diaries (1891) makes frequent reference to actors who drank themselves to death in the 1840s.
38. Op. cit., p. 76.
39. Op. cit., pp. 114-15.
40. Cf. the Crummles family in *Nicholas Nickleby* (1839) and Mr Wopsle in *Great Expectations* (1862); the dramatist Glenalvon Fogg and Mrs Rossett in Smith's *The Fortunes of the Scattergood Family* (1845); Miss Kemble and Vasty Vaughan in Elizabeth Lynn's *Realities* (1851); and Celest La Thionville – 'always natural, except off the stage' – in Mrs Annie Edwards' *The Morals of Mayfair* (1858).
41. *The World Behind the Scenes*, p. 213.
42. Paterson relates how strolling companies would send forward in advance to their next destination the best dressed actor among them in order to make a favourable impression: his less presentable colleagues would then arrive under cover of darkness. Op. cit., p. 53.
43. E. and E. Johnson, *The Dickens Theatrical Reader*, 1964, 207. It is significant that the theatre was a favourite subject of popular woodcuts and ballads in the early Victorian period. See Louis James, p. 150, and J.W. Robinson, *Theatrical Street Ballads*, 1971 (Society for Theatre Research). Stage celebrities were also responsible for setting many fashions, notably 'Jim Crow' hats and gin, Polka jackets and cigars, Taglioni coats, 'Dundreary' waistcoats and Gladstone collars (which were popularised by the burlesque 'The Wicked World' at the Haymarket in 1873). During her American tour of 1832-4, Fanny Kemble became the model for women's bonnets and riding habits. See Dorothie de Bear Bobbé, *Fanny Kemble*, 1932, pp. 76-7.
44. Op. cit. pp. 40-1.

45. R.M. Sillard, *Barry Sullivan*, 1901, vol. I, p. 180; vol. II, pp. 134-5.
46. Op. cit., p. 47.
47. 'On Novelty and Familiarity' (1826), in P.P. Howe (ed.), *Complete Works*, 1931, vol. XII, p. 299.
48. *The Adventures of Mr. Ledbury*, 1844, vol. II, p. 214.
49. W.B. Megson ('Trim'), *'Old Wild's': A Nursery of Strolling Players*, 1888, p. 49.
50. Wild's popularity in Lancashire ensured lenient judicial treatment there. Ibid. p. 182. Where actors were being pursued by the law, the local populace might well take positive steps to assist them. Cf. the case of the actor sought by bailiffs at Preston in 1837. Ibid. pp. 41-2.
51. J.K. Jerome, pp. 123-4.
52. R.M. Sillard, p. 141. This was a recollection of the mid-1840s.
53. *Works*, XXVIII, 52.
54. Op. cit., pp. 152, 196-7.
55. For a discussion of this theme, see Martin Meisel, 'Perspectives on Victorian and other acting', *Victorian Studies*, June 1963.
56. *The Examiner*, 15 January, 1817. Irving's appeal was similar, according to the critic A.B. Walkley, despite the greater sophistication of his audience. Cf. 'Playhouse Impressions' (1892) in George Rowell (ed.), *Victorian Dramatic Criticism*, p. 135.
57. G.O. Trevelyan, *Life and Letters of Lord Macaulay*, 1876, vol. II, p. 210.
58. Lewis Carroll found the realism of some theatrical scenes profoundly disturbing. See Ronald Pearsall, *The Worm in the Bud*, 1967, p. 334.
59. John Bailey (ed.), vol. II, p. 159.
60. *The Theatre in my Time*, 1933, p. 30.
61. John Forster, *Life of Dickens*, 1928, vol. I, p. 291.
62. The American actress Adah Isaacs Menken (1835-68) caused a furore in 1864 by appearing in the near-naked equestrian role of Mazeppa. Most critics were disconcerted by the performance, but by no means all were disgusted. See Bernard Falk, *The Naked Lady: A Biography of Adah Isaacs Menken*, 1934, pp. 80-6, 105.
63. The 'can-can' was of Parisian origin and first appeared in England at the Alhambra Music-Hall in the late 1860s. See M. Willson Disher, *The Personality of the Alhambra*, 1937, p. 9.
64. Cf. Fanny Kemble's shock at seeing 'decent Englishwomen' crowding night after night to the St James's in 1842 to see the French male impersonator Mademoiselle Déjazet. *Records of Later Life*, vol. II, p. 244.
65. *Journeys to England*, p. 123.
66. Dickens commonly employed this technique. Cf. the delight of the Nubbles children at Astley's in *The Old Curiosity Shop* (1841), 1950 (The New Oxford Illustrated Dickens), p. 293, and David's visit to Covent Garden in *David Copperfield* (1850), 1947, p. 286.
67. *The Fortunes of the Scattergood Family*, vol. I, p. 85.
68. Hence the anxiety of the music-hall proprietors before the Select Committee of 1866 on Theatrical Licences and Regulations to establish that their entertainment was popular with working men *and* their families. Cf. the evidence of the Alhambra manager, *Parl. Papers*, 1866, XVI, Q. 1616. The patronising view that working-class audiences needed protection from the vulgarity of the halls, while upper and middle-class spectators could attend the 'disreputable' French-imported dramas of the regular theatre undisturbed, suitably reflects the official tendency of the time to equate the working man's needs with those of children and to treat him accordingly.

CHAPTER 4

1. This did not go unnoticed in the theatre. Irving's 'Beefsteak' suppers were a conscious attempt to galvanise influential support behind the profession. Frances Donaldson, *The Actor-Managers,* 1970, p. 93.
2. Op. cit., vol. II, p. 544.
3. Charles Wyndham's Criterion Theatre, which he ran from 1876, was the first to sell coffee and strong liqueurs in the interval. See J.W. Donohue (ed.), *The Theatrical Manager in England and America,* 1971, p. 202.
4. T.H.S. Escott spoke of the West End theatre as being 'not only a place in which to sit still and laugh or wonder . . . but a lounge where cigarettes may be smoked, friends met and chatted with, and the news of the evening obtained'. Op. cit., vol. II, p. 543. The French actor Coquelin described the Haymarket under the Bancrofts (1880-5) as 'le rendez-vous de l'aristocratie'. See Mr and Mrs Bancroft, *On and Off the Stage,* 1886, vol. II, p. 22.
5. Districts with a distinctive artistic character continued to exist, however. One such in the 1880s and 1890s was Bedford Park, which was almost designed as a separate community and was peopled by a close society of artists, actors, academics, journalists and cultivated members of the professional classes. See 'Bedford Park: Aesthetes Elysium?' in Ian Fletcher (ed.), *Romantic Mythologies,* 1967.
6. See W.J. Reader, *Professional Men,* pp. 208, 211 (Appendix I, Tables 1 and 2).
7. Actresses will be dealt with in chapter 5.
8. Belton was a provincial actor-manager of some repute in the fifties and sixties. His parents had died while he was still a child. For his life, see his autobiography *Recollections of an Old Actor,* 1880.
9. Don stood 6 feet 7 inches in height and was eccentric to boot. See Lester Wallack, *Memories of Fifty Years,* 1889, pp. 42-4.
10. Our knowledge of the working-class theatre would tend to support this conclusion. Cf. evidence of this tradition among travelling theatre folk in W. B. Megson ('Trim'), pp. 36-7; among street exhibitors in Henry Mayhew, p. 94; and among dancing 'supers' at the regular theatres in Albert Smith's *Natural History of the Ballet-Girl,* p. 91.
11. The lower-class and lower-middle-class background of the great majority of stage aspirants in the first half of the nineteenth century is also suggested by Dickens's portrait of the patrons of private theatres in London. See 'Private Theatres' in *Sketches by Boz,* 1957 (New Oxford Illustrated Dickens). Dramatic ambitions were commonplace among shop workers and office clerks in the metropolis, many of whom were members of amateur clubs and elocution classes. The Whittington Club, founded by Douglas Jerrold in 1846 to afford lower-class families the advantages of club life, drew exactly this clientele, and its elocution class was extremely popular. See Christopher Kent, 'The Whittington Club: A Bohemian Experiment in Middle-Class Social Reform', *Victorian Studies,* XVIII, September, 1974, p. 32.
12. See Kenneth Richards and Peter Thomson (eds.), ch. I *passim.*
13. Cf. Thomas Marshall, *The Lives of the Most Celebrated Actors and Actresses,* 1847, pp. 163-6. This work is really Volume I of Marshall's intended National Dramatic Biography.
14. Select Committee Report, 1832, Q.2362.
15. Op. cit., vol. I, p. 99. Renton Nicholson's Judge and Jury Society, founded in 1841, toured the country in the 1840s and 1850s presenting mock trials, apparently to afford students at the Bar practice in 'eloquence,

aptitude of response, and ingenuity of reply'. See Nicholson, *An Autobiography*, 1861, pp. 286-7. In fact, many of the participants in the 'Baron's' charades were lawyers who had been struck off the rolls. See Theodor Fontane, p. 114.

16. The Bancrofts, *Recollections of Sixty Years*, 1909, p. 425.
17. See Joe Graham, *An Old Stock-Actor's Memories*, 1930, p. 5.
18. Before 1830 it was of little significance what school you had been to. Between 1840 and 1870, however, education became an important element in the struggle for social status, and the public schools were an increasingly significant passport into the professional ruling classes. See Geoffrey Best, pp. 150-1.
19. Although the *Theatre* in 1879 rejected any suggestion that actors were recruited from the 'lowest of middle class and artisan life', it is important to bear in mind that a rise in the number of middle-class recruits was quite compatible with an ever-increasing proportion of newcomers from socially inferior backgrounds – although the latter were increasingly the source of supply for music-hall entertainment rather than the theatre proper.
20. *The World Behind the Scenes*, p. 213.
21. Arthur Goddard, *Players of the Period*, 1891, vol. II, p. 87.
22. Percy Fitzgerald, p. 150.
23. Ibid. p. 134.
24. Quoted ibid. p. 128. The exaltation of actors as men of refinement and culture mirrored the rise of interest in players as social personalities in the 1870s and 1880s, fostering a profusion of theatrical memoirs, anecdotes and gossip. Edmund Yates's *Celebrities at Home* (1877/78) is a typical example of the genre. See First Series (1877), chs. V and XXIII, and Second Series, (1878) ch. VI.
25. Henry James, *The Scenic Art, Notes on Acting and the Drama, 1872-1901*, ed. Allan Wade, 1948, p. 135.
26. These developments are now well documented. See George Rowell, *The Victorian Theatre*, pp. 83-4; and Allardyce Nicoll, vol. V, pp. 54-7.
27. In the twentieth century the creation of drama schools strengthened this bias, the effects of which strongly shaped the social tone of the British theatre for several generations, Cf. Philip Godfrey, *Back-Stage*, 1933, p. 56; and Richard Findlater, *The Unholy Trade*, 1952, p. 83.
28. Squire Bancroft noted that many of his colleagues would never have entered the theatre had they not had the means to pursue so precarious an occupation. *Recollections of Sixty Years*, p. 33.
29. The famous music-hall comic Arthur Roberts commented sarcastically in his memoirs: 'I have always considered the dignity of my profession . . . for was I not one of the first music-hall artists to ride to business in their own broughams?' *The Adventures of Arthur Roberts*, 1895, p. 49. An insight into the upper-middle-class upbringing which the child of successful theatrical parents could expect at this date can be found in Edward Gordon Craig's recollections of his boyhood in the *Index to the Story of my Days, 1872-1907*, 1957, pp. 1-90 *passim*.
30. *On and Off the Stage*, vol. I, p. 281. The comic entertainer George Grossmith parodied this practice in theatrical reminiscences by including 'A Very Snobbish Chapter' in his own autobiography, *A Society Clown*, (1888). A rather earlier example of this practice can be found in Paul Bedford's *Recollections and Wanderings*, 1864, pp. 159-60.
31. See *On and Off the Stage*, vol. II, p. 34.
32. The ballet world, in its heyday before 1850, was particularly keen on a hierarchy of greenrooms for the different grades of performers. See P.H. Fitzgerald, pp. 145-6.
33. Sam Wild's strollers were treated with great condescension by the leading actors at Drury Lane in the 1840s. Megson, pp. 73-4.

34. St Vincent Troubridge, p. 48.
35. Cf. John Coleman, *Players and Playwrights I have Known*, vol. I, p. 199, and W. Marston, pp. 45-6. The banquet given for Charles Kean by fellow-Etonians at St James's Hall in 1859 was quite as socially distinguished as any of Irving's theatrical dinners. See J.W. Cole, pp. 354-5.
36. The rarity of actors' sons being found at public schools in the early Victorian period is well illustrated by Edmund Yates in *His Recollections and Experiences*, 1884, vol. I, pp. 36-7.
37. It also suggests that a public-school education was socially important even before 1830, as indicated by T.W. Bamford in *The Rise of the Public Schools*, 1967.
38. James Jupp tells us that at the Gaiety in the 1880s chorus-girls were often chosen not only for their beauty, but on the strength of their social connections, as this was reckoned the surest way of filling the stalls and boxes. *The Gaiety Stage Door*, 1923, p. 50.
39. Anon., *The Stage, with the Curtain Raised*, 1881, p. 14. See also *Random Recollections of the Stage*, by 'An Old Playgoer' (P. Hanley), 1883, p. 48.
40. See Henry James, p. 135; and W.H. Pennington, *Sea. Camp and Stage*, 1906, p. 121.

CHAPTER 5

1. See Rosamond Gilder, pp. 149-50.
2. *Saturday Review*, 22 March 1862, vol. XIII, p. 321.
3. The Matrimonial Causes Act of 1857 plainly enshrined such a philosophy. See J.A. and O. Banks, *Feminism and Family Planning in Victorian England*, 1965, p. 107.
4. See Banks, ibid. pp. 22-3.
5. A trend which coincided, significantly, with a rapid rise in the availability of domestic servants. See Banks, pp. 65-6.
6. John Ruskin, 'Of Queens' Gardens', *Sesame and Lilies* (1865), 1882 edn, p. 149. For a discussion of Ruskin's philosophy of womanhood, see Kate Millett, 'The Debate over Women: Ruskin versus Mill', *Victorian Studies*, September 1970.
7. 26 March 1859, vol. VII, p. 368.
8. Banks, p. 50.
9. The social position of the governess is discussed in M. Jeanne Peterson, 'The Victorian Governess', *Victorian Studies*, September 1970.
10. H.C. Shuttleworth, p. 18.
11. Vol. II, pp. 18-19.
12. Cf. the performances of the Elocution Class of the Hackney Literary and Scientific Institution, as reported in the *Shoreditch Observer*, 30 April 1864: here the parts of Portia and Hippolyta were taken by 'young gentlemen who certainly looked the characters, if they did not altogether deceive us as to their real sex'. Dickens's famous amateur group commonly hired professional actresses, which explains how he first met the actress Ellen Ternan (for a discussion of their liaison, see Ada Nisbet, *Dickens and Ellen Ternan*, 1952); where other women were used, strict conditions prevailed, even to the point of refusing to perform at Court, as happened in 1857, on the grounds that the ladies in the cast should not appear as actresses there.
13. Sir Frederick Pollock, vol. II, p. 266.
14. 'The Actress: Her Position and her Influence upon Society', *The Theatrical*

Times, 29 August 1846, vol. I, p. 92.

15. A Lady, *An appeal to the Women of England to Discourage the Stage,* 1855, pp. 9-10.
16. The familiar muslin dress of ballerinas was first seen in the 1830s. Its tight-fitting bodice, bare neck and shoulders, and skirt ending midway between ankle and knee, was popularised by Marie Taglioni in the title-role of *La Sylphide* (1832). See Daniel Nalback, *The King's Theatre, 1704-1867,* 1972, p. 126 (Society for Theatre Research).
17. Op. cit., p. 5.
18. See Steven Marcus, *The Other Victorians,* 1966, pp. 29-33, for a discussion of some of these themes.
19. See J.W. Calcraft, *A Defence of the Stage,* 1839, pp. 170-1, and 'Free Thoughts on the Ballet' in *The Theatrical Times,* 13 March 1847, vol. II, p. 75.
20. See Ivor Guest, *Fanny Cerrito,* p. 24.
21. Beatrice Headlam, *The Ballet,* 1879 (a paper read to the Church and Stage Guild).
22. The production was 'Vert, Vert' in December 1847: Frances Kemble, *Records of Later Life,* vol. III, p. 322.
23. Bernard Falk, pp. 13, 80-3.
24. A caution reflected in contemporary literary criticism of these characters. Cf. the *Shakespeare Variorum* to 'Twelfth Night', ed. Furness, 1901, pp. 382, 392.
25. Edward Gordon Craig, p. 22.
26. See N. Smither, 'Charlotte Cushman's second New York engagement: a new lady-actor of gentlemen', *Bulletin of the New York Public Library,* June 1970, p. 393.
27. *The Stage,* p. 23.
28. Cf. the heroine of Charlotte Brontë's *Villette* (1853) whose reluctance to play a male part in amateur theatricals is grounded in the fact that, 'to be dressed like a man did not please, and would not suit me. I had consented to take a man's name and part; as to dress – halte la!' (vol. I, p.27). In the event, she allows herself to wear women's dress with the addition of 'a little vest, a collar, and cravat, and a paletôt, of small dimensions' (vol. I, p. 273), a compromise which must have looked odd indeed!
29. Cf. W.H. Hudson, *The Church and the Stage,* 1886, p. 37, note.
30. Cf. the 'well-dressed, highly-painted' women soliciting in the saloons of Drury Lane, described by Jehangeer Nowrojee and Hirjeebhoy Merwanjee, p. 106.
31. The Terry girls were taught early on to observe this rule. See Marguerite Steen, p. 77.
32. Lucy Cohen, *Lady de Rothschild and her Daughters, 1821-1931,* 1935, p. 161.
33. Courtneidge, p. 32.
34. *Fifty Years a Showman,* 1938, p. 270. Arthur Goddard makes the same point in his *Players of the Period,* 1891, vol. II, p. 117.
35. See Michael Ryan, *passim,* and W. Logan's *The Great Social Evil* (1871), which blamed theatricals for habituating the public to 'the presence and sight, and almost to the touch of prostitution' (p. 231).
36. Cf. 'Corin', pp. 51, 79.
37. See Select Committee Report, 1866, Qs. 1696-1700.
38. See Elizabeth Fagan, *From the Wings,* 1922, 106. Sexual titillation was an implicit ingredient in many music-hall acts.
39. Select Committee Report, 1866, Q.966-1217.

40. Quoted in Ivan Bloch, *Sexual Life in England,* 1967, p. 264 (Corgi Books).
41. Raymond Blaythwayt, *Does the Theatre make for Good? A talk with Mr. Clement Scott,* 1898, p. 14.
42. *Our Recent Actors,* vol. II, p. 157.
43. Theodore Martin, pp. 125-6.
44. 'Theatrical Reform', December 1879, p. 646.
45. Lady Martin, *Some of Shakespeare's Female Characters,* 1885, ix.
46. Mrs Anna Jameson, *Shakespeare's Female Characters,* 1840, p. 195.
47. Lady Martin, p. 289.
48. Mrs Jameson, p. 355.
49. Ibid. p. 346.
50. See Banks, pp. 36-7.
51. Figures quoted by Madame R.A. Caplin, *Women in the Reign of Queen Victoria,* 1876, p. 103.
52. From C. Booth, 'Occupations of the People of the United Kingdom, 1801-1881', *Journal of the Statistical Society,* XLIX, Part II, June 1886, Appendix A(1), England and Wales, pp. 362-5.
53. March 22, 1862, vol. XIII, p. 321.
54. Walter Donaldson, *Recollections of an Actor,* 1865, p. 247.
55. This was an added reason why actors resented the music-halls. See Select Committee Report, 1866, Q. 6923.
56. John Coleman, *Players and Playwrights,* vol. II, p. 190.
57. Fanny Stirling, the daughter of a captain in the Horse Guards, had been withdrawn from a French convent on account of family misfortunes, and was put on the stage at the age of fourteen. Such cases seem to have been rarer than among actors, and where they did occur there was often some prior theatrical connection, as in the case of Frances Kelly, who was the niece of the famous singer Michael Kelly.
58. The Bancrofts recalled that most of their well-known female contemporaries in the profession had started life in the theatre, by contrast with most of their male colleagues who had hardly known an actor before they went on the stage: *Recollections,* p. 34.
59. A. Bailey and M. Whitley, *Women's Work,* 1894, p. 32.
60. *The Victoria Magazine* lamented the low educational standards of English actresses, arguing that the theatre's traditional preference for stage-bred girls kept out the more educated aspirants: August 1867, vol. IX, p. 365.
61. Though many touring companies were in fact run under appalling conditions, a prospect of which Bulley and Whitley give stage aspirants fair warning. Op. cit., pp. 32-3.
62. The *Theatre* complained that, as a result of Langtry's stage success, there was a veritable craze among amateur actresses to foist their performances on the public. April 1883, New Series, vol. I, p. 259.
63. Actresses such as Lilian Braithwaite, Sybil Thorndike, and the Vanbrugh sisters – all of them daughters of clergymen – epitomised the pre-1914 generation of middle-class actresses.
64. In George Gissing's *Isabel Clarendon* (1886) Rhoda wants to get a job and believes she is most suited to a stage career, but she is warned off this course in no uncertain terms: 'Like it or not, we have to consider our neighbour's opinion, and that doesn't yet regard the stage as a career open to gentlemen's daughters'. Vol. I, pp. 47-8. The actress Constance Featherstonhaugh (who married Frank Benson in 1886) relates how she took to the stage when her widowed mother lost most of her money through bad investments, but because of family opposition she had to apply for her engagements in secret. Lady Constance Benson, *Mainly Players: Bensonian Memories,* 1926, p. 23-4.
65. Emily Faithful and Bessie Rayner Parkes are the only two prominent

'feminists' who appear to have championed the actress's cause. See the *Victoria Magazine*, August 1871, vol. XVII, pp. 364-5, and April 1872, XVIII, 553; and Bessie Rayner Parkes, *Essays on Women's Work*, 1865, pp. 127-8.

66. Cf. Bessie Rayner Parkes, pp. 221-2. For this element in Victorian feminism, see Banks, pp. 47-8.

CHAPTER 6

1. *The Road to the Stage*, 1836 edn, pp. 5-9. In the preface Rede refers to the acting profession as 'fraught with toil, anxiety, and misery, beyond any other'.
2. Ibid. pp. 12-13. Rede's estimate here seems to be accurate, for it tallies with Professor Nicoll's list of London theatres open in the mid-thirties. See Allardyce Nicoll, vol. IV, pp. 222-33. This increases one's confidence in Rede's other statistics.
3. Ibid. p. 14. In the 1827 edition this figure was 6,000. I am unable to explain the wide discrepancy between the two estimates.
4. Occupation Abstract 1841, Part 1, England and Wales, *Parl. Papers*, 1844, vol. XXVII, p. 31.
5. The Theatre Royal, Hull, contained a resident company of about 30, a dozen of them actresses, in the 1820s; this figure was about the same in 1850. See K. Richards and P. Thomson, p. 31. The St James's company in London numbered 34 in 1854. See Barry Duncan, *The St. James's Theatre*, 1964, p. 98. Leman Rede mentioned the Scarborough company as containing 20 permanent members in 1827: op. cit., 1827 edn, p. 9. But these were established theatres of some repute; many companies, especially the itinerant 'sharing' companies, would have had a smaller membership so that overheads could be kept to a minimum. High unemployment in the 1830s was reported in the Select Committee Report, 1832, Q. 2618, and by the *Era*, 5 May 1839, vol. I, p. 375.
6. See census reports 1841-91. These proportions remained constant throughout the period. Compare, for instance, the proportion of London actors and actresses in 1851 (Table XXVIII, *Parl. Papers*, 1852-3, LXXXVIII, Part 1, ccxliv, cclvi) with the proportion in 1881 (Table X, *Parl. Papers*, 1883, LXXX, 12).
7. Rede, 1827, p. 8.
8. See Reader, *Professional Men*, p. 208, Appendix I, Table 1.
9. A slow turnover was deliberate policy at the Gaiety, according to James Jupp, being designed to keep the same company together to facilitate the job of authors and composers. Op. cit., 1923, p. 24.
10. See Alan Hughes, 'The Lyceum Staff: A Victorian Theatrical Organisation', *Theatre Notebook*, 1974, No. 1, p. 16.
11. Among the older guard, satirised by Pinero in *Trelawney of the Wells* (1898), there was a strongly held belief that to accept parts other than those to which one was accustomed was infra dig.
12. See Anon., *The Stage, with the Curtain Raised*, 1881, p. 12. Agencies, which were evident in London from the 1820s and numbered some nine major concerns by 1870, were a by-product of the intense competition for theatrical jobs. Actors frequently condemned them for exploitation and unscrupulousness. Cf. Anon, ibid. and 'Corin', p. 88.
13. In the 1890s, when recruitment shot up by another 70 per cent, unemployment reached the chronic proportions which were to characterise the theatre in the twentieth century. Cf. the actor Charles Warner's warnings in J.A.

Hammerton (ed.), *The Actor's Art*, 1897, pp. 169-70. The level of unemployment in the theatre was put as high as 80 per cent in the 1950s. See Richard Findlater, *The Unholy Trade*, 1952, p. 87. In the 1970s, Equity has recently estimated that 60 per cent of the profession earns less than £1,000 a year. See Ronald Hayman, *The Set-Up*, 1973, pp. 46-7 (Eyre Methuen).

14. Casual labour was not difficult to find. 'Dismal Jemmy' the 'stroller' in Dickens's *Pickwick Papers* (1837), refers to the 'host of shabby, poverty-stricken men' who regularly hung about the larger theatres hoping for parts in the Christmas pantomime or the Easter piece or any spectacular production. New Oxford Illustrated Dickens, 1947, p. 35.
15. Cf. T.P. Cooke's complaints of this practice. Select Committee Report, 1832, Qs. 2618-19.
16. Alan Hughes, p. 16. According to 'Corin', 1*s* to 1*s* 6*d* was the standard nightly wage for 'extras' in the sixties and seventies: op. cit., p. 78.
17. See George Grossmith, *A Society Clown*, 1888, p. 107.
18. The versatility expected of stock actors also enabled managements to operate on reduced manpower, for the same performers could be cast in several different parts in a variety of pieces. Doubling in the same piece was also common. See A.C. Sprague, *The Doubling of Parts in Shakespeare's Plays*, 1966, Society for Theatre Research.
19. See J.K. Jerome, pp. 88-9.
20. Ibid. p. 90.
21. Cf. Albert Smith, *The Adventures of Mr. Ledbury*, 1844, vol. II, p. 220; Mrs E.J. Burbury, *Florence Sackville, or Self-Dependence*, 1851, vol. II, p. 247; Albany Fonblanque, *Cut Adrift*, 1869, vol. I, pp. 247-8; Harriet Jay, *Through the Stage Door*, 1873, vol. I, p. 37; and Florence Marryat, *My Sister the Actress*, 1881, vol. I, p. 171.
22. Sir Theodore Martin, pp. 61-2.
23. Report of the Select Committee on Theatres and Places of Entertainment, *Parl. Papers*, 1892, XVIII, Qs. 2517-22. 'Corin' noted that back-stage facilities were invariably cramped with five or six performers crowded into a single dressing-room. Touring companies often had to make do with hastily improvised arrangements such as changing areas in the wings. Op. cit., pp. 99-100.
24. Ibid. p. 180. See also Lady Constance Benson, p. 41.
25. R.J. Broadbent, p. 170.
26. W.E. Roth found that lung and throat infections were even more common among music-hall performers, which he put down to the fact that they performed at several different venues each evening. *Theatre Hygiene*, 1888, p. 49.
27. W.E. Roth, ibid. p.32. For the use of gas in Victorian theatres, see Richard Sothern, *The Victorian Theatre: A Pictorial Survey*, *passim*; and J.R. Wolcott, 'The Genesis of Gas Lights', *Theatre Research*, 1972, XII, No. 1. Electricity superseded gas on a wide scale only in the 1880s, but it was costly to install and several managements, notably Irving's at the Lyceum, favoured gas lighting for many years.
28. Harriet Jay, vol. I, p. 22.
29. See Ivor Guest, *Victorian Ballet-Girl*, p. 3.
30. J.H. Chute, lessee of the Bristol Theatre Royal 1853-78, was obliged to connect the theatre's water supply at his own expense in 1854 in the interests of better sanitation because of the proprietor's own recalcitrance. K.M.D. Barker, 'The Theatre Proprietor's Story', *Theatre Notebook*, vol. XVIII, pp. 79-91 *passim*.
31. The Actors' Association of 1891 was a direct response to managerial irresponsibility in the area of back-stage conditions. See Select Committee

Report, 1892, Qs. 3505, 3509.

32. 'Fringe benefits', owing to the nature of theatrical work, played a much less important part in the actor's standard of living than in the major working-class occupations such as farm labouring, coal-mining, shop-work, and domestic service. 'Free tickets' to the performance for an actor's family and friends was a standard 'perk', but there are also signs that actors occasionally received free medical care. Cf. John Coleman, *Memoirs of Samuel Phelps,* 1886, p. 97. The Actors' Benevolent Fund seems to have had the free services of two doctors. See The *Era*, 31 January 1891, LIII, No. 2732, p. 8.
33. See Thomas Marshall, p. 164.
34. Ibid.
35. Ibid. p. 165.
36. 'Salaries of Actors and Actresses', the *Era Almanack,* 1871, p. 50.
37. Percy Fitzgerald, p. 126.
38. By the end of this period the American theatrical profession was becoming seriously concerned at the extent of English infiltration. See 'The Drama in America', *Punch,* 1889, Vol. LIXVI, p. 39.
39. Some of the more famous included Frances Kelly (1790-1882) at the Dean Street theatre in the 1840s (later to be the Royalty); Mrs Warner (1804-54) at the Marylebone from 1847; Charles Dillon at the Lyceum 1856-8; and Walter Montgomery (1827-71), whose losses at the Gaiety in 1871 so preyed on his mind that he shot himself.
40. Cf. the account of the development of the Theatre Royal, Hull, up to 1850, in Richards and Thomson, pp. 27-31.
41. The lavishness of productions at the patents entailed crippling costs. See G.G. Urwin, 'Alfred Bunn 1796-1860: A Revaluation', *Theatre Notebook,* 1957, vol. XI, pp. 96-102.
42. See Richards and Thomson, ch. 3 *passim.*
43. See Alan Hughes, op. cit., p. 16.
44. By contrast, many early Victorian 'stars' had relatively short careers and could show a spectacular decline. Not a few had died in penury. Westland Marston recorded the case of one Covent Garden 'star' of the 1830s, Henry Gaskell Denvil, who never recovered from the bad press he received as Othello and degenerated into a purely 'physical' actor at the 'minors', ultimately becoming a check-taker and dying in obscurity in 1866. Marston, op. cit., vol. I, p. 16.
45. For the list of distinguished guests at his farewell dinner in the London Tavern on 1 March 1851, see Sir Frederick Pollock, vol. II, pp. 372-3.
46. G.H. Lewes, *On Actors,* p. 50.
47. See Thomas Marshall, p. 165.
48. Ben Webster ran a newsagent's on the side while engaged at Drury Lane in the early 1820s on 30*s* a week. For salary levels at Drury Lane at this date, see also Rede, 1827 edn, p. 75.
49. Cooke was earning £60 a week at the Surrey in 1829, and Liston a similar sum at the Olympic in the 1830s.
50. Rede, pp. 9-14.
51. See Baxter's 'Hierarchy of Labour', reproduced in Geoffrey Best, pp. 95-7.
52. Op. cit., 1827, p. 8. However, at the Edinburgh Theatre Royal in 1841-2, the manager W.H. Murray was earning only £4 a week, and his leading actor Edmund Glover only £3. On the other hand, salaries overall were fairly equable, the lowest in the company being £1 5*s*. See J.C. Dibdin, p. 380.
53. See Best, p. 58, and chapter 3 of this study.
54. Select Committee Report, 1832, Qs. 4169-79.
55. Before the Theatres Act of 1843 the risk was considerable. For example, in 1835 two actors performing at an unlicensed 'minor' were each fined £50

by the Middlesex magistrates, 'rather hard upon a man probably earning five or six pounds a week'. Lord William Pitt Lennox, *Plays, Players and Playhouses,* 1881, vol. II, pp. 12-16. In general, however, prosecutions against the 'minors' were unpopular and rarely successful by this date.

56. Georgina Pauncefort, a 'character' actress in Irving's Lyceum company, drew £8 a week for twenty years. See Alan Hughes, p. 16.
57. See Geoffrey Best, pp. 75-6.
58. Thus a leading tragedian was expected to supply his own complete dresses for Hamlet, Richard III, Macbeth and Rolla. See Leman Rede, 1827, p. 20.
59. Cf. Paterson, p.91.
60. Laurence Irving, p. 60.
61. See George Arliss, p. 166.
62. J.K. Jerome implies as much. Op. cit., pp. 123-4.
63. R.M. Sillard, p. 84. Samuel Phelps recalled how he walked 30 miles to take up one of his first engagements in the mid-1820s. Coleman, *Memoirs of Samuel Phelps,* pp. 49-50.
64. See Geoffrey Best, p. 71.
65. See the fares quoted in *Butler's Dramatic Almanac* for 1853.
66. Op. cit., p. 84.
67. Sillard, p. 85.
68. See St Vincent Troubridge, p. 58. This is the most comprehensive study of the benefit system available.
69. It is not unreasonable to assume that the image of conviviality which early Victorian actors gave out was in part an occupational habit resulting from long practice in the art of 'chatting up' prospective supporters.
70. Unknown performers usually tried to obtain the services of a well-known favourite on their benefit night. Phelps's first benefit was a disaster in this respect. See Coleman, *Memoirs of Samuel Phelps,* pp. 98-9.
71. Op. cit., p. 73.
72. Liverpool, for instance, was reckoned second only to London by the mid-fifties in the scope and scale of its musical and theatrical activities. See Broadbent, p. 167.
73. Op. cit., p. 166.
74. H. Byerley Thomson, p. 335.
75. Cf. Best, p. 90.
76. Joe Graham, p. 7.
77. Cf. the Theatre Royal, Hull, in Richards and Thomson, p. 29.
78. Laurence Irving, p. 80. When he talked in later years about the rise in actors' salaries, Irving mentioned that 'leads' in the 1850s received only some two guineas a week, out of which 'necessities' had to be provided. Ibid. pp. 379-80.
79. Op. cit., p. 69.
80. Op. cit., pp. 80-1.
81. See W.N.M. Geary, *The Law of Theatres and Music-Halls,* 1885, pp. 102-3.
82. Laurence Irving, pp. 172, 180.
83. Geary, p. 107.
84. Select Committee Report, 1866, Qs. 4375, 5051.
85. Ibid. Q. 7701.
86. Ibid. Q. 4375.
87. Ibid. Q. 3862.
88. Paterson, p. 191.
89. Select Committee Report, 1866, Q. 1369.
90. Ibid. Q. 5382.
91. Ibid. Q. 5061.
92. *On and Off the Stage*, p. 395.

93. Laurence Irving, p. 380. The 'minors' showed corresponding increases. At the Surrey, second only to the Lyceum as the home of melodrama, actors were being paid £5 a week under George Conquest's management in the 1880s.
94. Alan Hughes, p. 16.
95. See Bulley and Whitley, pp. 34-5.
96. Ibid. p. 33. John Martin-Harvey was on £2 a week at the Lyceum in 1883, two years after his professional début. See Alan Hughes, p. 16.
97. Bulley and Whitley, p. 33.
98. Loc. cit.
99. Laurence Irving, p. 70.
100. *Theatre Notebook*, vol. XXVI, No. 4, p. 135.
101. Thus the theatrical agent H.J. Turner, before the Select Committee of 1866, estimated that there were few 'good actors' out of work and that it was more than he could do to supply theatres with the performers they needed; he added, however, that in fact theatrical journals contained the advertisements of a great many unemployed actors and actresses, but, he commented, 'they are not people of much esteem.' Q. 5210.
102. Not all 'gaffs' were so low, though they were always a source of controversy owing to the large numbers of children which patronised them. Cf. the report in the *Builder*, 5 June 1858. It was estimated that London had some 80 to 100 'gaffs' catering for a total audience of about 24,000 people. Grant, pp. 162-3.
103. Op. cit., pp. 165-6, 169. The full extent of poverty among 'gaff' actors can be measured by the fact that quarrels were frequent over who should eat the stage-food provided. Ibid. p. 165.
104. Cf. the 'gaff' clown whom Mayhew interviewed in the 1850s, who declared that 'gaff' productions were done in a style 'that would astonish some of the big houses'. Op. cit., vol. III, p. 121.
105. Op. cit., p. 213.
106. Ibid. pp. 91-3.
107. Ibid. p. 352.
108. See Edward Stirling, *Old Drury Lane: Fifty Years' Recollections of Author, Actor and Manager*, 1881, vol. I, p. 63.
109. The Lancashire wakes had a notorious reputation on this score. The famous circus impresario 'Lord' George Sanger described one notable incident at the Whitsun Fair in Walsall in 1849, when Wombwell's menagerie tried to intimidate an itinerant troupe off its fancied pitch: the actors finally drove off their attackers by assaulting the animals' cages with picks and crowbars. *Seventy Years a Showman*, 1908, p. 76.
110. Op. cit., p. 21.
111. Ibid. p. 42.
112. Cf. the intermittent acting experiences of two such individuals between the 1820s and the 1840s: Christopher Thomson, *Autobiography of an Artisan*, 1847; John Frederick Brent, *Memories of a Mistaken Life*, 1897.
113. Players only finally disappeared from St Giles's Fair, Oxford – one of the biggest provincial fairs – in the 1880s. See Sally Alexander, *St. Giles's Fair 1830-1914*, 1970, p. 44 (Ruskin College History Workshop).
114. Many of the varied street exhibitors Mayhew contacted in the 1850s showed clear signs of anxiety about the future of their occupations. Op. cit., vol. III, pp.89, 94 and 120.
115. See in particular 'Corin', *passim*, who claimed that his examples were representative of at least 60 per cent of the profession; Robert Courtneidge, *passim*; and J.K. Jerome, pp. 86-90.
116. Bulley and Whitley, pp. 32-3.
117. H.C. Shuttleworth, p. 43.

118. See Best, pp. 73, 80 and 94.
119. See W.J. Reader, *Victorian England,* p. 123.
120. See Leman Rede, 1836, Preface.
121. Bancroft's recollection of his stock days in the early 1860s. *On and Off the Stage,* vol. I, p. 166.
122. For improvements in workers' hours, see Best, p. 117, and Reader, *Victorian England,* pp. 136-7.
123. The phrase is Gordon Craig's, who remarked with reference to the seventies and eighties: 'I now see what an empty, *idle* life the stage (in England) offered us in those days'. Op. cit., p. 167. See also Max Beerbohm 'A Most Hard-Working Profession', *Around Theatres,* 1924, pp. 179-83.
124. For these contractual developments, see W.N.M. Geary, pp. 110, 117-21. For a typical list of rules in reputable theatrical companies of the 1880s, see Wilson Barrett's regulations for his theatres: ibid. pp. 122-3.
125. R.D. Baxter, *National Income,* 1868, Appendix IV, pp. 88-93.
126. See Reader, *Victorian England,* p. 123.
127. 'Corin' spoke of scores of 'capable actors and actresses' vainly seeking work in London in the early 1880s. Op. cit., p. 179.
128. The *Theatrical Times,* 1846, vol. I, p. 141 ('The Abuses of the Theatre'); ibid. 1846, vol. I, pp. 195-6 ('Sucking Actors'); ibid. 1848, vol. III, p. 2 ('Managerial Vampires'); ibid. 1847, vol. II, pp. 43-4 ('A Few Words About Theatrical Matters'); and ibid. 1847, vol. II, p. 99 ('The Destiny of the Drama').
129. See Reader, *Victorian England,* p. 144.
130. Bessie Rayner Parkes, op. cit., p. 129.
131. Philip Godfrey concluded that the 'various attempts to organise actors into a trade association disclose a history of depressing struggles against ingrained snobberies, childish petulance, and unbelievable stupidity'. *Backstage,* 1933, p. 58.

CHAPTER 7

1. In this category, numbers increased by over 300 per cent in the period 1841-81. See C. Booth, vol. XLIX, Part II, June 1886, Appendix A (1), p. 365.
2. Proper ventilation in theatres was enforced by the Towns Improvement Act (1847) and the Public Health Act (1875); fire and space regulations were improved by the Metropolitan Buildings Act (1855) and the Metropolis Management and Buildings Acts Amendment Act (1878); standards of public order and propriety were set by the Towns Police Clauses Act (1847), the Theatres and Public Houses Act (1850), and a host of local bye-laws, many of them established under Borough Acts of the 1860s.
3. See Watson Nicholson, *The Struggle for a Free Stage in London,* 1906.
4. See Acts 6 and 7 Vict., c. 68, *Parl. Papers,* 1843, IV, pp. 479-85.
5. See Select Committee Report, 1842, Qs. 1225, 3009.
6. See Reader, *Professional Men, passim.*
7. Charles Kean noted that under the patent system actors could think in terms of a stable career, for London was then 'a home for life; they became members of a fund and there was a settlement for old age'. Select Committee Report, 1866, Q. 6607.
8. See Select Committee Report, 1832, Qs. 4147-8.
9. Sir Frederick Pollock, vol. I, p. 27.
10. Acts 6 and 7 Vict., c. 68, *Parl. Papers,* 1843, IV, Sections XI and XV.
11. Ibid. Section XXIII.
12. 'Theatrical Regulation', *The Times,* 16 September 1843.

13. 'Trim', pp. 69-70.
14. Select Committee Report, 1832, Qs. 320-1, 440, 1360, 1414, 2362, 2394, 2630-3, 2817-19, 3781, 3805, 3915.
15. See Richards and Thomson, pp. 16-23.
16. Report of the Select Committee on Public Houses, *Parl. Papers*, 1854, XIV. Its recommendations are outlined on pp. 231-47.
17. Select Committee Report, 1866, Q. 7701.
18. One opponent of a change in the law asserted in the Commons debate of 1865 that the proposed Bill (to give dramatic licences to music-halls) would turn every pothouse into a theatre and vice versa. Theatres Bill (Second Reading, 13 June 1865), *Parliamentary Debates*, 12 June-6 July 1865, CLXXX, p. 183.
19. Select Committee Report, 1866, Q. 2929; see also Qs. 2936, 2992, 3367, 3612, 4793, 6604.
20. Ibid. Q. 4867.
21. Ibid. Qs. 4595-6.
22. Ibid. Qs. 2937-9, 3405, 3427, 4375, 5382.
23. The critic Henry Morley concluded at this date that the 'playgoer who would find in our London theatres a dramatic literature . . . fitly housed may be indignant at much that he sees in them'. *Journal of a London Playgoer*, p. 6.
24. Select Committee Report, 1866, Qs. 4163-5.
25. Ibid. Q. 5382.
26. Select Committee Report, 1892, Qs. 975, 1081, 3518.
27. See Reader, *Professional Men*, p. 54.
28. Ibid. p. 67.
29. Data from C.J. Stratman, xii-xiii.
30. At the fourteenth anniversary festival dinner of the Royal General Theatrical Fund (RGTF), Buckstone spoke of the College's hopes for a future dramatic school for actors: the *Era*, 24 April 1859, vol. XXI, p. 11.
31. *The Theatrical Times* criticised the RGTF for excluding Leman Rede's widow, an actress of thirty years' standing, from its support: 'A Few Words on the General Theatrical Fund' 29 April 1848, vol. III, pp. 138-9.
32. Clement Scott thought the Dramatic College fêtes 'the most degrading exhibitions ever patronised by the dramatic profession'. Clement Scott and Cecil Howard (eds.), *The Life and Reminiscences of Edward Leman Blanchard*, 1891, vol. I, p. 243, note 2.
33. See the *Era*, 6 May 1855, vol. XVII, p. 11.
34. See the *Saturday Review*, 24 July 1858, vol. VI, p. 83.
35. The *Era*, 11 April 1863, p. 20.
36. See *The Drama Addresses by Henry Irving*, 1893.
37. *A Defence of the Stage*, 1839, p. 163.
38. 'Position of the Actor', 11 November 1848, vol. III, p. 434.
39. J.W. Cole, p. 13.
40. Laurence Irving, p. 56.
41. See H. Dodd, *Royal Dramatic College: Correspondence respecting proposed gift of land*, 1859.
42. See Edward Stirling, pp. 306-8.
43. These problems were summarised by the *Saturday Review*, 13 October 1888, vol. LXVI, pp. 433-4, and 3 November 1888, vol. LXVI, pp. 522-3.
44. *The Victoria Magazine*, August 1871, vol. XVII, pp. 362-5.
45. Ibid. September 1872, vol. XIX, p. 445.
46. See 'Corin', p. 174. Also W.A. Chevalier, *A Tribute to the Shakespeare Memorial at Stratford-on-Avon. Outlines of a Scheme for Reforming the Stage*, 1875.

47. 2 May 1875, vol. XXXVII, p. 13.
48. 'The French Play in London', *Nineteenth Century*, August 1879, vol. VI, pp. 239-40.
49. November 1880, New Series, vol. II, pp. 274-9.
50. The *Theatre*, February 1882, New Series, V, pp. 73-6. See also the *Era*, 7 October 1882, XLV, No. 2298, p. 5.
51. The whole subject was reviewed by the *Era*, 14 February 1891, vol. LIII, p. 15.
52. Ibid. 14 April 1900, vol. LXIII, p. 11.
53. J.C. Trewin, p. 18.
54. Op. cit., p. 155.
55. See the *Theatre*, August 1890, New Series Vol. XVI, pp. 63-7.
56. See John Coleman, *Memoirs of Samuel Phelps*, p. 276.
57. See the *Theatre*, August 1878, New Series, vol. I, pp. 7-11; September 1878, N.S. vol. I, pp. 109-12; December 1878, N.S. vol. I, 346-52; and the *Era*, 2 November 1879, vol. XLI, p. 12; 12 October 1879, vol. XLI, p. 12.
58. 30 July 1876, XXXVIII, 10, and 23 July 1876, vol. XXXVIII, p. 10.
59. *The Victoria Magazine*, August 1871, vol. XVII, pp. 364-5.
60. February 1879, New Series, vol. II, p. 28.
61. *The Fortnightly Review*, 1889, vol. XLV, pp. 610-26.
62. 'Dramatic Patronage', 31 October 1846, vol. I, p. 175.
63. *The World Behind the Scenes*, p. 163.
64. The *Theatre*, August 1890, N.S. vol. XVI, pp. 63-7.
65. 24 November 1888, vol. LXVI, p. 615.
66. November 1879, N.S. vol. III, p. 184.
67. Ibid. December 1879, N.S. vol. III, p. 292.
68. Laurence Irving, p. 359.
69. P. 132.
70. Ibid. vii.
71. For a discussion of this trend in Victorian life, see D.J. Olsen, 'Victorian London: Specialisation, Segregation, and Privacy', *Victorian Studies*, March 1974, vol. XVII, pp. 265-78.
72. J.C. Trewin, p. 69.
73. The *Era*, 7 February 1891, vol. LIII, p. 12.
74. For a report of the Association's inaugural meeting at Manchester, see ibid.
75. Ibid. 31 January 1891, vol. LIII, p. 8.
76. Ibid. 7 February 1891, vol. LIII, p. 12.
77. Select Committee Report, 1892, Q. 3500.
78. The *Era*, 7 February 1891, vol. LIII, p. 12.

CHAPTER 8

1. 'The Actor's Social Position' (1834), reproduced in T.E. Pemberton, *The Kendals*, 1900, pp. 24-6.
2. Mrs Kendal, *The Drama*, 1884, pp. 8-9 (a paper read to the Congress of the National Association for the Promotion of Social Science).
3. See Laurence Irving, p. 410. Cf. also the frontispiece cartoon to the *Entr'acte Annual*, 1883, showing Irving being knighted by the Queen above the caption 'Why Not? In the event Irving declined the offer on the grounds that the time was not ripe, but it is also apparent that the move was the subject of some dispute inside the Cabinet, not least because of the actor's rather awkward domestic difficulties. See D.W.R. Bahlman (ed.), *The Diary of Sir Edward Walter Hamilton*, 1972, vol. II, pp. 451, 453, 883. Irving had

finally separated from his wife in 1872, and in the 1880s there were strong rumours of his 'too close intimacy with Ellen Terry'.

4. 'Behind the Scenes', *The Fortnightly Review,* 1885, vol. XXXVII, pp. 84-94.
5. Dutton Cook, *On the Stage,* 1883, vol. I, p. 84.
6. For a discussion of these developments, see Elizabeth Burns, *Theatricality: A Study of Convention in the Theatre and in Social Life,* 1972, pp. 174-83.
7. See C. Booth, 'Occupations of the People of the United Kingdom, 1801-81', in the *Journal of the Statistical Society,* XLIX, Part 2, June 1886, Appendix A (1), p. 365.
8. These figures appear in Reader, Appendix 1, Table 1, p. 208.
9. The description belongs to John Gross in his excellent *The Rise and Fall of the Man of Letters,* Pelican, 1973, p. 148. See Ch. 3 for the growth of the Victorian periodical press.
10. 'The Spirit of the Age', an essay which first appeared in the *Examiner* in five instalments, unfinished, January-May 1831. See J.B. Schneewind (ed.), *Mill's Essays on Literature and Society,* 1965, p. 32.
11. 'The First Edinburgh Reviewers', an article which first appeared in the *National Review,* October 1855. See N. St John Stevas (ed.), *Walter Bagehot, Collected Works,* vol. I, Literary Essays, pp. 310-11.
12. Select Committee Report, 1892, Q. 1188.
13. Wade, pp. 119-20.
14. *Mid-Victorian Memories,* 1914, p. 296.
15. *Edmund Yates, His Recollections and Experiences,* 1884, 2 vols.
16. *The World Behind the Scenes,* 1881, p. 126.
17. *Labour, Life and Literature,* 1913, pp. 132-6.
18. Francis Warre Cornish (ed.), *Extracts from the Letters and Journals of William Cory,* 1897, p. 504. Most of the top periodical journalists – Leslie Stephen, Charles Appleton (first editor of the *Academy,* a literary weekly founded in 1869), John Morley, R.H. Hutton (literary editor of the *Spectator*), Andrew Lang and George Saintsbury – were also dons at one time or another.
19. Ian Fletcher, pp. 190-205.
20. See John Gross, Ch. 5.
21. Bulley and Whitley judged there were growing opportunities for women in minor fiction and journalism, especially in topics such as dress, society and the home. A woman of letters, they advised, could earn as much as £400 a year, with much larger rewards for the well known. Op. cit., pp. 4-7.
22. George Gissing, *New Grub Street,* Penguin, 1976, p. 38. (First published 1891).
23. Malcolm Elwin, *Charles Reade: A Biography,* 1931, p. 176.
24. The description is Sir Walter Besant's in his manual for aspiring writers *The Pen and the Book* (1899), and is reproduced in Gross, p. 220.
25. Arliss, p. 149. Mrs Calvert observed that 'young ladies and gentlemen' took to the stage in shoals when long runs did away with the need for long and laborious periods of rehearsal, attracting not only those anxious to do something for a living, but 'many who simply desired to while away the time'. Op. cit., pp. 269-70.
26. 'The Renaissance of the Drama' (Part III), *Saturday Review,* 22 December 1888, LXVI, p. 742.
27. *Backstage,* 1933, p. 56.
28. Ronald Hayman, Ch. 3 *passim.*

APPENDIX I: Tables Showing the Principal Biographical Details of Three Generations of Actors and Actresses who Appeared on the Stage in the Period 1830-90

The data in the following tables relate to performers who spent an important or major part of their careers on the English stage; in some cases individuals were of American extraction or started on the Australian stage, but I have recorded only their English débuts; in others, where the provincial débuts are as yet unknown, I have recorded their London débuts only. Many actresses began their careers as children – this was usually the case where they had theatrical parents – but unless the exact date of their débuts is known, I have referred only to their regular or adult débuts.

Most of the following cases have never been the subject of memoirs or biographies. Their details are therefore often sparse, uncertain and incomplete, particularly before 1860. As one would expect, the last generation (1860-90) has left a fuller record, and I have by no means included every performer of this era whose career is known; those who do appear are representative enough. A word about sources. Early Victorian theatrical newspapers frequently carried short biographical sketches of the leading players of the day, and *The Theatrical Times* (June 1846-March 1849) has been particularly valuable in this respect. I would also mention, among other notable works, Thomas Marshall, *Lives of the Most Celebrated Actors and Actresses* (1847), Charles Eyre Pascoe, *The Dramatic List* (1879), John Coleman, *Players and Playwrights I have Known* (1888), Westland Marston, *Our Recent Actors* (1888), and Clement Scott and Cecil Howard (eds.), *The Life and Reminiscences of Edward Leman Blanchard* (1891) (which contains many biographical references in its copious footnotes). The best-known Victorian celebrities have usually had their careers rather better recorded, but even in these cases there is often relatively little information about their private lives. The same might also be said of Phyllis Hartnoll's *The Oxford Companion to the Theatre* (3rd edn., 1967), which on the whole is a disappointing biographical source for this period.

The performers in the following tables are not arranged alphabetically, but according to the year of their professional débuts.

Table 1: Actors who Made Their Professional Débuts 1800-30

ACTOR	Dates	Father's Occupation	Initial Occupation	Début	Further Theatrical Connections
Charles Young	1777-1856	Surgeon (early death)	City Clerk	1802	Married actress
T.P. Cook	1786-1864	Surgeon	Naval Officer	1804	
James Wallack	1791-1864	Actor	Actor	1804	Married actress; a son on stage
Edmund Kean (Irish)	1787?-1833	? (Actress mother)	Actor	1806 (London)	Married actress; a son on stage
John Vandenhoff	1790-1861	Dyer	Schoolmaster	1808	Several children on stage
William Macready (Irish)	1793-1873	Actor-manager	Actor	1810	1st wife actress; a son, 2 daughters on stage
Richard Smith	1786-1855	Theatre Treasurer	Solicitor's Clerk	*c.*1810	
John Cooper	1793-1870	Bath Tradesman	?	1811	
Robert Keeley	1793-1869	Watchmaker	Printer's Apprentice	1813	Married actress; 2 daughters on stage
J.P. Warde*	1792-1840	?	2nd Lt., Royal Artillery	1813	
Joseph Cowell*	1792-1863	Army Colonel	Naval Officer/ Portrait Painter	*c.*1815	Married actress; son, a daughter on stage
Benjamin Webster	1797-1882	Dancing Master	Actor	1815	1st wife actress, (adopted) son on stage, another a dramatist
J.P. Harley	1786-1858	Draper	Solicitor's Clerk	1815 (London)	
Tyrone Power (Irish)	1795-1841	Actor	Army/Navy	1815	A son on stage
Frederick Calvert	1793-1877	Duke of Norfolk's Agent	? (Intended for Catholic priesthood)	1816	A son on stage

Table 1 (Continued)

ACTOR	Dates	Father's Occupation	Initial Occupation	Début	Further Theatrical Connections
D.W. Osbaldiston	1794-1850	Manchester Tradesman	? (Intended for Church)	1817	Married actress
Frederick Yates	1797-1842	Tobacco Manufacturer	Army Officer	1817	Married actress
William Farren	1786-1861	Actor	Actor	1818 (London)	2nd wife actress; 2 sons on stage
George Bennett	1800-79	Actor	Naval Midshipman	1818	
John B. Buckstone	1802-79	? ('Respectable')	Solicitor's Clerk	*c.* 1820	
J.R. Anderson	1811-95	Actor	Actor	1820s?	
Edmund Glover	1813?-60	Actor (mother was Mrs. Glover, actress)	Actor	1820s?	Married actress; a son and daughter on stage
Edmund Falconer* (Irish)	1814-79	Actor	Actor	1820s?	2nd wife actress
John Douglass	1814-74	Actor	Actor	1822	Married actress
William Chippendale	1801-88	Actor	Printer's Apprentice	1823	3rd wife actress
William Leman Rede	1802-47	Barrister	Lawyer's Clerk	1823	Married actress
Edward Elton*	1794-1843	Schoolmaster	Actor (Intended Barrister)	*c.* 1823	
Robert Honner	1809-52	Publican	Ballet-dancer	1824	Married actress
Newton T. Hicks	*b.* 1812	Actor	Actor	1824	
Henry Marston	1804-83	Doctor	Trainee Barrister	1824	Married actress; 2 daughters on stage
William Oxberry	1808-52	Actor	Surgeon's Apprentice	1825	
George Rignold	*b.* 1813	Customs Surveyor	Actor	1825	Married actress

Table 1 (Continued)

ACTOR	Dates	Father's Occupation	Initial Occupation	Début	Further Theatrical Connections
George Wild*	*b.* 1805	?	Medical Student	1825	
Henry Compton*	1805-77	Clergyman	Clothier's Clerk	1826	Married actress; 9 children on stage
Charles Kean	1811-68	Actor	Actor (intended for East India Company)	1827	Married actress
Henry Mellon (Irish)	*b.* 1808	Irish Landowner (disinherited)	Naval Midshipman	1827	
Samuel Phelps	1804-78	Devonport Wine-merchant	Compositor	1826	A son on stage
Thomas Lee	*b.* 1810	Actor	Goldsmith's Apprentice	1828	
James Vining	1795-1870	Hatton Garden Silver-smith	?	1828	
George Cooke	1807-63	?	Commercial Clerk	1828	Married actress
A. Younge	*b.* 1806	Watchmaker	Commercial Clerk	1829	
John Parry	*b.* 1810	Solicitor	Shipbroker	1829	
Harry Carles	*b.* 1815	Actor	Actor	1829	
Henry M. Lewis	*b.* 1816	Army Officer (family misfortune)	Actor	1830	
John Brougham	1810-80	?	Medical Student	1830	

*Stage name.

Table 2: Actors Who Made Their Professional Débuts 1830-60

ACTOR	Dates	Father's Occupation	Initial Occupation	Début	Further Theatrical Connections
Joseph Collier	*b.* 1818	Stage-manager	Actor	1830s?	
T. Johnson*	*b.* 1815	Brewery Collector	Brewery Clerk	1830s?	
Lysander S. Thompson	*b.* 1818	Theatre Manager	Merchant Seaman	1830s?	
Charles Dillon*	*b.* 1819	Actor	Actor	1830s?	Married actress; a son on stage
William Creswick	1813-88	?	Commercial Clerk	1831	Married actress
John Herbert	?	City of London Librarian	Trainee Architect	1831	
Edward Wright	1813-59	?	City Businessman	1832	
Thomas Lyon	*b.* 1812	Liverpool Merchant	?	1832	
James Munyard	*b.* 1817	Seaman	Lawyer's Clerk	1832	
E.F. Saville	*b.* 1811	Actor-manager	Trainee Surgeon	*c.* 1832	
H.L. Bateman (American)	1812-75	?	Engineer's Apprentice	1832	Married actress; 4 daughters on stage
G.V. Brooke (Irish)	1818-66	?	Actor (intended for Bar)	1833	2nd wife actress
Frederick Belton	1815-89	Militia Captain (early death)	Actor	1833	Married actress
Alfred Wigan	1814-78	Schoolmaster	Itinerant Musician	1834	Married actress
Samuel Emery	1817-81	Actor	Stockbroker's Clerk	1834	Married actress; a daughter on stage
Charles Mathews	1803-78	Actor	Trainee Architect	1835	1st and 2nd wives actresses
Thomas Fredericks	*b.* 1812	Camberwell Architect	Trainee Architect	1836	

Table 2 (Continued)

ACTOR	Dates	Father's Occupation	Initial Occupation	Début	Further Theatrical Connections
Henry Howard	*b.* 1820	?	Bar Student	1836	
William Davidge	*b.* 1814	London tallow-merchant	Commercial Clerk	*c.* 1836	
Barry Sullivan (Irish)	1821-91	Private soldier	Attorney's Clerk	1837	A son on stage
Henry Betty	*b.* 1819	Actor	Actor (intended for the Church)	1836	
Dion Boucicault (Irish)	1822-90	Banker/Brewer	Actor	1838	2nd and 3rd wives actresses; 4 children on stage
Henry Leigh Murray*	1820-70	?	City Clerk	1839	Married actress; a daughter on stage
George Vandenhoff	1813-85	Actor	Liverpool Solicitor	1839	Several children on stage
Henry Craven*	1818-1905	Schoolmaster	Publisher's Clerk	1840	Married actress; a son on stage
Samuel Houghton*	1820-64	Actor	Actor	1840	Married actress; several children on stage
Charles Rice	1819-80	Contractor	Engraver's Apprentice	c. 1840	
Henry Scharf	*b.* 1822	German Lithographer	Assistant Curator Royal College of Surgeons	1842	
Tom Robertson	1829-71	Actor-manager	Actor	1843	Married actress; several children on stage
Frederick Robson*	1821-64	?	Engraver's Apprentice	1844	2 sons on stage
George Vining	1824-75	Actor	Bank Clerk	1845	
Rowley Cathcart	*b.* 1832	Actor	Actor	1845	A daughter on stage

Table 2 (Continued)

ACTOR	Dates	Father's Occupation	Initial Occupation	Début	Further Theatrical Connections
Sir William Don	1825-62	6th Bnt. of Newtondon, Berwicks.	Lt., 5th Dragoons	1845	2nd wife actress
John Coleman (Irish)	1831-1904	Craftsman	Accountancy Clerk/ Trainee Architect	1846	
Edward Sothern*	1826-81	Liverpool Shipowner/ Colliery Proprietor	Father's Business	1847	2nd wife actress; 2 sons and a daughter on stage
Charles Horsman	*b.* 1825	Actor	Scene-painter	1847	
Albert Smith	1816-60	Surgeon	Medical Student/ Journalist	1850	Married actress
Hermann Vezin	1829-1910	Pennsylvania Businessman	Trained for Bar	1850	1st and 2nd wives actresses
Walter Montgomery	1827-71	?	Commercial Clerk	1850s?	Married actress
John S. Clarke (American)	1833-99	?	Solicitor's Clerk	1851	Married actress; 2 sons on stage
Charles Calvert	1828-79	London merchant	Mercer's Clerk/ Solicitor's Clerk	1852	Married actress; 8 children on stage
J.L. Toole	1830-1906	Court Usher	Vintner's Clerk	1852	
Horace Wigan (brother of Alfred)	1818?-85	Schoolmaster	?	1853	
George Conquest*	1837-1901	Actor-manager	Actor (intended as violinist)	1855	Married actress; 3 sons on stage
Gaston Murray* (brother of Henry)	1826-89	?	?	1855	Married actress
Henry Irving	1838-1905	Tailor's salesman	Lawyer's Clerk/ Commercial Clerk	1856	2 sons on stage

Table 2 (Continued)

ACTOR	Dates	Father's Occupation	Initial Occupation	Début	Further Theatrical Connections
Montague Williams	1835-92	Barrister	Officer, Royal South Lincs. Militia	1856	Married actress
Edward Saker	1831-83	Actor	Trainee Architect	*c.* 1856	Married actress; several sons on stage
Henry Neville	1837-1910	Theatre Manager	Actor (intended for Army)	1857	

*Stage name

Table 3: Actors Who Made Their Professional Débuts 1860-90

ACTOR	Dates	Father's Occupation	Initial Occupation	Début	Further Theatrical Connections
Thomas Thorne	1841-1918	Actor-manager	Actor	*c.* 1860	
Squire Bancroft*	1841-1926	Oil-merchant (early death)	Actor	1861	Married actress
William Kendal*	1843-1917	Artist	?	1861	Married actress
Charles Warner*	1846-1909	Actor	Trainee Architect	1861	A son and daughter on stage
Charles Wyndham*	1837-1919	Surgeon	Surgeon	1862	2nd wife actress; a son theatre manager
Wilson Barrett	1846-1904	Essex Farmer (family misfortune)	Printer's clerk	1864	Married actress
John Hare*	1844-1921	? (early death of parents)	Civil Service Trainee	1864	
Lionel Brough	1836-1909	Dramatist	Journalist	1864	4 children on stage
Augustus Glover*	*b.* 1846	Author/Educationist	?	1864	
Edmund Lyons	*b.* 1851	Theatre Manager	Actor	1864	
Lewis Wingfield	1842-91	6th Viscount Powerscourt	Intended for the Army	*c.* 1865	
John Clayton*	1845-88	?	Indian Civil Service Trainee	1866	Married actress; 1 son dramatist, 1 son actor, 1 son theatre manager
W.H. Pennington	?	Civil Servant	Officer, 11th Hussars	1866	
Charles Kelly*	1839-85	Clergyman	Officer, 66th Regiment	1867	Married actress
William Terris*	1847-97	Barrister	Naval Officer	1867	Married actress; a daughter on stage

Table 3 (Continued)

ACTOR	Dates	Father's Occupation	Initial Occupation	Début	Further Theatrical Connections
Henry Kemble	1848-1907	Army Captain	Privy Council Clerk	1867	
Charles Collette	*b.* 1842	Solicitor	Officer, 3rd Dragoons	1868	Married actress
Arthur Cecil*	1843-96	Solicitor	?	1869	
H.J. Byron	1834-84	Diplomat	Trained for Bar	1869 (London)	
Robert Lyons (bro. of Edmund)	*b.* 1853	Theatre manager	Actor	1869	
George Grossmith	1847-1912	Journalist	Journalist	1870	2 sons on stage
William Herbert*	*b.* 1844	Indian Army Colonel	Army Officer	1870	
Frederick Marshall	*b.* 1848	Actor	Actor	1870	
Clavering Power	*b.* 1842	Barrister	Indian Army Officer	1870	
Edward Compton	1854-1918	Actor	Actor	1870s?	Married actress; 4 children on stage
William S. Penley	1852-1912	Schoolmaster	Milliner's Apprentice	1871	
Edward S. Mott	*b.* 1844	Landowner	Indian Army Officer	1872	
G.B. Soane-Roby	?	Actor	Trainee Surgeon	1873	
Rutland Barrington*	1853-1922	London Sugar Dealer	City Clerk	1874	
Johnston Forbes-Robertson	1853-1937	Journalist	Art Student	1874	Married actress; a daughter on stage
A.W. Pinero	1855-1934	Solicitor	Trainee Solicitor	1874	Married actress
Harold K. Bellew	1855-1911	Clergyman	Naval Officer	1875 (England)	

Table 3 (Continued)

ACTOR	Dates	Father's Occupation	Initial Occupation	Début	Further Theatrical Connections
H. Beerbohm Tree*	1853-1917	Grain Merchant	Commercial Clerk	1878	Married actress; a daughter on stage
Fred Leslie*	1855-92	Military Outfitter	Army Contractor's Clerk	1878	
George Alexander*	1858-1918	Commercial Traveller	Draper's Clerk	1879	
Charles Brookfield	1857-1913	Clergyman	Trained for Bar	1879	Married actress
Ben Greet	1857-1936	Naval Captain	Schoolmaster	1879	
Fred Terry	1863-1933	Actor	Actor	1880	Married actress; a son and daughter on stage
Charles Hawtrey	1858-1923	Clergyman	Private Tutor	1881	
John Martin-Harvey	1863-1944	Naval Architect	Trainee Architect	1881	Married actress; a daughter on stage
Frank Benson	1858-1939	Barrister	Actor	1882	Married actress
Lewis Waller*	1860-1915	Civil Engineer	Commercial Clerk	1883	Married actress
Cyril Maude	1862-1951	Army Officer	Intended for Army	1885	1st wife actress
Walter L. Bradfield	1866-1919	Post Office Official	Commercial Clerk	1885	Married actress; a son on stage
George Arliss*	1868-1946	Publisher	Commercial Clerk	1886	Married actress
Albert E. Mathews	1869-1960	Actor	Actor	1886	
Benjamin Webster	1864-1947	Solicitor	Trained for Bar	1887	Married actress; a daughter theatre director
Arthur Bourchier	1863-1927	Army Captain	Actor	1889	1st and 2nd wives actresses

*Stage name

Table 4: Known Education of Prominent Actors Who Made Their Débuts 1800-30 (in alphabetical order)

John Brougham	Trinity College, Dublin
Henry Compton	Academy School
Charles Kean	Eton
Henry Naishe Lewis	Academy school
William Macready	Rugby
William Oxberry (the younger)	Merchant Taylors
Samuel Phelps	Academy school
Lysander Steel Thompson	Academy school
John Vandenhoff	Stoneyhurst College
Benjamin Webster I	Academy school
George Wild	Academy school
Frederick Yates	Academy school
Charles Young	Eton and Merchant Taylors

Table 5: Known Education of Prominent Actors Who Made Their Débuts 1830-60 (in alphabetical order)

Dion Boucicault	Privately and at London University
Gustavus Vaughan Brooke	Edgworth's Town School
Charles Calvert	King's College School, London and at a theological college
George Conquest	Collége Communal, Boulogne
William Davidge	St Paul's School, London
Sir William Don	Eton
Thomas Fredericks	Academy school
Henry Irving	City of London Commercial School
Henry Marston	Winchester College
Charles Mathews	Merchant Taylors
E.F. Saville	Christ's Hospital
Henry Scharf	London University
Albert Smith	Merchant Taylors
J.L. Toole	City of London School
George Vining	St Peter's Grammar School, Eaton Square, and in France
Montague Williams	Eton

Table 6: Known Education of Prominent Actors Who Made Their Débuts 1860-90

George Alexander	Privately
Squire Bancroft	Privately in England and France
Rutland Barrington	Merchant Taylors
Frank Benson	Winchester College and Oxford University
Arthur Bourchier	Eton and Oxford University
John Clayton	Merchant Taylors
Frank Clements (*b.*1844, début 1861)	University educated
H.B. Conway (*b.*1850, début 1872)	Rossall and University of Berlin
Johnston Forbes-Robertson	Charterhouse
Charles Hawtrey	Eton, Rugby and Oxford University
Henry Kemble	King's College School, London
John Martin-Harvey	King's College School, London
Cyril Maude	Charterhouse
E.S. Mott	Eton and Sandhurst
A.Pinero	Privately and at the Birbeck Institution
Clavering Power	King's College School, London
Herbert Beerbohm Tree	Schnepfenthal College, Thuringia
Lewis Waller	King's College, London, and in Germany
Charles Warner	Westbury College, Highgate
Benjamin Webster III	King's College School, London
Lewis Wingfield	Eton and Bonn University
Charles Wyndham	King's College School, London, and the University of Giessen, Germany

Table 7: Actresses Who Made Their Professional Débuts 1800-30

ACTRESS	Dates	Father's Occupation	Adult or Regular Début	Husband
Frances Kelly	1790-1882	Army Captain	1807*	?
Kitty Stephens	1794-1882	Carver/Gilder	1813	Earl of Essex (1838)
Mrs Bunn (née Margaret Somerville)	1799-1883	Scots Biscuit Baker	*c.*1815	Alfred Bunn, theatre manager (1819)
Mrs Yates (née Elizabeth Brunton)	1799-1860	Actor	1815*	Frederick Yates, actor-manager (1823)
Mrs Wigan (née Leonora Pincott)	1805-84	Actor	1818*	Alfred Wigan, actor-manager (1841)
Mrs William Daly	*b.*1806	Actor	*c.*1820*	William Daly, occupation unknown (1813)
Madame Vestris	1797-1856	Italian Engraver	1820* (London)	1. Armond Vestris, dancer 2. Charles Mathews, actor-manager (1838)
Mrs Warner (née Mary Huddart)	1804-54	Actor	*c.*1820*	R.W. Warner, publican (1837)
Ellen Tree	1806-80	East India Company Official	1823	Charles Kean, actor-manager (1842)
Maria Honner (Irish)	1812-70	Actor	late 1820s?*	1. Robert Honner, actor-manager 2. Frederick Morton, stage-manager
Mrs W. Lacy (née Miss Taylor)	1807-74	?	1827	Walter Lacy, actor (1839)

Table 7 (Continued)

ACTRESS	Dates	Father's Occupation	Adult or Regular Début	Husband
Mrs Nisbett (Irish)	1812-58	Actor	1828*	1. Captain Nisbett (1831) 2. Sir William Boothby, Bt. (1844)
Fanny Kemble	1809-93	Actor	1829	Mr Butler (American) (1834)
Fanny Stirling	1815?-95	Captain, Horse Guards (family misfortune)	1829	1. Edward Stirling, actor and dramatist 2. Lord Gregory (1894)
Laura Honey	1816-43	? (mother Mrs Young, a Sadler's Wells actress)	*c.* 1829*	Mr Honey (occupation unknown)
Mrs Henry Compton (née Emmeline Montague)	?	Actor	1820s?*	Henry Compton, actor (1848)
Mrs Mary Keeley (née Goward)	1806-99	Actor	1820s?*	Robert Keeley, actor (1829)

*Appeared before this date as a child.

Table 8: Actresses Who Made Their Professional Débuts 1830-60

ACTRESS	Dates	Father's Occupation	Adult or Regular Début	Husband
Eliza Terrey	*b.* 1823	London Tradesman (early death)	1830s?	?
Emma Stanley	*b.* 1822	Actor	1830s? *	?
Madame Céline Celeste	1814-82	? (in reduced circumstances)	1830* (London)	Mr Elliott, American (occupation unknown)
Miss Rogers	*b.* 1821	Licensed Victualler	1832	?
Mrs T.H. Lacy (née Fanny Cooper)	*b.* 1819	Actor	1833*	T.H. Lacy, actor-manager (1842)
Priscilla Horton	1818-95	Actor	1835*	Thomas German Reed, actor (1844)
Helen Faucit	1817-98	Actor	1836	Theodore Martin, MP (1851)
Charlotte Cushman (American)	1816-76	Businessman (early death)	1836*	—
Mrs Alfred Mellon (née Sarah Jane Woolgar)	1824-1909	Actor (former tailor)	1836*	Alfred Mellon, musician
Charlotte Vandenhoff	1818-60	Actor	1836*	Tom Swinbourne, actor (1856)
Fanny Vining	*b.* 1823	Stage-manager	1838*	?
Jane Louisa Reynolds	*b.* 1824	Army Officer	1839	?
Mrs Bateman (née Sydney Frances Cowell)	1823-81	Actor	late 1830s? *	H.L. Bateman, actor-manager (1839)
Elizabeth Lee	?-1892	Actor-manager	late 1830s? *	Henry Leigh Murray, actor (1841)
Clare Conquest	1825-88	Actor	*c.* 1840*	Charles Dillon, actor

Table 8 (Continued)

ACTRESS	Dates	Father's Occupation	Adult or Regular Début	Husband
Julia Bennett	*b.* 1824	Actor	1841	?
Emma Stanley	1818-81	Actor	1842*	?
Laura Addison	?	London gentleman 'of independent means'	1842	?
Madame Anna Thillon	?	'English gentleman' (of reduced circumstances)	1844	M. Thillon (occupation unknown)
Isabella Glyn	1823-89	Scottish architect	1847	1. Edward Wills (occupation unknown) 2. E.S. Dallas, journalist
Mrs John Wood (née Mathilda Vining)	1831-1915	Actor	late 1840s*	John Wood
Clara Tellet	?	Actor	1848* (London)	Samuel Emery, actor
Agnes Robertson	1833-1916	Actor	*c.* 1850*	Dion Boucicault, actor-dramatist (1853)
Louise Keeley	1833-1877	Actor	*c.* 1850*	Montague Williams, actor (1858)
Caroline Heath	1833?-87	?	1852	Wilson Barrett, actor-manager (1866)
Lydia Thompson	1836-1908	Actor?	1852*	1. Mr Tilbury, Coachman 2. Alexander Henderson, manager
Lydia Foote (née Legge)	1844-92	Actor	1852	?

Table 8 (Continued)

ACTRESS	Dates	Father's Occupation	Adult or Regular Début	Husband
Mrs Howard Paul (née Isabella Featherstone)	1833-79	?	1853	Howard Paul, actor-dramatist (1857)
Eleanor Bufton	1840-93	Actor?	1854* (London)	Arthur Swanborough, actor
Marie Wilton	1839-1921	Actor	*c.* 1855*	Squire Bancroft, actor (1867)
Mrs Hermann Vezin (née Jane Thomson)	1827-1902	Merchant (actress mother)	1857*	1. Charles Young, American actor (1846)
Adelaide Calvert (née Biddles)	1837-1921	Actor	*c.* 1859*	Charles Calvert, actor-manager (1856)
Henrietta Hodson	1841-1910	? (actress mother)	mid-1850s	2. Hermann Vezin, actor (1863) 1. Mr Pigeon, Solicitor 2. Henry Labouchere, writer (1868)

*Appeared before this date as a child.

Table 9: Actresses Who Made Their Professional Débuts 1860-90

ACTRESS	Dates	Father's Occupation	Adult or Regular Début	Husband
Charlotta Leclercq	1840-93	Actor	1861*	John Nelson, actor (1877)
Ellen Farren	1848-1904	Actor	1862*	Robert Soutar, actor (1867)
Fanny Addison	*b.* 1847	Actor	1862*	Henry Mader Pitt, actor
Ellen Terry	1847-1928	Actor	1862*	1. G.F. Watts, painter (1862) 2. Charles Kelly, actor (1876) 3. James Carew, actor (1907)
Ada Cavendish	1839-95	Actor	1863	Francis Marshall, dramatist (1885)
Adelaide Neilson	1846-80	Actor	1865* (London)	P.H. Lee, clergyman's son
Marie Litton	1847-84	?	1868	Mr W. Robertson (occupation unknown)
Emily Fowler	*b.* 1849	Actor?	1868*	J.C. Pemberton (occupation unknown)
Rose Coghlan	1851-1932	Actor?	1869*	?
Clara Rousby	1852-79	Inspector General of Hospitals	1869	W. Rousby, actor-manager (1868)
Fanny Brough	1854-1914	Dramatist	1869	Richard Smith Boleyn, actor
Alma Murray	1854-1943	Actor	1870	Alfred Forman (occupation unknown)
Kate Vaughan	1852-1903	Musician	1870	Hon. F.A. Wellesley, son of Earl of Cowley
Jennie Lee	?	Artist	c. 1870	J.P. Burnett, actor-dramatist

Table 9 (Continued)

ACTRESS	Dates	Father's Occupation	Adult or Regular Début	Husband
Louise Hibbert	*b.* 1855	Actor	1874*	?
Winifred Emery	1862-1924	Actor	1879*	Cyril Maude, actor (1888)
Lilly Langtry	1853-1929	Dean of Jersey	1881	1. Edward Langtry (1875) 2. Sir Hugo de Bathe
May Whitty	1865-1948	Liverpool Journalist	1881	Ben Webster (1864-1947), actor (1892)
Janet Achurch	1864-1916	(Theatrical grandparents)	1883	Charles Charrington, actor
Mary Anderson (American)	1859-1940	?	1883 (England)	A. de Navarro (1890)
Marie Tempest	1864-1942	Stationer	1887	1. Alfred Izard, pianist (1885) 2. Cosmo Gordon-Lennox, dramatist (1898) 3. William Browne, actor (1921)
Mrs Patrick Campbell (née Beatrice Tanner)	1865-1940	Army Contractor	1888	1. Patrick Campbell, city clerk (1884) 2. Major George Cornwallis-West (1914)
Julia Neilson	1868-1957	Silversmith	1888	Fred Terry, actor (1891)

*Appeared before this date as a child.

APPENDIX II: Family Trees of Some Typical Victorian Theatrical Dynasties

Actors, actresses, and others connected with the theatre are set in italic, although in many cases non-theatrical members of the family have been left out for purposes of convenience. Further examples can be found in Bampton Hunt (ed.), *The Green Room Book, or Who's Who on the Stage,* 1906, 377-85.

1. The Kembles, Murrays, Cowells, Comptons, Batemans and Montagues

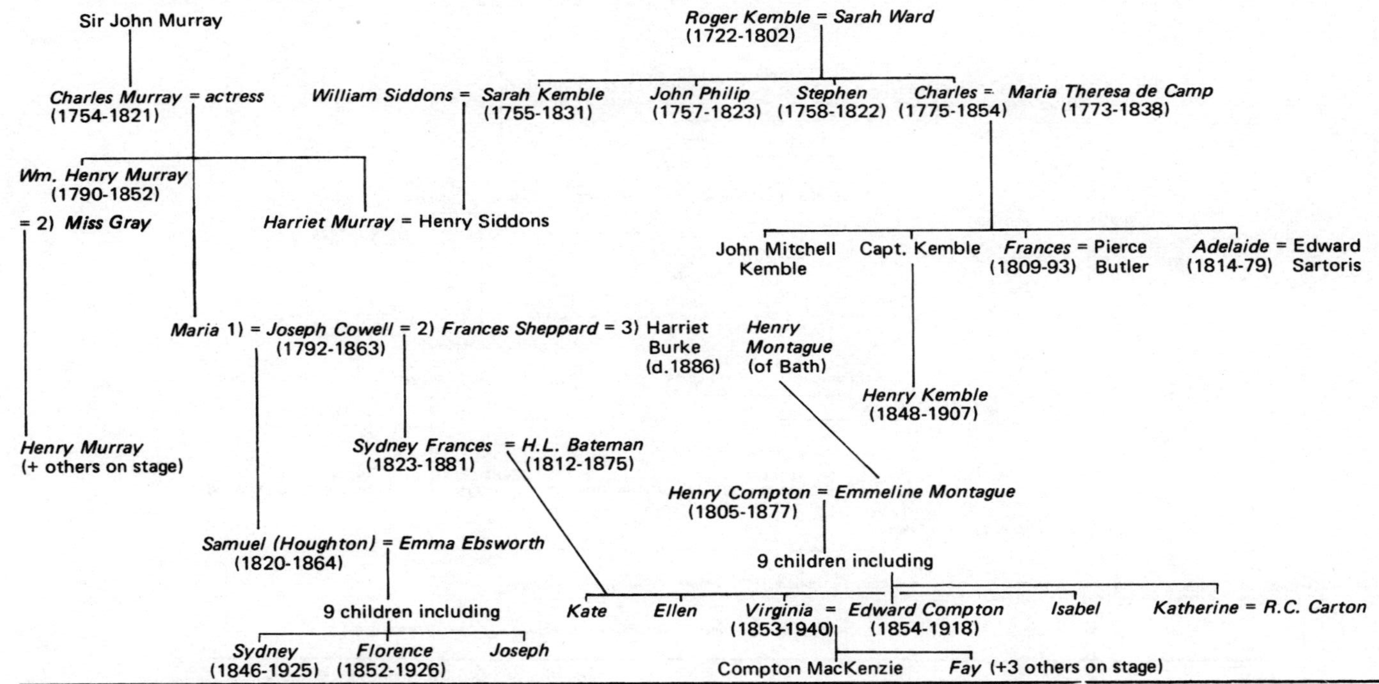

2. The Websters, Broughs, Whittys and Lupinos

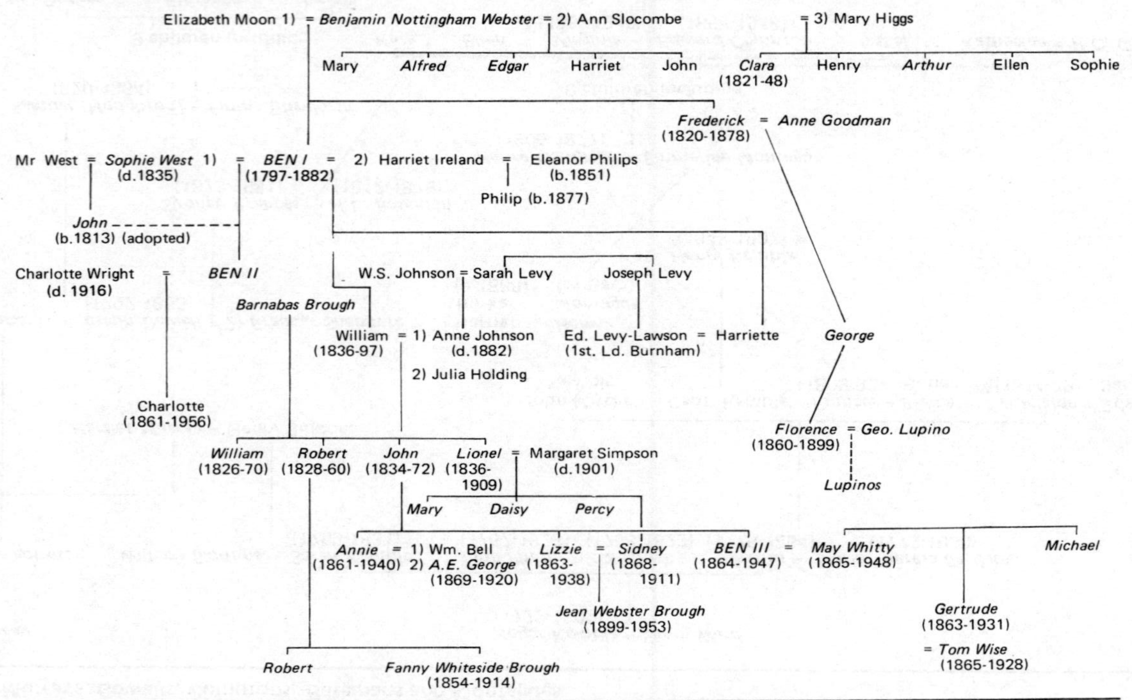

3. The Terry Family (adapted from the tree in Marguerite Steen's *A Pride of Terrys*, 1962)

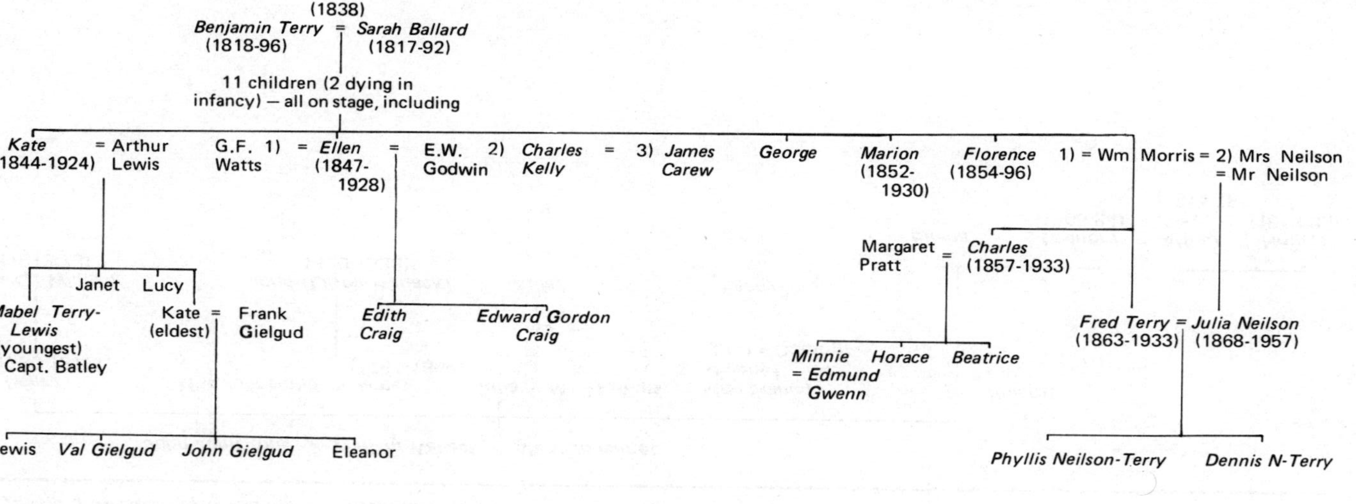

4. The Johnstones, Wallacks, Pincotts and Wigans

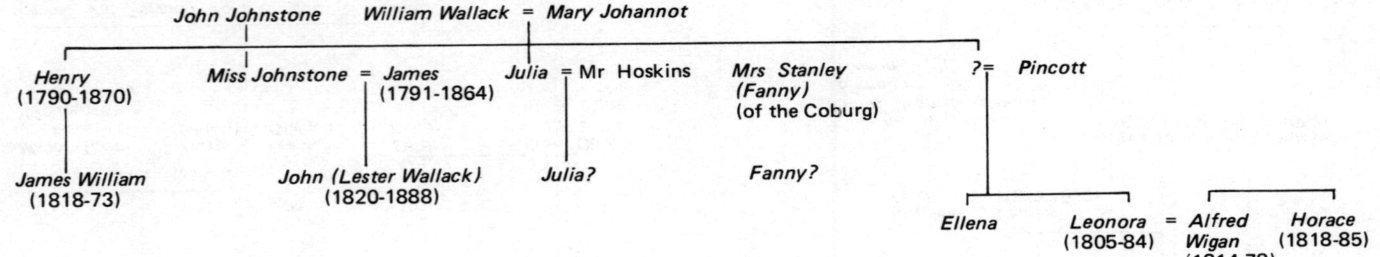

APPENDIX III: Increase between Censuses in the Recorded Numbers of Actors and Actresses in England and Wales, 1841-91

YEAR	ACTORS	ACTRESSES	TOTAL
1841	973	384	1,357
1851	1,218	717	1,935
1861	1,311	891	2,202
1871	1,899	1,693	3,592
1881	2,197	2,368	4,565
1891	3,625	3,696	7,321

It would be fair to say that these figures err on the conservative side and should therefore be used with caution. The proportional *rate* of growth, on the other hand hand, is probably fairly accurate from decade to decade.

BIBLIOGRAPHY

Primary Sources

General Works

Acton, Dr William, *Prostitution, Considered in its Moral, Social and Sanitary Aspects,* 1857.

Archer, William, *About the Theatre,* 1886.

——, *Masks or Faces?*, 1888.

Arnold, Matthew, *Culture and Anarchy: An Essay in Political and Social Criticism,* 1869.

Baker, Henry Barton, *The London Stage, 1576-1888,* 2 vols., 1889.

Blathwayt, Raymond, *Does the Theatre make for Good?,* 1898.

Booth, C., 'Occupations of the People of the United Kingdom, 1801-81', *Journal of the Statistical Society,* XLIX, Part II, June 1886, Appendix A (1).

Broadbent, R.J., *Stage Whispers,* 1901.

——, *Annals of the Liverpool Stage,* 1908.

Henry Butler's Theatrical Directory and Dramatic Almanac for 1853 (also *for 1860*).

Cook, Dutton, *The Book of the Play,* 2 vols., 1876.

——, *On the Stage,* 2 vols., 1883.

——, 'Corin', *The Truth about the Stage,* 1885.

Croker, Thomas, *A Walk from London to Fulham,* 1860 (revised and edited by T.F. Dillon Croker).

Davenant, Francis, *What Shall My Son Be?,* 1870.

Dibdin, J.C., *The Annals of the Edinburgh Stage,* 1888.

Escott, T.H.S., *England: Its People, Polity, and Pursuits,* 2 vols.,1885.

Fitzgerald, P.H., *The World Behind the Scenes,* 1881.

——, *Music Hall Land, An Account of the Natives, Male and Female, Pastimes, Songs, Antics, and General Oddities of that Strange Country,* 1890.

——, *Picturesque London,* 1890.

——, *The Art of Acting,* 1892.

Fontane, Theodor, *Journeys to England in Victoria's Early Days, 1844-59* (translated by Dorothy Harrison), 1939.

Furness, H.H. (ed.), *The Shakespeare Variorum to 'Twelfth Night',* vol. XIII, 1901.

Garcia, Gustave, *The Actor's Art,* 1882.
Geary, W.N.M., *The Law of Theatres and Music Halls,* 1885.
Gissing, George, *New Grub Street,* Penguin, 1976 (first published 1891).
Goddard, Arthur, *Players of the Period,* 1891.
Godwin, George, *On the Desirability of Obtaining a National Theatre not Wholly controlled by the Prevailing Popular Taste,* 1878. (A paper read to the Cheltenham Congress of the Social Science Association).
Grant, George, *The Science of Acting,* 1826.
Grant, James, *Sketches in London,* 1838.
Greg, W.R., *Literary and Social Judgements,* 1869.
Hammerton, J.A. (ed.), *The Actor's Art.* 1897.
'Hawk's-Eye', *The Stage of 1871 – A Review of Plays and Players,* 1871.
Hollingshead, John, *Footlights,* 1883.
Howe, P.P. (ed.), *The Complete Works of William Hazlitt,* IV (1930: 'On Actors and the Art of Acting') and XII (1931: 'On Novelty and Familiarity').
Irving, Henry, *The Stage,* 1878 (an address delivered at the Perry Barr Institute, Birmingham).
——, *English Actors, Their Characteristics and Methods,* 1886.
——, *The Drama Addresses by Henry Irving,* 1893.
James, Henry, *The Scenic Art, Notes on Acting and the Drama 1872-1901,* ed. by Alan Wade, 1949.
Jones, H.A., *Renascence of the English Drama,* 1895.
Kendal, Mrs., *The Drama,* 1884 (a paper read at the Congress of the National Association for the Promotion of Social Science).
Lamb, Charles, *The Essays of Elia,* 1823.
Lennox, Lord William Pitt, *Plays, Players and Playhouses, At Home and Abroad,* 2 vols., 1881.
Lewes, G.H., *On Actors and the Art of Acting,* 1875.
Logan, W., *The Great Social Evil,* 1871.
Lowe, R.W., *A Bibliographical Account of English Theatrical Literature,* 1888.
Lytton, Bulwer, *England and the English,* 1833.
MacKinnon, Alan, *The Oxford Amateurs,* 1910.
Marshall, Thomas, *Lives of the Most Celebrated Actors and Actresses,* 1847 (also known as *The National Dramatic Biography,* Vol.I., ed. by T. Marshall).
Marston, Westland, *Our Recent Actors,* 1888.
Mayall's Celebrities of the London Stage, 1863.
Mayhew, Henry, *London Labour and the London Poor,* Vol.III, 1861.

Mill, J.S., *Autobiography*, 1873.
Morley, Henry, *Journal of a London Playgoer*, 1866.
Newman, Henry, *Discourses Addressed to Mixed Congregations*, 1849.
Nowrojee, Jehangeer and Merwanjee, Hirjeebhoy, *Journal of a Residence of Two years and a Half in Great Britain*, 1841.
Pascoe, Charles Eyre, *The Dramatic List*, 1879.
——, *Where Shall I Educate My Son?*, 1884.
Planché, J.R., *Suggestions for Establishing an English Art Theatre*, 1879.
Rede, Leman Thomas, *The Road to the Stage*, 1827, 1836.
Robins, Edward, *Twelve Great Actresses*, 1900.
Rogers, Frederick, *Life, Labour and Literature*, 1913.
Roth, W.E., *Theatre Hygiene*, 1888.
Ruskin, John, *Modern Painters*, III (1856), *Works*, V, 1904.
——, Ibid., XXVIII, 1907. XXXIV, 1908.
——, *Stones of Venice*, 1899 edn.
Russell, W.C., *Representative Actors*, 1872.
Ryan, Michael, *Prostitution in London*, 1839.
Schneewind, J.B. (ed.), *Mill's Essays on Literature and Society*, 1965.
Smith, Albert, *The Natural History of the Ballet-Girl*, 1847.
Stone, H. (ed.), *Uncollected Writings of Dickens: Household Words, 1850-59*, Vol.I, 1969.
Talma, F.J., *On the Actor's Art*, 1883 (with an introduction by Henry Irving).
Thomson, H. Byerley, *The Choice of a Profession*, 1857.
Thornbury, Walter, *Haunted London*, 1880.
Tree, Herbert Beerbohm, *Some Interesting Fallacies of the Modern Stage*, 1892.
'Trim' (W.B. Megson), *'Old Wild's' – A Nursery of Strolling Players*, 1888.
Watts, G.T., *Theatrical Bristol*, 1915.
Wright, Thomas, *Some Habits and Customs of the Working Classes*, (by a journeyman engineer), 1867.
Yates, Edmund, *Celebrities at Home*, 1877 (1st series) and 1878 (2nd series).

Memoirs, Recollections, Diaries and Biographies

'An Actor', *The Stage with the Curtain Raised*, 1881.
Archer, Frank, *An Actor's Notebooks*, 1912.
Archer, William, *Henry Irving, Actor and Manager*, 1885.
Arliss, George, *On the Stage*, 1928.
Bailey, John (ed.), *The Diary of Lady Frederick Cavendish*, 2 vols., 1927.

Bahlman, D.W.R. (ed.), *The Diary of Sir Edward Walter Hamilton*, 2 vols., 1972.
Bancroft, Mr and Mrs, *On and Off the Stage*, 2 vols., 1886.
Bancrofts, The, *Recollections of Sixty Years*, 1909.
Beale, S. Sophia (ed.), *Recollections of a Spinster Aunt*, 1908.
Beckett, Arthur a, *Green-Room Recollections*, 1896.
Belton, Frederick, *Random Recollections of an Old Actor*, 1880.
Benson, A.C., *Memories and Friends*, 1924.
Benson, Lady Constance, *Mainly Players: Bensonian Memories*, 1926.
Brent, J.F., *Memories of a Mistaken Life, an Autobiography*, 1897.
Brett, M.V. (ed.), *Journals and Letters of Viscount Esher*, 1934.
Brookfield, Charles, *Random Reminiscences*, 1902.
Burnand, F.C., *Records and Reminiscences*, 2 vols., 1904.
Butler, Frances Anne, *Journal*, 1835.
Calvert, Mrs Charles, *Sixty-Eight Years on the Stage*, 1911.
Campbell, Mrs Patrick, *My Life and Some Letters*, 1922.
Clegg, James (ed.), *Autobiography of a Lancashire Lawyer, being the Life and Recollections of John Taylor*, 1883.
Cohen, Lucy, *Lady de Rothschild and her Daughters, 1821-1931*, 1935.
Cole, J.W., *The Life and Theatrical Times of Charles Kean*, 1859.
Coleman, John, *The Memoirs of Samuel Phelps*, 1886.
——, *Players and Playwrights I Have Known*, 2 vols., 1888.
——, *Fifty Years of an Actor's Life*, 2 vols., 1904.
Coleridge, Hon. Stephen, *Memories*, 1913.
Collingwood, S.D., *The Life and Letters of Lewis Carroll*, 1898.
Colvin, Sidney, *Memories and Notes*, 1921.
Compton, Charles and Edward, *Memoir of Henry Compton*, 1879.
Cornish, F.W. (ed.), *Extracts from the Letters and Journals of William Cory*, 1897.
Courtneidge, Robert, *'I Was An Actor Once'*, 1930.
Craig, Edward Gordon, *Index to the Story of my Days, 1872-1907*, 1957.
Donaldson, Walter, *Recollections of an Actor*, 1865.
Ervine, St John, *The Theatre in my Time*, 1933.
Fagan, Elizabeth, *From the Wings*, 1922.
Fitzgerald, P.H., *Sir Henry Irving*, 1895.
Francillon, R.E., *Mid-Victorian Memories*, 1914.
Ganthony, Robert, *Random Recollections*, 1898.
Gladstone, Mary, *Diaries and Letters*, 1930.
Graham, Joe, *An Old Stock-Actor's Memories*, 1930.
Grossmith, George, *A Society Clown*, 1888.
Hanley, P. (An Old Playgoer), *Random Recollections of the Stage*, 1883.

Hatton, Joseph, *'With a Show in the North' – Reminiscences of Mark Lemon,* 1871.
Hatton, Joseph (ed.), *Reminiscences of J.L. Toole,* 1889.
Hibbert, H.G. *A Playgoer's Memories,* 1920.
Howard, J.B., *Fifty Years a Showman,* 1938.
Jerome, J.K., *On the Stage – and Off,* 1885.
Jupp, James, *The Gaiety Stage Door,* 1923.
Kemble, Frances, *Records of Later Life,* 1882.
——, *Further Records, 1848-83,* 1890.
Kennedy, A.L. (ed.), *'My Dear Duchess' – Social and Political Letters to the Duchess of Manchester 1858-69,* 1956.
Kintner, Elvan (ed.), *The Letters of Robert Browning and Elizabeth Barrett Barrett, 1845-46,* 1969.
Laceby, Arthur, *The Stage Struggles of a Bad Actor,* 1904.
Martin, Sir Theodore, *Helen Faucit, Lady Martin,* 1900.
Mott, Edward Spencer, *A Mingled Yarn,* 1898.
Nicholson, Renton, *An Autobiography,* 1861.
Paterson, Peter, *Glimpses of Real Life,* 1864.
Paxton, Sydney, *Stage Seesaws,* 1917.
Pemberton, T.E., *The Kendals,* 1900.
——, *Sir Charles Wyndham,* 1904.
Pennington, W.H., *Sea, Camp and Stage,* 1906.
Philips, F.C., *My Varied Life,* 1914.
Plomer, William (ed.), *Kilvert's Diary – Selections from the Diary of the Rev. Francis Kilvert 1870-79,* 3 vols., 1960.
Pollock, Sir Frederick (ed.), *Macready's Reminiscences and Selections from his Diaries and Letters,* 2 vols., 1875.
——, *The Personal Remembrances of Sir Frederick Pollock,* 2 vols., 1887.
Pollock, Lady, *Macready As I Knew Him,* 1884.
Redesdale, Lord, *Memories,* 1915.
Reeve, Henry (ed.), *The Greville Memoirs, 1818-60,* 3 vols. (Vol. I, 1874, Vols. II and III, 1885).
Roberts, Arthur, *The Adventures of Arthur Roberts,* 1895.
Sanger, 'Lord' George, *Seventy Years a Showman,* 1908.
Scott, Clement, *Thirty Years at the Play,* 1892.
Scott, Clement and Cecil Howard (eds.), *The Life and Reminiscences of Edward Leman Blanchard,* 2 vols., 1891.
Scott, Mrs. Clement, *Old Days in Bohemian London,* 1919.
Shuttleworth, H.C. (ed.), *The Diary of an Actress or Realities of Stage Life,* 1885.

Sillard, R.M., *Barry Sullivan,* 2 vols., 1901.
Soane-Roby, G.B., *A Night of Change – My First Experience of Hamlet,* 1895 (from *Stage Stories by Actors and Actresses* No.1).
Soldene, Emily, *My Theatrical and Musical Recollections,* 1897.
Stirling, Edward, *Old Drury Lane,* 2 vols., 1881.
Stoker, Bram, *Personal Reminiscences of Henry Irving,* 2 vols., 1906.
Thomson, Christopher, *The Autobiography of an Artisan,* 1847.
Trevelyan, G.O., *Life and Letters of Lord Macaulay,* 2 vols. 1876.
Vernon-Harcourt, F.C., *From Stage to Cross,* 1902.
Vincent, W.T., *Recollections of Fred Leslie,* 1893.
Wallack, Lester, *Memories of Fifty Years,* 1889.
Williams, Montague, *Leaves of a Life,* 2 vols., 1890.
Windsor, The Dean of (ed.), *Letters of Lady Augusta Stanley – A Young Lady at Court 1849-63,* 1927.
Yates, Edmund, *His Recollections and Experiences,* 2 vols., 1884.

Newspapers and Periodicals

The Actor and the Elocutionist, 1881.
Actors by Gaslight, 1838.
All the Year Round, 1876.
Blackwood's Magazine, 1879.
The Dramatic Almanack, 1862.
The Dramatic, Equestrian, and Musical Sick Fund Almanack, 1862-71.
The Dramatic and Musical Directory of the United Kingdom, 1883-90.
The Dramatic Register for 1853.
The Entr'acte Annual, 1883.
The *Era*, 1838-1900.
The Era Almanack, 1868-87.
The Fortnightly Review, 1865-90.
The Green Room, 1880.
The Looker-On, 1851.
London Opinion, 1880.
Nineteenth Century, 1877-9.
Punch, or the London Charivari, 1841-90.
Saturday Review, 1856-90.
The Stage-Manager, 1849
Theatre, 1877-90
The Theatrical Times, 1846-9.
The Times, 1835-45.
Vanity Fair, 1868-90.
The Victoria Magazine, 1863-80.

Women and Womanhood

Bulley, A. Amy and Whitley, Margaret, *Women's Work,* 1894.
Caplin, Madame R.A., *Women in the Reign of Queen Victoria,* 1876.
Cobbe, Frances, *Essays on the Pursuits of Women,* 1863.
Ellis, Mrs S., *The Women of England,* 1839.
Jameson, Mrs Anna, *Shakespeare's Female Characters,* 1840.
Linton, Elizabeth Lynn, *The Girl of the Period and Other Essays,* 2 vols., 1883.
Martin, Lady, *Some of Shakespeare's Female Characters,* 1885.
Mill, J.S., *The Subjection of Women,* 1869.
Parkes, Bessie Rayner, *Essays on Women's Work,* 1865.
Ruskin, John, *Sesame and Lilies* (1865), 1882.
Sandford, Mrs E., *Female Improvement,* 1836.

Church and Stage

Baxter, Rev. A.J., *The Theatre – 'A Religious Institution',* 1865. (Bodleian Library, Oxford).
Calcraft, J.W., *A Defence of the Stage,* 1839.
Candlish, Robert S. (ed.), *Lovers of Pleasure More Than Lovers of God,* by Andrew Thomson, D.D. (1818), 1867.
Close, D.D., Francis, *The Stage, Ancient and Modern,* 1877.
Davies, J., *The Attitude of Society to the Stage, Past and Present,* 1879. (A paper read to the Church and Stage Guild).
Dixon, J.M., *The Pulpit and the Stage,* 1879, 1881.
Ferguson, Rev. R., and Morton Brown, Rev. A., *Life and Labours of John Campbell, D.D.,* 1868.
Fluck, A.W., *Theatrical Reform,* 1879. (A paper read to the London Theatrical Reform Association).
Fowler, J.H., *The Influence of the Theatre on Life and Character,* 1886.
Ham, J. Panton, *The Stage and the Drama in their relation to Society,* 1880 (published by the Sunday Lecture Society).
Haweis, Rev. H.R., *Shakespeare and the Stage,* 1878.
Headlam, Beatrice R., *The Ballet,* 1879. (A paper read to the Church and Stage Guild).
Hudson, W.H., *The Church and the Stage,* 1886.
Kingsley, Charles, *Plays and Puritans, and other Historical Essays,* 1873.
'A Lady', *An Appeal to the Women of England to Discourage the Stage,* 1855.
Lightfoot, J.B., *The Drama,* 1898.
Lyne, Rev. Augustus, *Theatres, Their Uses and Abuses,* 1881.
Pease, Alfred (ed.), *Diaries of Edward Pease,* 1907.

Roberts, Rev. R.E. (ed.), *Sermons on Theatrical Amusements,* by Rev. Thomas Best, 1865.

'A Visitor', *Observations on a Recent Pamphlet entitled 'The Pulpit Justified, and the Theatre Condemned',* by the Rev. John East, 1844.

Plays

Simpson, J. Palgrave, *World and Stage,* 1859. (Lacy's Acting Edition, Vol.97).

Pinero, A.W., *Trelawney of the Wells,* 1898.

Roberts, George, *Behind the Curtain,* 1870.

Stage Fiction

Anon., *Artist and Craftsman,* 1862.

Brontë, Charlotte, *Villette,* 3 vols., 1853.

Burbury, Mrs E.J. *Florence Sackville, or Self-Dependence,* 3 vols., 1851.

Black, William, *In Silk Attire,* 1869.

Chorley, H.F., *Pomfret,* 3 vols., 1845.

Coleman, John, *Curley, An Actor's Story,* 1885.

——, *The Rival Queens,* 1887.

Dickens, Charles, *Sketches by Boz,* (1833-6), 1957 (New Oxford Illustrated Dickens, OUP).

——, *Pickwick Papers* (1837), 1947 (NOID).

——, *Nicholas Nickleby* (1839), 1950 (NOID).

——, *The Old Curiosity Shop* (1841), 1951 (NOID).

——, *David Copperfield* (1850), 1947 (NOID).

——, *Hard Times* (1854), 1955 (NOID).

——, *Great Expectations* (1862), 1955 (NOID).

Eliot, George, *Middlemarch* (1871-2), 1965 (Penguin English Library).

Edwards, Mrs Annie, *The Morals of Mayfair,* 3 vols., 1858.

Francillon, R.E., *Olympia,* 1874.

Gissing, George, *Demos: A Story of English Socialism,* 3 vols., 1886.

——, *Isabel Clarendon,* 2 vols., 1886.

Hall, Mrs S.C., *A Woman's Story,* 3 vols., 1857.

Hatton, Joseph, *Christopher Kendrick,* 2 vols., 1869.

James, Edwin (Mrs) *Muriel, or Social Fetters,* 1867.

James, Henry, *The Tragic Muse,* 3 vols., 1890.

Jay, Harriet, *Through the Stage Door,* 3 vols., 1873.

Jewsbury, Geraldine, *The Half-Sisters,* 2 vols., 1848.

Lewes, G.H., *Ranthorpe,* 1847.

Marryat, Elizabeth, *My Sister the Actress,* 3 vols., 1881.

——, *Peeress and Player,* 3 vols., 1883.
——, *Facing the Footlights,* 3 vols., 1883.
McCarthy, Justin, *My Enemy's Daughter,* 3 vols., 1869.
Merrick, Leonard, *The Position of Peggy Harper,* 1911.
Moore, George, *A Mummer's Wife,* 1918 edn. (first published 1882).
Riddell, Mrs, *Home, Sweet Home,* 3 vols., 1873.
Smith, Albert, *The Adventures of Mr Ledbury,* 3 vols., 1844.
——, *The Fortunes of the Scattergood Family,* 3 vols., 1845.
Wilde, Oscar, *The Picture of Dorian Gray,* 1891.

Parliamentary Papers

Select Committee Reports
Report of the Select Committee on Dramatic Literature, *Accounts and Committees,* 1831-2, VII, 3.
Report of the Select Committee on Public Houses, etc. *Accounts and Committees,* 1852-3, XXXVII, 1.
——, 1854, XIV, 231.
Report of the Select Committee on Theatrical Licences and Regulations, *Accounts and Committees,* 1866, XVI, 1.
Report of the Select Committee on Theatres and Places of Entertainment, *Accounts and Committees,* 1892, XVIII, 1.

Debates
Dramatic Performances (House of Commons), *Parl. Debates,* 1833, XVI, 561.
——, *Parl. Debates,* 1833, XIX, 1220.
—— (House of Lords), *Parl. Debates,* 1833, XX, 270.
Theatres Bill (House of Commons), *Parl. Debates,* 1865, CLXXVII, 1529.
Theatres Regulation Bill (House of Commons), *Parl. Debates,* 1883, CCLXXIX (3rd series), 331.

Bills relating to the theatre (which did not receive the royal assent)
To amend Acts relating to Theatres and Public-houses, *Public Bills,* 1860, VI, 521.
Theatres Bill, *P.B.,* 1865, IV, 521.
Public Entertainments Bill, *P.B.,* 1875, V, 59.
Theatres Regulation Bill, *P.B.,* 1883, X, 1.
——, 1884, VII, 257.
——, 1886, VI, 35.
To confer Inspecting Powers on the Metropolitan Board of Works, *P.B.,*

1887, IV, 227.
London Theatres Regulation Bill, *P.B.*, 1887, VI, 327.
——, 1888, VII, 615.
——, 1890-91, X, 329.

Acts Affecting the Theatre
Metropolitan Police Act, 1839 (2 and 3 Vict., c.47).
Theatres Act, 1843 (6 and 7 Vict., c.68).
Refreshment Houses Act, 1860 (23 Vict., c.27).
Public Entertainments Act, 1870 (38 and 39 Vict., c.21).
Metropolitan Management and Buildings Acts Amendment Act, 1878 (41/42 Vict., c.32).
Metropolitan Board of Works Act, 1882 (45 Vict., c.56).
Local Government Act, 1888 (51/52 Vict., c.41).
Public Health Acts Amendment Act, 1890 (53/53 Vict., c.59).

Census Reports (Occupation Tables)
Parl. Papers, 1844, XXVII.
——, 1852-53, LXXXVIII, Pts. 1 and 2.
——, 1863, LIII, Pt.1.
——, 1873, LXXI, Pt.1.
——, 1883, LXXX.
——, 1893-94, CVI.

Secondary Sources

General and Miscellaneous Works

Alexander, Sally, *St. Giles's Fair, 1830-1914,* 1970 (History Workshop, Ruskin College, Oxford).
Amerongen, J.B. van, *The Actor in Dickens,* 1926.
Arnold, Matthew, *Letter of an Old Playgoer,* 1919.
Banks, J.A., and O., *Feminism and Family Planning in Victorian England,* 1965.
Beerbohm, Max, *Around Theatres,* 1924.
——, *Works and More,* 1930.
——, *More Theatres,* 1969.
——, *Last Theatres,* 1970.
Best, Geoffrey, *Mid-Victorian Britain 1851-75,* 1971.
Blakelock, Denys, *Round the Next Corner,* 1967.
Blanche, J-Emile, *Portraits of a Lifetime,* 1937.
Bloch, Ivan, *Sexual Life in England,* 1967 (Corgi Books).

Bobbé, Dorothie de Bear, *Fanny Kemble,* 1932.

Booth, M.R., *English Melodrama,* 1965.

Bostock, E.H., *Menageries, Circuses and Theatres,* 1927.

Bowman, W.P., and Ball, R.H., *Theatre Language. A Dictionary of terms in English of the drama and stage from medieval to modern times,* 1961 (New York, Theatre Arts Books).

Bradbrook, M.C., *The Rise of the Common Player,* 1964.

Briggs, Asa, *The Age of Improvement 1783-1867,* 1959.

Brown, Eluned (ed.), *Selections from the Diary of Henry Crabb Robinson – The London Theatre 1811-66,* 1966 (Society for Theatre Research).

Bruford, W.H., *Theatre, Drama, and Audience in Goethe's Germany,* 1950.

Burton, E.J., *The British Theatre; Its Repertory and Practice,* 1960.

Chadwick, Owen, *The Victorian Church,* Part 1 (2nd edn. 1970) & Part 2 (2nd edn. 1972).

Chesney, Kellow, *The Victorian Underworld,* 1970.

Chisholm, Cecil, *Repertory,* 1931.

Clunes, Alec, *The British Theatre,* 1964. (Illustrated)

Dalziel, E.M., *Cheap English Popular Fiction, 1840-60, and the Moral Attitudes reflected in it*, 1952 (Oxford D.Phil. thesis).

Darton, F.J. Harvey, *Vincent Crummles, His Theatre and His Times,* 1926.

Disher, M. Wilson, *The Personality of the Alhambra,* 1937.

Donaldson, Frances, *The Actor-Managers,* 1970.

Donohue, J.W. (ed.), *The Theatrical Manager in England and America,* 1971.

Duncan, Barry, *The St. James's Theatre,* 1964.

East, J.M., *'Neath the Mask,* 1967.

Elliott, Philip, *The Sociology of the Progessions,* 1972.

Elwin, Malcolm, *Charles Reade – A Biography,* 1931.

Falk, Bernard, *The Naked Lady – A Biography of Adah Isaacs Menken,* 1934.

Findlater, Richard, *The Unholy Trade,* 1952.

——, *Lilian Baylis: The Lady of the Old Vic,* 1975.

Fleetwood, Frances, *Conquest, the Story of a Theatre Family,* 1953.

Fletcher, Ian (ed.), *Romantic Mythologies,* 1967.

Gilder, Rosamond, *Enter the Actress,* 1931.

Godfrey, Philip, *Backstage,* 1933.

Granville, Wilfred, *Theatre Language,* 1952.

Grein, J.T., *The World of the Theatre,* 1921.

Gross, John, *The Rise and Fall of the Man of Letters,* Pelican, 1973.
Guest, Ivor, *Fanny Cerrito – The Life of a Romantic Ballerina,* 1956.
——, *Victorian Ballet-Girl. The Tragic Story of Clara Webster,* 1957.
——. *The Empire Ballet,* 1962.
Hardy, Florence E., *Life of Thomas Hardy,* 1962.
Hartnoll, P., *The Oxford Companion to the Theatre,* 1967 (3rd ed.).
——, *A Concise History of the Theatre,* 1968.
Hauser, Arnold, *The Social History of Art,* 2 vols., 1951.
Hayman, Ronald, *The Set-Up: An Anatomy of the English Theatre Today,* 1973.
Hillebrand, H.N., *Edmund Kean,* 1933.
Hoge, J.O. (ed.), *The Letters of Emily Lady Tennyson,* 1974. (Pennsylvania State University Press).
Houghton, W.E., *The Victorian Frame of Mind, 1830-70,* 1957.
Howard, D., *London Theatres and Music Halls, 1850-1950,* 1970.
Hunt, Bampton (ed.), *The Green Room Book,* 1906.
Hunt, Hugh, *The Director in the Theatre,* 1954.
Huxley, Gervas, *Lady Elizabeth and the Grosvenors,* 1965.
Irving, Laurence, *Henry Irving, The Actor and His World,* 1951.
James, Louis, *Fiction for the Working Man, 1830-50,* 1963.
Johnson, E. and E., *The Dickens Theatrical Reader,* 1964.
Joseph, B.L., *The Tragic Actor,* 1959.
Kermode, Frank, *Romantic Image,* 1957.
Clark, G. Kitson, *The Making of Victorian England,* 1965 (University Paperback).
Leacroft, R., *The Theatre Royal, Leicester, 1836-1958,* 1958 (Society for Theatre Research).
Lewis, Roy and Maude, Angus, *Professional People,* 1952.
Loewenberg, A., *The Theatre of the British Isles,* 1950.
Machen, Arthur, *Things Near and Far,* 1923.
Mander, R., and Mitchenson, J., *A Picture History of the British Theatre,* 1957 (Hulton).
Marcus, Steven, *The Other Victorians,* 1966.
Marshall, Norman, *The Producer and the Play,* 1962.
Mason, A.E.W., *Sir George Alexander and the St. James's Theatre,* 1935.
Mews, Hazel, *Frail Vessels – Woman's Role in Women's Novels from Fanny Burney to George Eliot,* 1969.
Millett, Kate, *Sexual Politics,* 1970.
Neuberg, Victor E., *Popular Literature, A History and Guide,* Pelican, 1977.
Nicholson, Watson, *The Struggle for a Free Stage in London,* 1906.

Nicol, Allardyce, *A History of English Drama, 1660-1900,* IV (1970, CUP) and V (1967, CUP).

Nisbet, Ada, *Dickens and Ellen Ternan,* 1962.

Pearsall, Ronald, *The Worm in the Bud,* 1972 (Pelican).

Pearson, Hesketh, *Beerbohm Tree, His Life and Laughter,* 1956.

Pollard, A. (ed.), *The Victorians,* 1970 (Sphere History of the English Language, Vol.6).

Reader, W.J., *Professional Men,* 1966.

——, *Victorian England, 1974* (Book Club Associates).

Richards, E. and Thomson, P. (eds.), *Nineteenth Century British Theatre,* 1971.

Robinson, J.W., *Theatrical Street Ballads,* 1971 (Society for Theatre Research).

Rosenthal, Harold (ed.), *The Mapleson Memoirs,* 1966.

Rowell, George, *The Victorian Theatre,* 1956.

Rowell, George (ed.), *Victorian Dramatic Criticism,* 1971 (University Paperback).

Saunders, A.M. Carr, *Professions – Their Organisation and Place in Society,* 1928.

Shattuck, C.H. (ed.), *Bulwer and Macready – A Chronicle of the Early Victorian Theatre,* 1958.

Southern, Richard, *The Georgian Theatre,* 1948.

——, *Seven Ages of the Theatre,* 1964.

——, *The Victorian Theatre: A Pictorial Survey,* 1970.

Sprague, A.C., *The Doubling of Parts in Shakespeare's Plays,* 1966 (Society for Theatre Research).

Steen, Marguerite, *A Pride of Terrys,* 1962.

Stokes, J., *Resistible Theatres,* 1972.

Stratman, C.J., *Britain's Theatrical Periodicals: A Bibliography,* 1972 (New York Public Library).

Thomson, Patricia, *The Victorian Heroine – A Changing Ideal, 1837-73,* 1956.

Trewin, J.C. *Benson and the Bensonians,* 1960.

——, *The Pomping Folk,* 1968.

Troubridge, St Vincent, *The Benefit System in the British Theatre,* 1967 (Society for Theatre Research).

Webster, Margaret, *The Same Only Different,* 1969.

Whitworth, G., *The Making of a National Theatre,* 1951.

Willey, Basil, *More Nineteenth Century Studies,* 1956.

Williams, Raymond, *Culture and Society, 1780-1950,* Penguin, 1963.

Woodward, Sir Llewellyn, *The Age of Reform 1815-70,* 1962.

Periodical Articles

Theatre Notebook

Armstrong, A., 'Madame Vestris: A Centenary Appreciation', XI, 1956-7.

Barker, K.M., 'The Theatre Proprietor's Story', XVIII, 1963-4.

Hughes, Alan, 'The Lyceum Staff – A Victorian Theatrical Organisation', XXVIII, 1974.

Macht, Stephen, 'The Origin of L.A.M.D.A.', XXVI, 1971.

Morley, M., and Speaight, G., 'The Minor Theatre in Catherine Street', XVIII, 1963-4.

Thompson, Marjorie, 'William Archer: Dramatic Critic 1856-1924', XI, 1956-7.

——, 'Henry Arthur Jones and Wilson Barrett: Some Correspondence 1879-1904', ibid.

Urwin, G.G., 'Alfred Bunn 1786-1860: A Revaluation', ibid.

Wearing, J.P., 'Pinero the Actor', XXVI, 1972.

Victorian Studies

Ellis, J. and Donohue, J., 'The London Stage 1800-1900: A Proposal for a Calendar of Performances', XVI, June 1973.

Kent, Christopher, 'The Whittington Club: A Bohemian Experiment in Middle-Class Social Reform', XVIII, September 1974.

Meisel, Martin, 'Perspectives on Victorian and Other Acting', VI, June 1963.

Millett, Kate, 'Ruskin and Mill: The Debate over Women', XIV, September 1970.

Olsen, D.J., 'Victorian London: Specialisation, Segregation, and Privacy', XVII, March 1974.

Peterson, M.J., 'The Victorian Governess', XIV, September 1970.

Smith, Sheila, 'John Overs to Charles Dickens: A Working-Man's Letter and its Implication', XVIII, December 1974.

Stottlar, J.F., 'A Victorian Stage Censor – The Theory and Practice of William Bodham Donne', XIII, March 1970.

Miscellaneous

Ades, J.I., 'Charles Lamb, Shakespeare, and Early 19th Century Theatre', *Publication of the Modern Languages Association,* LXXXV, May 1970.

Downer, A.S., 'Players and Painted Stage: Nineteenth Century Acting', ibid., LXI, June 1946.

Holland, Mary, 'Carry On, Equity', *New Statesman,* 23 August 1974.

Smither, N., ' "Charlotte Cushman's Second New York Engagement: A New Lady-Actor of Gentlemen" ', *Bulletin of the New York Public Library,* June 1970.

Sutcliffe, E.G., 'Charles Reade's Notebooks', *Studies in Philology,* XXVII, October 1930.

Taylor, L., and Williams, K., 'The Actor and his World', *New Society,* 29 July 1971.

Wolcott, J.R., 'The Genesis of Gas Lights', *Theatre Research,* XII, 1972.

INDEX

Further biographical information on many of the actors indexed may be found in the appendices.